A remarkable novel of our struggle for civil rights

"Engaging and suspenseful, this is contemporary fiction at its best. . . . Readers too young to remember Freedom Summer will find Bob Moses an enigmatic, admirable hero."
— *Dayton Daily News*

"Bob Moses was the kind of leader we sadly miss today, one of quiet, yet enormous moral strength: a genuine inspiration to the sometimes confused idealism of the young volunteers in the midst of a violent and passionate struggle. Perhaps now, more than ever, we need to remember the summer of 1964. This novel is wonderfully instructive, it has a great deal of moral energy, and it tells an important story sensitively, carefully, thoughtfully."
— Robert Coles, author of *Farewell to the South*

"The Children Bob Moses Led is an important and timely book, one that is being published at an extremely pivotal period in our national history. The reader will experience the raw courage, the personal discipline, and the reliance on transcendent values, whether philosophical or religious, that were at the basis of this historic period of transformation in Mississippi."
— James A. McPherson, Pulitzer Prize-winning
author of *Battle Cry of Freedom*

"Heath has created a novel that holds true to the actual heroic events of Freedom Summer. *The Children Bob Moses Led* is an illuminating account of a period from our history that is too little known and too little understood."
— Claybourne Carson, editor of the papers of
Dr. Martin Luther King, Jr. and author of *In Struggle:
SNCC and the Black Awakening of the 1960s*

"The large cast of characters gives voice to the complexity of the era's issues, and Heath's clear chronicle of this poignant moment in our nation's recent past is often compelling."
— *Publishers Weekly*

Also by William Heath

The Walking Man (Icarus Books)

The Children
Bob Moses Led

William Heath

MILKWEED
EDITIONS

This is a work of fiction. Although it was inspired by real persons and events, the characters, incidents, and dialogue are products of the author's imagination and, except for appearances by some public figures, Bob Moses in particular, do not portray actual persons. Some of the historical events have been fictionalized in their details. McComb, for example, is a real town, and the Freedom House and Society Hill Baptist Church incidents actually occurred, but the author has changed some dates and other details for dramatic purposes. Historical characters, such as Bob Moses, are real people in a fictional work. The author has received written approval from the Martin Luther King Center and from the Wisconsin Historical Society for the way in which he has made use of and acknowledged their archives.

©1995, Text by William Heath
Cover photo of Bob Moses by Danny Lyon.
Cover design by Adrian Morgan, Red Letter Design.

Published 1995 by Milkweed Editions
Printed in the United States of America
Book design by Will Powers. The text of this book is set in Monotype Calisto.
96 97 98 99   5 4 3 2 1
First Edition

Milkweed Editions is a not-for-profit publisher. We gratefully acknowledge support from the Bush Foundation; Target Stores, Dayton's, and Mervyn's by the Dayton Hudson Foundation; Ecolab Foundation; General Mills Foundation; Honeywell Foundation; Jerome Foundation; John S. and James L. Knight Foundation; The McKnight Foundation; Andrew W. Mellon Foundation; Minnesota State Arts Board through an appropriation by the Minnesota State Legislature; Challenge and Literature Programs of the National Endowment for the Arts; I. A. O'Shaughnessy Foundation; Piper Jaffray Companies, Inc.; John and Beverly Rollwagen Fund of the Minneapolis Foundation; The St. Paul Companies, Inc.; Star Tribune/Cowles Media Foundation; Surdna Foundation; James R. Thorpe Foundation; Lila Wallace-Reader's Digest Literary Publishers Marketing Development Program, funded through a grant to the Council of Literary Magazines and Presses; and generous individuals.

Library of Congress Cataloging-in-Publication Data

Heath, William, 1942–
    The children Bob Moses led / William Heath. — 1st ed.
        p. cm.
    ISBN 1-57131-008-8 (cl); ISBN 1-57131-012-6 (pb)
    1. Moses, Robert Parris—Fiction.   2. Civil rights movements—Mississippi—
History—20th century—Fiction.   3. Afro-Americans—Civil rights—Mississippi—
Fiction.   4. Civil rights workers—Mississippi—Fiction.   5. Afro-Americans—
Mississippi—Fiction.   6. Mississippi—Race relations—Fiction.   I. Title.
PS3558.E269C48 1995
813'.54—dc20   95–16349
                                                                            CIP

This book is printed on acid-free paper.

This book is dedicated to my parents

Louise Elizabeth Saywell and Ralph Mason Heath

and to my sister

Alice Heath Baker

The Children Bob Moses Led

The world is real. It is there.
ROBERT PENN WARREN

The Children Bob Moses Led

Tom Morton

Summer 1963

In those days I believed that America could be made safe for democracy, from the grassroots up, with just a little help from me and my friends. And so I served as a summer soldier to fight for civil rights. We were neophytes who thought that we could redeem our nation by holding hands and singing freedom songs. But when you toe the asphalt, stick out your thumb, and become a hitchhiker of history, currents beyond your control sweep you to destinations not of your devising. By the time I left the Movement, the world had not changed much, but at least I had not sat on the sidelines with the lip-service liberals; rather I had become my own contemporary and acted on my ideals. I had gone in search of America, and myself. What I found was Mississippi.

During the summer of 1963 I worked at a tennis camp in the Adirondacks for Jewish kids from Long Island. "We're from Great Neck," they used to chant, "couldn't be prouder. If you don't believe us, we'll buy you out!" Each cabin counselor was a college tennis player, and we spent long afternoons shouting "Racquet back; eye on the ball!" to our awkward pupils. They practiced hard, whether to satisfy their own dreams of athletic prowess or to please their parents, but only a few displayed the skills to excel.

The boy I remember best was a manic perfectionist who sometimes flipped out when he failed. Mostly he was quiet and kept to
himself, speaking in soft monosyllables and rarely smiling. Asked
to make his bed or to police the grounds for inspection, he did it
impeccably: a dime bounced on his taut sheets and all the gum
wrappers were gone. He used to sit on the front steps of the cabin
strumming the same folk tune by the hour, until some web-footed
demon in his fingers slipped up. I found his guitar, back broken, left
for dead in the weeds. Once, during a softball game, when a pitch
caught the inside corner of the plate and I called him out on
strikes, he whirled, white-eyed, and swung for my skull.

Palm Sunday (our name for parents' weekend) came in mid-
July that year. The moms and dads pontooned up to the dock in
their own seaplanes or parked swank machines on the outfield
grass. The rule was no tipping. (Ten spots changed hands on the
sly, a small offering to redeem a boy's second serve or forgive his
faults.) That evening at the intracamp basketball game, the parents
protected themselves from the splinters in the bleachers by sitting
on foxes and mink, on Scottish tweed, ready to praise the least sign
of grace in their ungainly offspring. As referee, my job was to spot
infractions. "Two shots," I shouted, "in the act," raising two fingers and pointing out the culprit, my camper. When I turned
toward the foul line, he suddenly pounced on my back and
clamped my throat with a merciless grip, which I unpried, smiling,
while the parents smiled back: boys will be boys. At the bench he
wept and pleaded, "I didn't do it! I didn't do it!" He left the next
day. I said good-bye to the family: his mother, face salvaged by
plastic surgery, her bouffant living a peroxide life of its own; the
father, pudgy and puzzled; and the son, grinning. I watched them
walk down to the dock; their plane skimmed the lake, gathering
speed, and ascended into heaven.

I couldn't help identifying with that boy who wanted to be perfect. I didn't have his fits of violence, but I fell into moody brooding
and self-pity when life didn't meet my expectations. I wanted to be
a top tennis player, but I had only made the Hiram team as a

sophomore, and the moves I brought to the game were better suited to basketball: I had quick hands, covered a lot of court, and my best stroke was a kind of walk-on-air leaping lunge that resembled a fallaway jump shot more than an overhead smash. At Camp Idylwold I soon realized that I was out of my league. Most of the other counselors beat me decisively, and the camp pro, Joe Fishback, demolished me. No matter how hard I hit the ball, he returned it with ease, and the wonder of it was, I never saw him run. He seemed to be waiting at the exact spot long before even my most sharply angled shots arrived. At the end of the match I slammed my racquet to the ground, and to make my humiliation complete, it bounced back up and smacked me in the face.

Nothing had gone the way I wanted that summer. My tennis game improved, but not as much as I had wished. When my girlfriend, Michelle, arrived unexpectedly, and the whole camp stood on the hillside cheering as I shouldered my sleeping bag and walked toward her car, I learned that she had come not because she wanted my body but because she had decided to go to Africa with the Peace Corps and was bound for Dartmouth to study Swahili. I'd been jilted before, but never by a continent.

Two weeks later I received letters from both my parents, bearing different addresses. "Your mother and I have decided to separate," my dad wrote, and he added with characteristic elusiveness, "I can't tell you how much I loved that house. Don't think for a minute I didn't hate to leave, but it got to a point where I couldn't stand it any more." I knew that was all he'd ever say, and for a moment I saw the stone fireplace and oak bookcases he had constructed with his own hands, and I wondered if he loved those better than he loved me. After years of listening to Mom's monologues and Dad's silences, I was not surprised. I thought of the photos of them when they were my age. He was a six-foot-two, well-muscled track star, and she a bright and patrician lawyer's daughter: an all-American couple walking arm-in-arm across the Oberlin campus with the world before them.

I had planned to drive straight back to Ohio as soon as camp closed, but I felt bitter and betrayed, as if they had staged all this just to hurt my feelings. *I have no home,* I thought, *I'm on my own.* I called my friend Lenny Swift in Washington. I admired his unflappable cool, his smart remarks at the passing scene; he could always make me laugh. Lenny had a heart, but he never wore it on his sleeve, and I found comfort in his caustic wit. He urged me to come to D.C. and join him for the March on Washington. That sounded like fun to me, especially after Lenny told me that Bob Dylan and Joan Baez would be singing. On the way, I decided to stop off in New York to scout out a suitable garret in Greenwich Village. Like most people my age I was auditioning identities: I saw myself at the time as something of a dandy, an aristocratic Q flaunting his foppish tail at the monotonous world of Os. Rather than go to graduate school as my favorite history professor had urged, I resolved to become a famous writer. I had read enough Jack Kerouac to assume that the place to find *Real Life* was with the hoboes huddled around flaming trash cans and the dark-skinned folk who worked the fields and sang the blues. I would write about them, the down-and-out and dispossessed, and when I returned to my hometown with a best-seller to my credit, a sheaf of rave reviews in my pocket, and an exotic beauty on my arm, the local yokels would go slackjawed with desire and Michelle would bite her lip in envy. That was my American Dream, the I-told-you-so fantasy of a callow know-it-all who was a stranger to himself.

That was before I met Bob Moses.

Bob Moses

McComb and Liberty, Mississippi

August–September 1961

1

I am Bob Moses. I first came to McComb in August of 1961 with a simple purpose: to break the Solid South by applying pressure at its strongest point. I sought out the worst part of the most intransigent state, placed myself on the charity of the black community, located a few brave souls who would support civil rights workers, and set up a voter registration school. If enough people could find the courage to go down to the courthouse, confronting the system designed to oppress them, then blacks all over the South would take heart, the country would take notice, and maybe, one hundred years too late, the federal government would take action. Was my effort a success? I would be reluctant to say that. When I started out, I hoped that no one would be killed.

A few years earlier I was headed down a different path. With an M.A. in philosophy from Harvard and a job teaching mathematics at the prestigious Horace Mann School in Riverdale, New York, I was a part of what W. E. B. DuBois termed "the talented tenth"—a black man who could succeed in the white world playing by white rules. I had had an elitist education since I was eleven, passing a citywide competitive exam to attend Stuyvesant High School in downtown Manhattan. President of my senior class, I received an academic scholarship to Hamilton, where I was one of three black students at the college.

It was at Hamilton, thanks to my French professor, that I discovered Camus. I read *The Rebel* and *The Plague* and began asking hard political questions: "Can revolution be humane?" "Can the 'victim' overthrow the 'executioner' without assuming his office?" For a time I believed that the only change worth working for was a change of heart, and so I joined a group of campus Pentecostals who traveled on weekends to Times Square to testify to the coming of the Kingdom. I considered becoming a preacher like my grandfather, but my father had his doubts. "That's not just any job," he said. "You've got to be called." The pacifism of the Society of Friends also impressed me. One summer I attended an American Friends Service Committee international work camp in France, where I met people who had been part of the Resistance during the Nazi occupation. The following summer I went to Japan, where I helped build wooden steps up a slippery hillside for the children of a nearby mental hospital. Before I flew home, a Zen Buddhist monk invited me to spend a week at his home. Through my travels and study I learned to think before I spoke and to mean what I said, but I wasn't the serious brooder people took me for. What I loved best about the Quakers was their folk dancing and hootenannies. Back in my room I listened to Odetta, and out on a date I would strut down Amsterdam Avenue whistling show tunes.

In the fall of 1956 I began graduate work in philosophy at Harvard. I was convinced that the analytic method, with its insistence on clarity and precision, represented a significant advance in thought. Previous philosophers had relied on metaphor and rhetoric to make muddy water appear deep. I sat in the back of the class during Paul Tillich's lectures, shaking my head and muttering, "It's all poetry." More to my taste was Wittgenstein's axiom: "Whereof one cannot speak, thereof one must be silent." If philosophy could streamline its language and define its terms, then it could attain the accuracy of mathematics with its postulates and proofs. Before long, however, I tired of thinking about thinking and the meaning of meaning. In that remote realm of tautologies, indexes, and surds, I was in danger of forgetting that the meaning of life was no abstract speculation but my immediate and concrete concern. I returned to Camus's dictum "I rebel, therefore we exist" and to Lao-tse, who taught that the way to wisdom consists in living one life well—starting small, a step at a time, with what is near, with what is at hand.

Then in the spring of 1958 my forty-three-year-old mother died of cancer; my father was so distraught he had to be hospitalized at Bellevue for several months. I dropped out of Harvard, accepted a job teaching math at Horace Mann High School, and moved back to Harlem to look after him. My father and I had always been close; we used to have long talks about what America denied and offered. Like many of his generation, he had been hamstrung by the depression. Intelligent, articulate, and handsome, he sacrificed his talents for the sake of his family, accepting a low-paying job as a security guard at Harlem's 369th Division Armory. He and my mother scrimped and saved to ensure that my brothers and I would get ahead. The stress and strain took their toll: my mother once suffered a minor breakdown, and my father would sometimes slip into fantasies that his name was not Gregory Moses but Gary Cooper—a man brave enough, in spite of his cowardly town, to stand up for what was right.

My only civil rights activity at that time was to participate in the Youth March for Integrated Schools that Bayard Rustin sponsored in Washington. Then, one day in February 1960, I saw a picture in the *New York Times* of the sit-ins that had just begun in Greensboro, North Carolina: a row of neatly dressed black students sat at a Woolworth's lunch counter, while a crowd of white toughs in ducktails and sleeveless T-shirts waved a Confederate flag and shouted at their backs. Some of the students tried to read books, others stared calmly at the camera. I was struck to the core by the determination on their faces. They weren't cowed, and they weren't apathetic—they meant to finish what they had begun. Here was something that could be done. I simply *had* to get involved.

Over spring break, I visited my father's brother, a teacher at Hampton Institute in Virginia. One day I saw some students picketing stores in Newport News. I slipped into the line of march and suddenly felt a great release. All my life I had repressed my resentments and played it cool. Now the sense of affirmation and the surge of energy that came from this mere gesture at protesting were exhilarating. I had had a taste of action and wanted more. That evening I went to a mass meeting where Reverend Wyatt Tee Walker of the Southern Christian Leadership Conference spoke. He talked about the need to collect money to defend the Reverend Martin Luther King from legal harassment, mentioning that Bayard Rustin was directing a fund drive in New York.

When I got back to Harlem, I volunteered my services to the Committee to Defend Martin Luther King, and so every day after school, I devoted time to organizing a Harry Belafonte fund-raising rally at the armory where my father worked. But I didn't feel right licking envelopes while others were putting their lives on the line. I confided my discontent to Bayard Rustin, whose advice I respected.

"Go down to Atlanta, Bob," he told me. "I'll write to Ella Baker to tell her you're coming. She and Martin will find something for you to do."

As soon as my teaching duties were over for the summer, I packed my bags and took a bus headed south.

The Southern Christian Leadership Conference office wasn't much: a small room, three women, three desks, three telephones. They were in the midst of a voter registration project and wanted me to do the same boring tasks I had done in New York. I soon found myself talking a lot to Jane Stembridge, a short, peppy blond with piercing blue eyes, a fiery spirit, and a crazy haystack of unruly hair. She was a southern girl, a minister's daughter, who had left Union Theological Seminary to become the Student Non-Violent Coordinating Committee's first executive secretary, a job she carried out with dispatch from her desk stuck in a corner of the SCLC office. We spent animated afternoons discussing Kant's categorical imperative, Tillich's ultimate concern, Sartre's terrible freedom, and Camus's authentic versus inauthentic existence. More pressing were our debates about the civil rights tactics of Martin Luther King and the SCLC, which we called "Slick." They were in the process of replacing Ella Baker with Wyatt Tee Walker—part of a larger plan to promote Dr. King as *the* leader and spokesman of the black revolt. Jane and I thought the whole approach was too hero-worshipping, media-centered, preacher-dominated, and authoritarian. We agreed with Ella Baker, the midwife of SNCC, which we called "Snick," who had very definite ideas about organizing. She believed that the Movement ought to seek out the small farmers, sharecroppers, and plantation workers and start building at the grassroots instead of posturing in front of cameras. Jane suggested that I should make a field trip to the Deep South to recruit students for an upcoming SNCC conference in October. I would pay my own way and see for myself what conditions were like.

At this time I wasn't even on the SNCC staff. In fact, several of the SNCC people in Atlanta eyed me with suspicion. Who was this soft-spoken guy in horn-rimmed glasses with a Harvard degree? Why would someone so well educated (and with that name!) just happen to show up from New York? Was he an FBI spy? A Communist agent provocateur? Although I never tried to impose my views, from the start I made it clear that I thought the Movement in America was part of a larger world picture. Ella Baker, whose impact on all of us was enormous, argued that what we were after was much more than equal access to greasy burgers at the five-and-dime. That didn't stop me, however, from joining any picket line I saw. I marched for hours with Julian Bond and the other Atlanta University students in front of a local A&P that served mostly blacks but refused to hire even one. Another time I was arrested while picketing for the Southern Conference Educational Fund.

"How did you get involved with the SCEF?" Julian asked.

"I heard about it at a lecture."

"On what?"

"Ramifications of Goedel's Theorem."

"Oh," he said, raising one eyebrow.

As a result of my arrest, Martin Luther King summoned me to his study at Ebenezer Baptist Church. I knew that some people in SNCC had been expressing doubts about me to King; he wanted to see for himself. Face to face, I felt less in the presence of a national symbol than of a troubled man a few inches shorter than I was and a few years older. After some painful silences and a smattering of small talk, King finally said, "We have to be careful. The FBI thinks the whole Civil Rights Movement is a Communist plot. I'd advise against picketing with the SCEF."

I didn't like his advice, but I took it. Then I changed the subject. Could I move my operations for the SCLC over to the Butler Street YMCA where I was staying?

"Of course, of course," King answered, and we parted on that cordial note of agreement.

When Ella Baker heard about my visit to Ebenezer, she was upset.

"Why, Martin himself is friends with Anne and Carl Braden and several of the other SCEF people. What right does he have to tell you to stay away from them?"

"It doesn't matter," I said. "I'm heading south in a few days anyway."

"Well, I wish I could join you. Wyatt Walker just evicted Jane from the SCLC office, and I'm being sent to New York. When you get to Mississippi, make sure you talk to Amzie Moore. Before I leave I'll give you his address, and I'm going to give those snooty Atlanta students a piece of my mind about the dangers of red-baiting. I won't have that. When I've finished with them, they won't say another word against you, Robert."

The next day Julian came by and apologized. I told him about my plan to tour the South.

"So 'Moses' is finally going to Mississippi," he said, inspecting my face for signs of insanity. "I wish you luck."

One day in late August I knocked on the door to Amzie Moore's house in Cleveland, Mississippi. He was an NAACP organizer who had been working to change things in the Delta ever since he came home from World War II. The floodlights that radiated out from his brick house and the rifle he held on his lap as we talked testified to how precarious his position was. But he was dug in like a tree by the water and determined to defend himself. A strong, broad-shouldered man who looked like he could handle himself in a fight, Amzie made me welcome immediately, and for a week, we reconnoitered the area and discussed strategy. We went from shack to shack, and he showed me scenes that I'll never forget: children with swollen ankles, bloated bellies, and suppurating sores; children whose one meal a day was grits and gravy; children who didn't know the taste of milk, meat, fruits, or vegetables; children who drank contaminated water from a distant well, slept five in a bed, and didn't have the energy to brush the flies from their faces. We were in the Delta, but it might as well have been Haiti.

"What can be done?" he asked me simply.

I mentioned the sit-ins and demonstrations going on elsewhere.

"No. No. That won't work here. They'd squash that like a bug and nothin' more would be heard. It's the politicians who control things in this state. If you can hurt them, things will change. The key is the vote."

Amzie convinced me that the best tactic was not to attack segregation head-on, but to focus exclusively on voter registration. Unlike the other NAACP leaders I had met, he was enthusiastic about bringing in SNCC workers and recruiting local students to help.

"It's the young people who are gonna carry this thing through," he said. "The adults are too afraid. But if the students show enough courage and commitment, they'll back them up."

Amzie showed me a booklet put out by the Southern Regional Council that outlined the voting situation. Mississippi, as usual, was the worst: although 40 percent of the state was black, only 5 percent of those eligible were registered, and most didn't dare vote. We taped a map of Mississippi on the wall and hauled out Amzie's old Underwood. He extemporized on life in the Delta while I typed up a rough draft of a voter registration project to present to SNCC. A few years earlier, Amzie and a Catholic priest in Mound Bayou—Father John Lebouvre—had set up a voting school in his church. That would be our model. We would run off copies of the state constitution, and SNCC workers would teach the local people how to register. We knew we faced a tough, dangerous job, but my eyes gleamed with the vision of thousands of black people descending on local courthouses and gaining control of the Delta.

"Don't get starry-eyed," Amzie would caution. "Things are gonna get real ugly round here before they get pretty. I've seen how mean these whites folks can be."

At the conference in October, Amzie Moore outlined our voter registration proposal. SNCC, which could never resist a dare or a challenge, was impressed with Amzie's presentation and decided to go ahead. I was named director of a voter registration project to start the following summer.

I taught one more year at Horace Mann, saving as much money as I could for what was ahead. Each night I read up on the South, studied the Mississippi constitution and maps of the state, planned, meditated, and then, before going to bed, listened to Odetta sing "I'm Going Back to the Red Clay Country."

When summer came, I returned to Mississippi, but it looked like the project wouldn't get off the ground. SNCC was in disarray over the question of whether voter registration wasn't a diversion from "direct action" demonstrations against segregation; Amzie was swamped with personal problems. Then a letter came from Curtis Bryant in McComb. He had read about SNCC's voter registration plans in *Jet* and wanted us to set up a project in Pike County.

"White folks around here are really upset about these Freedom Riders," Amzie said. "Maybe things down there won't be so tight."

So one day in early August I moved my base of operations to

McComb, a tough railroad town in the southwestern part of the state.

Bryant, a brusque, energetic man with a high-pitched voice and a warm handshake, was one of the stalwarts of the Movement. He ran a barbershop in front of his house in Baertown, a small black community the city fathers had deliberately zoned outside the town limits. He also operated a loading crane for the Illinois Central, whose tracks, along with the Gulf, Western & Ohio, cut right through the heart of McComb. On the west side of town were paved streets; a few blocks of retail stores, and the white suburbs, spread out under a canopy of shade trees and embroidered with flowers. On the east, Burgland, the all-black town with its shabby stores, ramshackle houses, and dirt roads. The general air of grinding poverty was broken by the occasional brick house of somebody who worked for the railroad.

Bryant took me in and introduced me to as many people as he could. "This is my friend, Bob Moses," he'd say. "He's here to help us, so I want you to help him." Ernest Nobles, who ran the local laundry, said he'd keep me looking good; Aylene Quin promised food at her restaurant; Mama Cotton provided housing; and Webb Owens, "Supercool Daddy," volunteered to go door-to-door with me to raise money for the Freedom School.

At first, children stopped playing hopscotch and huddled together as I walked by. "He's a Freedom Rider," they whispered. Their wary parents would pass me on the road without meeting my eyes, but I could feel their stares and questions jabbing into my back. Many were frightened; I meant nothing but trouble. I would tell them, "Get ready, the Movement is coming your way," but that wasn't anything they wanted to hear. One man stooped down behind the tomato plants in his garden to avoid me. Another time, a little girl came to the front door and said, "Mama say she not here."

It was hard work, but a few listened. I would take out a registration form and ask, "Have you ever filled one of these out?" They would shake their heads and look uneasy. Voting was white folks' business. "Would you like to sit down now and try?" I would encourage them to imagine themselves at the county courthouse in Magnolia actually answering the twenty-one questions, interpreting a section of the Mississippi Constitution, and stating in a paragraph the duties and obligations of citizenship. Whether they passed or not was at the discretion of the registrar, whose job was to see that they didn't.

People listened and gave what they could—a nickle, a dime, a quarter—to support a handful of SNCC workers. Soon I was joined by John Hardy, Reggie Robinson, Travis Britt, and a few others who had been in jail in Jackson for taking part in the Freedom Rides. Also, several of the local students got involved. One in particular, Brenda Travis, always bright-eyed and brimming with questions, would sit on a family's porch talking to them for hours if necessary until they were convinced of the need to register. Thanks to Curtis Bryant, who, in addition to being head of the local NAACP, a deacon in his church, a Sunday school teacher, and a scoutmaster, was also a high official in the Freemasons, we were able to set up a Freedom School in the Masonic Hall over the Burgland grocery store. Saint Paul's Methodist Church, across the street, agreed to let us hold meetings there too.

One day in early August I was at the Freedom School preparing for class when a slim, serious-faced young man, who was about twenty, came in. He scrutinized me with wide-eyed intensity.

"Are you Martin Luther King?"

"No. I'm Bob Moses. Why did you think I was King?"

"I heard talk about some big secret thing goin' on, so I come to see for myself."

"Where are you from?"

"Summit."

"What's your name?"

"Hollis Watkins."

"Are you in school?"

"No. But I got plans."

"I've got plans too."

I told him about the voter registration project, and even though

I wasn't Martin Luther King, he wanted to help. His friend Curtis Hayes would help too. They began to recruit. People related to them as the sons of local farmers who dressed and acted in down-home ways. I soon learned to scrap my suit and tie for boots, bib overalls, and a chambray shirt; the other SNCC workers did the same. Those of us from the North learned to slow down to the rhythms of the South.

The people flocked to our school. When we explained the power of the vote, they squirmed in their chairs and glanced at each other. One heavyset woman up front fanned herself harder every time I mentioned the word *freedom*. Within a few days we sent several students to the Pike County courthouse in Magnolia. When they learned that they had passed, we held a party that lasted long into the night. It seemed for the moment as if everything would be easy. Then the local paper, the *Enterprise-Journal,* ran an article on what we were trying to do. Whites became alarmed. The next day, the registrar rejected our students, and that evening one of them, in an incident apparently unrelated to voter registration, was shot at. As the news spread, I noted the panic in people's eyes; they saw a connection. Fewer and fewer came to the Freedom School.

Meanwhile, farmers in nearby Amite and Walthall counties heard about SNCC and asked if we could help them, too. As dangerous as McComb was, the surrounding areas, with long histories of violence, were much worse. In Amite only one black was registered; in Walthall, none. If we had serious difficulties in McComb, what chance did we have in those places? But I knew that if we turned down the farmers, we would lose the trust and destroy the hope of the people. If we shied away from the toughest areas, everyone would know we could be intimidated, and the fragile project would fall apart. We decided that John Hardy should take on Walthall while I went into Amite, a name that meant "friendship" in French and "trouble" to me.

On Saturday evening Curtis Bryant drove me to the farm of E. W. Steptoe, a small man with prominent ears, a wide smile, a weather-beaten face, and as I was soon to learn, an indomitable spirit. A few other farmers were there. One was Herbert Lee, short, self-effacing, with a touch of gray in his hair. He had grown up down the road, married a girl from nearby St. Helena Parish, raised a large family, and made enough money planting cotton to buy some land, a house, and a car. Only men like Steptoe and Lee, with the self-sufficiency of the independent farmer, had the courage to stand up to the threat of white reprisals.

In the fifties, Steptoe had single-handedly started an NAACP chapter in Amite County. He bought a batch of membership cards and sold them to the local farmers for two dollars each until more than the necessary fifty signed up. When the sheriff found out, he and twenty men surrounded the meeting place, confiscated the secretary's membership list, and frightened people so much that even Steptoe's friends turned their backs on him.

"You're goin' too fast," one said. "Why don't you quit that mess?"

"Ah, we are one hundred years too slow now," Steptoe replied.

"But you're just gonna go get yourself killed."

"I know my life is at stake," he said. "I know they wants me dead. But if they kill me, I would hate to know nobody else was workin' for the young peoples, for the unborn generation, but me."

Steptoe made an immediate and lasting impression on me. Sometimes he spoke so slowly it seemed it would take him all day to finish one sentence, but I always felt sure it would be worth the wait. No one convinced me more that the common man knew through hard-earned experience truths that few politicians heeded.

"I spent years tryin' to win the friendship of white folks," Steptoe told me. "I drove them places and waited hours until they was finished; I swam in creeks to rescue their cattle; I chopped wood for an old widow woman. Anything folks wanted done, I done it. I didn't ask for no money; all I wanted was thanks and appreciation. But folks just took advantage. The more I helped them, the more they hated me.

"These people here don't have no conscience. The only thing

they wants is to keep the Negro down. I come to the conclusion that it wasn't no friendship that you could gain from the white people by tryin' to do what they say, or tryin' to obey their laws, and rules, or whatnot; one day I said, `Now, look, Steptoe, you must take a stand and try to gain the vote, that seems to be the importantest thing that you can do.'"

"Do you think these people will work with me?" I asked Steptoe. "Do you think they really want to register?"

"Oh, yes, they wants to redish. I know that they are very anxious to redish so they can vote."

"Okay then, if you think we'll be successful, I'll come back tomorrow at ten o'clock and go to church with you."

"Good. I'll be expectin' you."

Sunday morning we drove down to a small church where several of Steptoe's cousins were deacons. It was an old clapboard church with gingerbread trim and wooden benches for pews. The people clapped and A-mened and shouted "Yes, Jesus!" and "Praise the Lord!" to everything the preacher said. He got so pleased with himself he began to dance in place, the signal for everyone to stand up and dance and sing and make some glorious noise. After the service, Steptoe asked to speak; the preacher looked doubtful. Finally they let him make a plea for the voter registration school starting seven-thirty Monday morning at the Mount Pilgrim Church. I stood by the door and distributed leaflets as people left. Many had fear in their eyes, but still they reached out with eager hands.

The next morning we woke with the dawn and walked over to Mount Pilgrim, a tiny pine-board place that from the road probably looked like a chicken coop with a cross on the roof. I was filled with apprehension. What if nobody showed up? The appointed time came and went. Finally, around eight, the first car arrived, bringing five people. Then a few more cars, until the little church was filled. What a relief! They, too, were willing to take a stand.

I introduced myself, explained the purpose of the school, and for the rest of the morning, we worked on how to fill out the forms and answer questions about the state constitution. The class went well, I thought, but afterward Steptoe looked worried.

"What's wrong?" I asked. "Didn't you like the class?"

"It was lovely," he said. "It ain't that. Whilst you was teachin', the sheriff was watchin' from across the road. I saw him, but I didn't say nothin'."

"They would have been frightened."

"That's right. He was lookin' at tags, people's cars."

"How did he know we were here?"

"Someone from church."

"But they're your friends."

"There is always a Judas," Steptoe said sadly.

The next day the people came back, and the day after that, until we decided that three—an old man from the Tangipahoa community, Ernest Isaac, and two middle-aged women, Bertie Lee Hughes and Matilda Schoby—were ready to register to vote.

3

Liberty, the county seat of Amite, was a back-road farming community of about six hundred. The tree-shaded town square was distinguished by a white-brick courthouse from the 1820s with four massive square columns in front supporting a double-tiered set of porches and a small-windowed octagonal cupola on its shingled roof. Whoever built the courthouse had big plans. But even though Liberty was the home of Borden's Condensed Milk and Tichenor's Antiseptic and had been important enough to merit a raid during the Civil War, the town clearly had not prospered. In spite of its name, Liberty was a stringent, oppressive place whose spirit was epitomized by a remark that Tichenor, a Civil War doctor, made about his famous antiseptic: "All you need for our boys," he said, "but not one drop for the damn Yankees!"

Early the next morning, we set out for the courthouse. Mr. Isaac and the ladies were dressed in their Sunday best. The night before it had rained; misty haze hung over the House of Justice. A plaque on the front door proclaimed the town's motto: Liberty . . . it works.

It almost didn't work for us.

When we presented ourselves to the registrar, he looked up, stunned; then his face reddened.

"What do you want?" he demanded.

I stood aside, waiting for someone to speak, but all three were frozen with fear.

Finally, I broke the long silence.

"They would like to register."

"Who the Sam Hill are you?"

"My name is Bob Moses."

"Are you here to register too?"

"No. I am here to assist these people who would like to fill out registration forms."

"Is that right? Well, you'll have to wait."

He nodded toward a bench on the far wall, gave a sickly grin to someone standing in the doorway, then turned his back on us.

All day we waited. The sheriff, his deputies, people coming for tax assessments or driver's licenses, the whole town it seemed, gawked and gave us hate stares and muttered remarks. Not until late afternoon were the three, who hadn't had anything to eat all day, allowed to fill out the forms. As they struggled with the questionnaire, a highway patrolman entered, leaned back in a chair, and watched them go through the whole painstaking process. They smiled with satisfaction when they finished, but weren't surprised when the registrar, after a cursory glance at their answers, announced the results.

"None of you passed," he said. "The law says you gotta wait at least six months if you want to try again."

When we left the courthouse, the patrolman and one of the Liberty deputies followed. As we drove out of town, they pulled up close and tailed us down the road. Ernest Isaac's hands shook so badly on the steering wheel he could barely keep the car under control.

"I knowed we shouldn't oughta done this," he said.

"Slow down to the side," I said, "and let him pass."

The patrol car sped by, but only to make a U-turn, and then another, in order to follow us again. For about ten miles we crept down the highway with his car nosing our bumper until he flicked on his flashers and pulled us over.

"Get out of your car and come here," he ordered. Mr. Isaac gave me a forlorn look and did what he was told.

I walked over to provide moral support.

"What's the trouble?"

"Go back to your car," the patrolman said. "I'll let you know if I need you."

"I just want to know what the problem is."

"You're the problem, coming down here and stirring these people up."

"I only want to know why you stopped us."

"That's none of your business. Now get back in your car."

I took out a small pad and wrote down the information on their badges.

"What the hell do you think this is?" He threw open his door and grabbed me by the arm. "You're interfering with what I'm doing here."

He and the deputy manhandled me back to the car.

"Get in, nigger." He pressed one hand down on my head and shoved. "Follow me."

The justice of the peace held forth at his blacksmith shop on Highway 51 south of McComb. I was charged with interfering with an arrest.

"But I'm the only one you arrested," I pointed out.

They exchanged perturbed glances, then conferred in a corner.

"We're charging you with obstructing justice. Are you ready to stand trial?" the justice of the peace asked.

"Right now?"

"Yes."

"Can I make a phone call?"

"I guess you can. Where to?"

"Washington."

"Washington! Who the hell do you know in Washington?"

"John Doar, at the Civil Rights Division of the United States Department of Justice."

"You want to call *them* over a little thing like this? Boy, we can't afford to let you dial long distance."

"I'm calling collect."

"Collect!" the justice of the peace scoffed. "You can go right ahead and try."

The call went through; their faces dropped.

"It's a case of intimidation," I told John Doar, "in clear violation of the Civil Rights Acts of 1957 and 1960."

"Call the FBI collect," Doar told me, "and tell them the story too."

And so I did.

"Boy, you've sure got some friends," the deputy said. "Too bad they're all the way up there in Washington."

The trial was swift; I was guilty as charged.

"The fine is fifty dollars plus five in court costs," the justice of the peace said, "but I'll suspend the fine and charge you only court costs if you'll agree not to return to court for ninety days."

"I'm not guilty. I won't pay a penny."

"Boy, are you sure you know what you're about? You leave me no choice but to order that you be remanded to the Pike County Jail."

I stayed in jail two days while all of McComb talked about the "New York Negro" who was too stubborn to pay five dollars in court costs. I would have stayed in jail longer, but without my knowledge, Jack Young, an attorney for the NAACP, came down from Jackson and paid my fine and I was free.

The next morning I resumed the citizenship school at Mount Pilgrim Church.

By the following Tuesday, five people were ready and willing to go to the courthouse. They returned all smiles. Nothing had happened. But later that day we received word that the whites of

Liberty had held a secret meeting where they drew up a list of "uppity" blacks and vowed to kill me if I came to town.

4

The situation in Liberty was so tense, I didn't press anyone at citizenship classes to volunteer. But about a week later, Curtis Dawson, a dependable man whom Steptoe vouched for, and Reverend Alfred Knox, a powerfully built farmer and part-time preacher, said they were ready to register. If they had the courage, others would follow their example. Curtis Dawson picked me up at Steptoe's, and we drove to the Liberty courthouse, where Preacher Knox was supposed to be waiting. We didn't see him on the lawn, so we parked and looked around. We found him outside the post office, where he felt less conspicuous. We were walking back to the courthouse when suddenly three men strode across the street and blocked the sidewalk.

A big, burly man grabbed a fistful of my T-shirt and demanded, "Where do you think you're goin', nigger?"

"To the courthouse."

"Like hell you are," and he slugged me on the side of my head with the blunt end of a folded jackknife. Blood spurted from my scalp and ran down my face; I fell to my knees and threw up my hands to protect my skull.

"Leave him alone," Alfred Knox cried, reaching out to help. "Let him be."

"You stay out of this, uncle," one of the other men warned.

He clobbered me again on the top of the head and my face slammed the sidewalk. For a moment I felt as if my soul had ascended and I were a disembodied spirit hovering above with a bird's-eye view of my own beating. I watched what had been my body on the ground tuck up its legs and try to protect its groin. A man bent over the curled form, kicking and punching it until he was winded. Finally, he stepped back.

"Nigger," he panted, "you're leavin' town."

I watched the three men walk away.

Then I was back in my body, with a stabbing pain behind my eyes, while Alfred Knox pressed a large handkerchief to my head until the bleeding stopped.

"Come on," he said, helping me to my feet, "you've had enough for one day."

I stood as still as I could, waiting for the nausea to pass.

"No," I said. "I want to see the sheriff."

We crossed the courthouse lawn to the office of Sheriff E. L. Caston.

"I've been assaulted," I said. "I want you to swear out a warrant.

"Do you know who?"

"It was Billy Jack," Curtis Dawson volunteered.

"Billy Jack, you say?"

"Do you know him?" I asked.

"He's my first cousin." The sheriff put a hand up to his mouth to hide the smirk on his face. "If you want to waste your time filin' a complaint, go see the county prosecutor. I can't help you."

"Can I use your phone?"

"Can't help you there either. I'd advise you to get out of town and forget the whole thing."

Dawson, Knox, and I left the sheriff's office to the sound of snickers and a burst of laughter.

"What was so funny?" I asked as we stepped outside.

"You know those other two men?" Dawson explained. "One of them was Billy Jack's brother, and the other was the sheriff's son."

"Nice."

I found a phone booth across the street and asked the local operator to call the Justice Department; it seemed she couldn't make the connection. There was nothing to do but return to Steptoe's farm and lick my wounds. I wasn't about to let the black people of Liberty and McComb see me covered with blood.

When he heard our car rattling up the dirt drive, Steptoe came out of the barn carrying a pail of milk. He took one look at me and grimaced.

"Bob, is that you?"

"Don't worry," I said. "I'm not hurt that bad."

Unconvinced, he patted my shoulder, gazing at me with troubled eyes.

Two of his daughters came out of the house, saw my blood-soaked shirt and started screaming. They ran to their father, clutching him and crying, "Do something! Do something!"

Steptoe helped me off with my shirt and wrung the blood out, which made the girls gasp and cry harder. Then he led me to the kitchen, washed me off with a wet cloth, found a change of clothes, and drove me to the office of the only black doctor in McComb, who stitched me up while Steptoe wiped my face with his handkerchief.

Early the next morning, Steptoe approached me as I was dressing and looked apprehensively at the three bandages on my scalp.

"Bob," he asked with deep concern in his voice, "where are you goin'?"

"To Liberty."

"Bob, you can't go back there."

"I have work to do," I said. "There are people who are counting on me to help them register, and I need to see the county prosecutor."

"The people will understand," he said, "and the county prosecutor won't help you."

"It's something I have to do."

"Bob, listen to me. I know those people. Don't go back there. They will be expectin' you today. They will kill you up there today. Don't go."

"If I don't go back," I said, "I'm finished. They'll figure they've won. The people want to register; they're counting on my help."

"I don't want to see you dead."

"Look, don't worry. If anything happens to me, someone else will take my place."

"I feel like you're one of my own kids," Steptoe said with tears in his eyes and his voice choking. "You're just that close to me."

"I know," I said, putting my arms around him. "I'll be back."

In Liberty I told the county prosecutor I wanted to swear out a complaint against Billy Jack Caston for criminal assault. He looked at me as if my brains were oozing out from under my bandages. Then he explained that no Negro had ever done anything like that around there and that all I would probably accomplish would be to get myself killed, but he agreed to file a complaint and call the justice of the peace.

N. T. Bellue, a tottering, toothless old gent with watery eyes, showed up an hour later. When I told him I had filed assault and battery charges against Billy Jack Caston, his tobaccoless pipe nearly fell out of his mouth.

"I want a trial," I said. "I've got witnesses."

"You'll get one," he grumbled, tapping his cane for emphasis, "as soon as I eat my lunch."

Two hours later I brought Curtis Dawson and Alfred Knox into Liberty. Pickup trucks lined the town square; an angry crowd milled around on the courthouse lawn; the second-floor courtroom was packed with men brandishing shotguns to ensure that the niceties of southern justice were observed.

"Oooah, I never see so many peoples," Alfred Knox exclaimed. "This ain't good. This ain't a good sign at all."

Dawson, Knox, and I were kept in a back room and brought out one by one to tell our story to the six-man jury. By pressing my ear to the wall, I caught a part of Billy Jack's version: "We was just walkin' along when this brash nigger bumped me off the sidewalk. When I told him to watch where he was goin' he jumped into one of them Jap fightin' stances and forced me to defend myself."

While we waited for the verdict, some shots were fired outside.

"If I was you, I wouldn't stick around," the sheriff said. "Billy Jack is pretty well liked around here. Y'all better follow me out the back way."

The sheriff took us to our car and escorted us to the Amite County line. The next day the McComb paper read:

Court Acquits White Man On Negro Beating Charge.

"There's no turning back," I told a rally at the McComb Masonic Hall that evening. "We have to keep going down to the courthouse until we get our rights."

Tom Morton
Orientation

Oxford, Ohio

June 21–27, 1964

1

Oxford is one of those quaint college towns built by transplanted
New Englanders, which add a grace note to Ohio's endless farm-
lands, look-alike suburbs, and smokestack cities. The campus of
Western College for Women, two hundred acres of designed seren-
ity, was a landscaper's dream of woodlands, lawns, and gardens,
dramatically divided by an overgrown ravine spanned by a series of
stone footbridges. The main building, Peabody Hall, a U-shaped,
five-storied, cupola-crowned pile of brick and ivy, overlooked the
scene from its commanding hilltop. Lenny and I pulled off to the
side of the soft tar driveway and parked. Other than stalling at the
occasional red light, my Edsel had made the three-hundred-mile
catercorner jaunt across Ohio without incident. Crayoned arrows
on cardboard slabs directed us to a long table where name badges,
meal tickets, and room assignments were handed out, along with a
thick packet of info about the Summer Project.

Why had I chosen this way to spend my summer? Mississippi,
everyone agreed, was a nasty place, a hopeless case; it would be
a fool's errand to go there. My decision, no doubt, dated back
to the March on Washington, when, amid that straggling army
of shuffling feet, I had felt an overwhelming sense that biracial

brotherhood was no idle dream. As I was being pressed on all sides by strangers, it occurred to me that maybe being a lone individual was not what life was about: the important thing was to be part of mankind. I wanted the world to be a better place because I had passed through it. Then came the assassination of Kennedy. For days I sat in a daze in front of the TV, watching and rewatching. If anything seemed clear in that chaotic time, it was that the work Kennedy started had to be completed. I made my decision to join the Mississippi Summer Project one spring weekend when I stayed up half the night listening to a long interview Lenny's SNCC friend Hal Zizner had taped with Bob Moses. I was struck by his courage and resolution. While I was still seeking my identity, here was a person who knew what to do with his life. There was something compelling about a man named Moses walking into a town named Liberty where no one with a dark skin was free. I felt certain that he was doing what needed to be done, and I wanted to join him.

At the end of the registration table I was asked to sign over powers of attorney and pose for two pictures—one front, one side—with numbers propped under my chin. Lenny hummed a few bars of the *Dragnet* theme, but I didn't laugh. They even asked me to write down the name of my dentist.

"What's that for?" I asked Lenny. "My cavities can wait."

"Like if you were missing, they'd distribute your photo. But if they had to fish you out of some river . . ."

"That's grisly!" a girl said in a squeaky voice. "Don't even joke about it."

"I agree," I said. "Leave my body out of this."

Suddenly I felt a lump in my throat.

"Don't worry about Tom," Lenny said, trying to sound cheerful. "He can take it."

"I'm not so sure," I said. "As a fighter, I'm capable of boxing's first no-hitter."

"That's the whole point of nonviolence," a guy with pale blue eyes said. "We turn the other cheek."

His cheeks were too sunken to offer much of a target. He was as thin as a Giacometti stickman; one swift kick and he'd snap like a dry twig.

I wondered how much violence I *could* take. In high school there'd been the usual James Dean stuff. The guys from Poland would beat up the guys from Boardman and tell them to stay the hell out of their territory and leave our girls alone; the guys from Boardman would reciprocate. One night, after a sock hop, there was a near rumble outside our school. During the face-off, I positioned myself behind our champion shot-putter and hoped for the best. Luckily, some teachers broke it up. That only delayed the inevitable. The next night our corner gang (looking spiffy in their pegged pants, black leather jackets, and DA cuts) fought their corner gang to a draw on the Poland field. Belts and bicycle chains were the weapons of choice, and more than one guy was dragged face-first down the cinder track.

Lenny and I took our bags over to our dorm room in Clawson Hall and then joined a circle of people singing on the hillside in front of Kumler Chapel. Although my voice fit a frog pond better than a concert hall, I loved music. I had been brought up on droning Methodist hymns, deliberately pitched, it seemed, to constrict the vocal cords—only at Christmas did we achieve full-throated joy. Compared to that, even the corny crooners on *Lawrence Welk* and the bland renditions of the top twenty on *Your Hit Parade* sounded good. Our family felt genuine sadness when Rosemary Clooney signed off the show with *"So long for a while, That's all the songs for a while, So long for your hit parade, And the tunes that you picked to be played . . . "* Then came Elvis the Pelvis, rock 'n' roll was here to stay, and we no longer assembled around the TV. My sister and I were up in our rooms, portable record players at full blast, listening to our favorite singles.

In college, my taste ran to moody make-out music (Johnny Mathis, The Platters) and then to folk (The Kingston Trio, Bob Dylan, Joan Baez). In the evenings a group of us would troop down to the Hiram sugar camp in the woods, build a bonfire, sit in a circle, and sing "Come By Here" and "Michael, Row the Boat Ashore," feeling vague cause for celebration. We all knew the words by rote, so we sat on our beach towels and blankets in the middle of Ohio and sang along as if they represented our deepest beliefs.

This music was different. A heavyset black woman with a limp was leading a gathering of volunteers in "It Ain't No Crime to Have Our Minds on Freedom," and thanks to a few blacks among the hesitant whites, they were belting out enough soul force to make the walls of Poland Memorial Methodist come tumbling down.

Lenny gave me a nudge. "That's Fannie Lou Hamer."

I looked at her with new respect. Her sunken eyes and puffy cheeks confirmed what I had heard about how badly she'd been beaten in the Winona Jail.

"Now y'all gonna hafta sing bettern that," Mrs. Hamer said to us self-conscious whites. "They's gonna be times this summer when these songs is all we got to hold us together. And as we sing them this week, we better think hard about what they mean and about what we doin'. My daddy taught me that 'faith is the substance of things hoped for and the evidence of things not seen.' Now if we can love a God we don't see, then we had better learn how to love the neighbor we do. You got to understand we wasn't raised on hate but on love, and love is the onlyist thing we got to keep us goin'. Now first off, if y'all gonna sing, y'all gotta suck in some air and open yo mouths like you meant it. And for God's sake, white folks, don't just stand there. This here's a movement, so *move* yo bodies, clap yo hands, and come on now, sing with yo whole self."

We sang "Ain't Gonna Let Nobody Turn Me Around," "We'll Never Turn Back," and "O Freedom." With each song, I loosened up a little more, gaining tone and volume and rhythm, but I couldn't get the knack of how to clap. We whites tended to clap on the first and third beats, the *on* beats of every measure. Blacks preferred the second and fourth beats. Looking around the circle, I could see most of the white hands clapping together to the opposite beat from the black hands. But what we white students lacked in skill we began to make up in enthusiasm. By the time we got to "Go Tell It on the Mountain," a song I thought I already knew, they probably could hear us over on the Miami University campus a half-mile away.

"That's more like it," Mrs. Hamer said, her perspiration-drenched face breaking out in a smile. "Let's sing it again."

> *"Who's that yonder dressed in black?*
> *Let my people go.*
> *Must be the hypocrites turning back . . ."*

The second time around, she improvised a few lines:

> *"Who's that yonder dressed in red?*
> *Let my people go.*
> *Look like the children Bob Moses led.*
> *Let my people go.*
> *Go tell it on the mountain, over the hills and everywhere,*
> *Go tell it on the mountain, to let my people go."*

I felt proud to be one of the people who knew who Bob Moses was.

At dinner Lenny and I took a table near the end of the cafeteria line. I wanted to inspect the troops one by one, trying to guess by their looks and dress their politics and where they were from. At first glance they seemed to break down into bearded beatniks and sandaled radicals from both coasts and wholesome homebaked liberals from the Midwest. On closer scrutiny and after a few conversations, my off-the-cuff categories didn't always fit. One storm-the-Bastille type, with the black-blended eyebrows of a satyr, itching, no doubt, to regurgitate half-chewed hunks of dialectic, proved to be a swimming instructor from Muncie, Indiana. And a sandy-haired kid with an ear-to-ear, *What, me worry?* grin was a community organizer from Newark, New Jersey, who had already been arrested five times. And what, for example, to make of me, with my butch-waxed flattop and Rod Laver tennis shoes, my brand new blue jeans and freshly washed Maynard G. Krebs sweatshirt, hacked off at the elbows and honeycombed with holes? Actually, most of the guys were clean-cut, wearing sports shirts and pressed chinos. The Dean's List; Who's-Who-on-Campus set.

"I don't see as many weirdos as I thought I would," Lenny observed.

"You could be lonely."

"Up yours. What do you think of the chicks?"

"I'm still looking."

There were a lot of pert pretty types, all bounce and curls, whose exuberance gave them an inner glow. Equally prevalent were thin, spiritual girls with circles under their eyes and prim, pinched mouths that looked as if they were tasting one of life's bitter pills. Several had tense, fervid faces and spoke with shrill petulance. Here and there I spotted someone special—a tall blonde with a majorette's muscle tone and a jaunty stride; her sandals and sack dress in their simplicity stressing her lean legs and high breasts; long wisps of crispy hair half-hid her face.

"She looks like Connie Stevens."

"Everybody prefers blondes," Lenny said. "Look for somebody who couldn't be from Poland, Ohio."

"How about that one over there?"

I nodded toward a shapely girl with a glorious mass of thick dark curls that fell halfway down her back. She was wearing hoop earrings, an embroidered Mexican blouse, a thin skirt that clung to her hips, and clogs. Her black, lustrous eyes had an intense expectant look, while her lips held a moody pout that seemed to be the prelude to a smile.

"She looks Mediterranean," Lenny said. "Probably Jewish."

"That body could sure set Solomon to singing."

"You're not the only one who thinks so. Don't turn around right away."

I slowly shifted in my chair and glanced back. I had been so busy ogling the student volunteers I had forgotten all about the

SNCC staff. Several of the men were clustered at the table behind us, looking stern and formidable in their blue denim jackets and black boots. One, with the chipped-flint face of an Iroquois warrior and the wide go-to-hell mouth of a hipster, began to whisper heavily: "Oh, baby, if you were mine, I'd stroke you like velvet and sip you like wine!"

That brought a general chuckle, but also a warning from somebody at the table to drop the subject.

"Where have they been hiding?"

"They've been here all along," Lenny said. "You just haven't been noticing."

"Invisible men, right?"

"Check out where they're sitting?"

"Over in the corner. So what?"

Alexander Dining Hall, Lenny pointed out, was actually circular. There weren't any true corners. "Look again," he insisted.

"They're over against the wall. I don't get it."

"This room is almost all windows," Lenny explained. "That's the only place where they can cover their flanks and keep an eye on the door."

"But that's paranoid; this is Ohio."

"There's nothing paranoid about thinking people are trying to kill you when people really are trying to kill you."

What must it be like, I wondered, *to live every day on the razor's edge?*

At seven-thirty that evening in Leonard Hall there was an "optional" session addressing the question "Why go to Mississippi?" The three-hundred-seat auditorium—which had no air-conditioning—was packed with sweating volunteers who didn't let the heat stifle their enthusiasm. Bruce Hanson of the National Council of Churches opened the meeting with a refrain we would hear all week: "If anybody doesn't want to go to Mississippi, they are free to leave." He went on to announce that the first contingent of volunteers, who left Oxford the day before, had reached Mississippi without incident.

Then Vincent Harding, a stocky, bespectacled black man who was both a scholar and a Mennonite missionary, came forward to lead the discussion. He spoke with thoughtful compassion, instantly establishing a tone that made it clear he considered us neither heroes nor fools, but serious people engaged in serious business that required total honesty, discipline, and commitment on our part.

"You can consider what you are doing in two ways," he said. "You can see yourselves as an 'in group' trying to help an 'out group' enjoy the dubious pleasures of middle-class life, or you can see yourselves as outsiders, seeking the basic restructuring of society. Are we Ins or Outs? Do we want liberal reforms or basic change?"

Several volunteers took this as in invitation to stand up and testify.

"I can't sit idly by," one said, "knowing that injustice exists. I cannot merely be concerned; I must also be effective. Empathy without action is impotent."

Then the striking Jewish girl I'd noticed at dinner spoke out: "There's not enough justice and not enough liberty. There's not enough truth and not enough beauty. Who will work for these things? It's everybody's job."

"The fight for civil rights is our fight," a well-tanned guy in a flowered shirt said. "We must combat racism as our parents combated Hitler. There is a moral wave building for this generation, and I mean to catch it."

"Very well-spoken," Harding interjected. "We were wondering what kind of kooks would be crazy enough to spend a summer in Mississippi, but you appear to be people of sensitivity and intelligence."

We volunteers, who obviously thrived on praise, beamed.

"But I wonder," Harding added, "whether your big words and fine sentiments will be enough. How will you enter into humanizing relationship with the people of Mississippi? It is hard sometimes for those of us who have had an education, who *believe* in education, to realize that education might not do it."

"That's right," a goateed volunteer asserted. "Schools aren't the answer. This is a political question. The whole damn country has gone to hell, and we've got to overthrow the system to save it."

Harding glanced with a hint of disdain at the earnest young man.

"Some of us believe in education and some of us in politics," he said coolly.

"I don't want to know why you're coming," Fannie Lou Hamer said, "but I do wonder what took you so long. I'm just thankful you're here."

After that we stood up, crossed arms and gripped hands, and sang "We Shall Overcome." Each stanza—*"black and white together," "we'll walk hand in hand," "we are not afraid"*—tolled in me like a bell and filled me with a sense of conviction that I couldn't possibly have mustered on my own.

Later that evening about a dozen of us gathered in a dorm room to down a few beers and discuss the big questions. At first, we steered clear of what awaited us in Mississippi, foraging instead through a smorgasbord of topics: Can stateways change folkways? Would you rather be red than dead? ("Hell yes!" from the back of the room.) What did Bob Dylan's lyrics mean? Who made the best foreign films? (I was torn between Fellini's peacock splendor and Bergman's fiordic angst.) Where have you hitchhiked to? (I once thumbed a ride to Lake Placid in a hearse.) Who makes the best car? (I knew who made the worst.) Who's going to win the pennant? (The Indians of course.) What was your first political act? (When I was ten, I ripped down my neighbor's Taft sign and replaced it with my own hand-drawn "I Like Ike" sign.) What was your first protest? (On May 2, 1960, I stood up in my high school civics class at the moment Caryl Chessman was executed.)

Meanwhile, Lenny sat glumly in a corner getting a good buzz on. When someone brought up the Cuban Missile Crisis, he suddenly broke in.

"I thought it was great," he announced. "I told my girl, 'Darling, we haven't much time,' or words to that effect, and bingo, I was home free. I could stand a crisis like that every weekend."

"You're so cynical; I don't understand why you're here."

I looked over. It was the same sepulchral beanpole who had given us a homily earlier in the afternoon.

"My palm reader told me I was going to live a long and purposeless life," Lenny drawled out of the corner of his mouth. "I want to prove her wrong."

As if to clear the air of Lenny's sarcasm, people began making self-righteous statements about why they were going to Mississippi. Everybody was spouting position papers and reciting received ideas as if this were a senior seminar. I think we assumed in our well-intentioned souls that our erudition and idealism would somehow save us when we went South: we were too good to kill.

2

A light-brown man of medium height in a dazzlingly white T-shirt and freshly pressed bib overalls walked slowly to the front and mounted the stage. This could only be Bob Moses. He spoke in a voice soft as mist. "Mississippi is unreal when you're not there." He paused a long while before he added, "And when you're there, the rest of the world is unreal."

He took a piece of chalk and drew a crude map of Mississippi on the blackboard, adding a crescent line to mark off the northwest corner.

"This is the Delta," he said. "And here is Mrs. Hamer's Sunflower County, which is also the home of Senator Eastland and the place where the White Citizen's Council originated."

Moses marked the spot in the center of the Delta with a square. Then he added a dot and labeled it "Greenwood."

To the right of the Delta, in the northeastern part of the state, Moses indicated there were fewer Negroes, little industry, the moderating influence of the TVA, and, therefore, less threat. The most dangerous area was the southwestern part of the state. In contrast to the Delta, with its plantations and last vestiges of aristocracy, the Klan ruled supreme in the hill country.

Moses chalked a large-lettered "KKK" in the lower, left corner of his map and made dots for Liberty and McComb. Since the March on Washington, he said, this area had been undergoing a reign of terror.

"The situation there," he stated solemnly, "is one of guerrilla warfare. If the country realizes that fact, then the federal government has to act. We have to make this nation face up to the reality that the struggle going on there is pressing and crucial. When we tried to speak to President Johnson about Mississippi, we were told he was busy with Vietnam."

While Moses was speaking with calm deliberation, I took advantage of my front-row seat to scrutinize him closely. He was lean and muscular, by no means frail, and he stood up straight, shoulders back, so that he looked taller than he was. At first I found his heavy, black farmer's boots and bib overalls incongruous with his horn-rimmed glasses and scholarly air, but the thoughtful assurance of his voice and the forthright dignity of his presence made everything fit. His face was a study in contrasts. He had a strong jaw, not protruding, but firm and defined; a well-shaped, sensuous mouth; and thick, dark eyebrows—all suggestive of a down-to-earth, realistic stance. On the other hand, his large, tranquil eyes seemed to see beyond, into the far distance. His high forehead and elongated skull, slightly tapered at the top, conveyed something mystical and otherworldly. When he spoke, he drew up from a deep inner well the distillate of his thought, uttering each carefully considered word as if it were a separate decision. His prophetic aura held me in thrall. And yet there was a sad beauty in his face that was almost childlike, reminding me of a bright, sensitive kid who is lost.

"When you come South," Moses said, "you bring the rest of the country with you. You bring their concern, which usually doesn't extend to Negroes. To accomplish something very real, we are going to try to do something very limited. Don't expect big results. If we all go and come back alive, that will be an important accomplishment. If we can simply talk to Negroes and stay in their homes, that will be a huge job. We won't engage in direct action— no sit-ins—nor will we encourage local people to do so. There's no point in integrating a lunch counter if you can't afford a hamburger. But we *are* willing to risk our lives so that Negroes can receive a better education and participate in free elections. Mississippi has been called a closed society. It is more than that; it is a padlocked police state. We think the key to opening it is the vote."

As Moses laid down the basic ground rules for the summer, I scanned the faces of my fellow volunteers until I saw the dark-haired girl who caught my eye the day before. When she saw me look her way, I tried out my best trouble-is-my-business smile, but I don't think she bought it.

"We will not allow any staff members or volunteers to carry a weapon," Moses stressed. "This is absolutely bedrock. If the police thought we were armed, they would simply use that as an excuse to murder us."

He gave us a hypothetical case:

"What would you do if you were in a farmhouse under attack and the owner, firing back in self-defense, had been shot, and his children were crying for help? You can't walk away, say 'I'm nonviolent,' and find out what happened the next morning. You have to be a part of it. You'd have to make an on-the-spot decision. Should you pick up the gun? If you do, you violate our commitment to nonviolence; if you don't, you leave yourself and the children exposed. What should you do? I can't answer that. There is no clear answer. What I can say is be cautious, avoid arrest. The work we're doing can't be done in jail—or in the grave."

I tried to picture what I would do in those circumstances. It was all too easy for me to simulate the fear I would feel, but what decisions would I make? How would I act? Would I meet the test?

"I see an analogy in Camus's *The Plague* to what is happening in this country," Moses continued. "The sickness pervades the whole society, but nobody will admit it. We are all victims of the plague of prejudice, but we refuse to diagnose our symptoms because recognition would make action necessary. Unless we have the courage and lucidity to face facts and openly and honestly discuss our own racism, the Summer Project could blow up in our faces. And unless this country . . ."

At that point Moses broke off in midsentence; one of the SNCC staff was motioning to him from the side of the stage. Moses walked over, bending down on one knee to hear what the man was urgently whispering. He remained there for a moment, rocking gently back and forth, then he rose wearily to his feet and stood silently before us, shrouded in thought. Finally, he looked up and spoke in a flat, inflectionless voice.

"Yesterday morning, three of our people left Meridian, Mississippi, to investigate a church bombing in Neshoba County. They haven't come back, and we haven't had any word from them. We spoke to John Doar in the Justice Department. He promised to order the FBI to act, but the local FBI claims they've been given no authority."

Moses paused, absorbed in his own brooding.

Waves of shock and dismay swept the auditorium. Who was missing? Where was Neshoba? Are they already dead? Do they mean to kill us all? I sat stunned in my chair, paralyzed by a sudden surge of sheer terror.

A frail, birdlike woman in a sleeveless blouse and cutoff blue jeans took the stage. Her thin face was pale and distraught, and she fidgeted constantly with the filter tip in her hand, but her voice was composed.

"My husband, Michael Schwerner; a fellow CORE worker, James Chaney, of Meridian; and a Summer Project volunteer, Andrew Goodman, of New York, have to all-present knowledge 'disappeared' on a mission to investigate a church burning in Neshoba County. A thorough check of all jails and hospitals produced no clue. Our appeals to local and federal officials—the FBI and the Justice Department—have been in vain. We were told the matter is 'out of the province' of federal concern. The Mississippi State Patrol told us bluntly, 'Why should we care?' Finally, at seven o'clock this morning, we were told by the jailor's wife in Philadelphia, Mississippi, that the three were arrested for speeding Sunday afternoon and released at 6:00 P.M. after paying a fine. Sheriff Rainey has confirmed that his deputy, Cecil Price, made the arrest and saw them leave town."

Rita Schwerner then went to the blackboard and wrote the names of the missing men over the map Moses had drawn of Mississippi.

> *James Chaney–CORE staff*
> *Michael Schwerner–CORE staff*
> *Andrew Goodman–Summer Project Volunteer*
> *Neshoba County–Disappeared*

"Go wire your congressman to do something," she pleaded. "Demand that the FBI start searching for these men. Even though we have contacted them repeatedly, so far they've done nothing. If we can get some action from these law enforcement officials, there is still hope."

Moses came back and said a few words about how crucial the first twenty-four hours were. We then broke up into groups according to states. In a daze, I drafted telegrams to Ohio legislators while I wished I were back in my room packing my bags. *This is a mistake,* my brain kept telling me. *Leave now or you will die.* All around me people were cursing and vowing a little too loudly that they were undaunted and more determined than ever to go.

As I walked across the campus on my way to the Western Union office on High Street, I saw Moses, sitting alone on the steps of the dining hall. When I returned an hour later, he was still there, lost in polar solitudes.

At lunch I picked at my food like most of my companions. Cigarette smoke hung in the room as thickly as storm clouds. Everybody talked about the disappearance, but nobody seemed to have any new information.

"Why won't they tell us anything?" the girl sitting across from me asked. I could see her lips quivering.

"I don't think they know very much," I said.

"But I heard they were up all night calling people in Mississippi," she replied. "They must know more than they're saying."

I glanced over to where the SNCC staff were gathered at one long table.

"I knew it was going to be bad," I said, "but I didn't think it would be this bad."

"Cheer up," Lenny chipped in. "The worst is yet to come."

Nobody laughed.

At two o'clock I went to a large meeting on the Freedom Schools. The person in charge was distant and disorganized, and everyone's mind was on the missing civil rights workers anyway. Afterward we received our assignments. Lenny and I were being sent to McComb.

I broke out into a cold sweat and headed for the bathroom.

Our group was already gathered in a semicircle under a large sycamore tree near the chapel. Among the dozen volunteers I immediately recognized the girl I had noticed the day before at dinner. Our project director, leaning back against the tree trunk with his legs stretched out in front of him, was the man who had also had his eye on her.

"I see you're already on CPT," he said to me as soon as I sat down.

"I'm a little late," I apologized. "I didn't catch what you said."

"That's 'colored people's time,'" he replied sardonically, giving me a granite look. "Why don't y'all say who you are?"

The girl was Esther Rappaport.

"My name is Raymond Fleetwood," he continued after the introductions, "but my friends call me 'Feelgood.' We ain't friends yet, but you can call me Feelgood too. Now listen up, we got things to discuss. I know y'all are scared because of what happened, but I want you to calm down and cool yourselves 'cause they's a lot of people those crackers plan to kill before they get around to you. To survive this summer, we're gonna hafta learn to love each other. Now that'll be real easy for you, 'cause I'm very loveable." He paused a moment to smile a splintered smile, which exposed a chipped front tooth. "But it's gonna be a lot harder for me, you dig, because I was brought up to hate whites. Down South the people that've been beatin' on me and abusin' my people has all got white faces just like yours, so if you want to work with me, you're gonna have to make your position very clear. I won't trust you an inch until you show me why I should."

"If we didn't care," Esther said, "we wouldn't be here."

"That's right," another volunteer added. "I'm more determined to go to Mississippi than ever."

"What's happened proves that something needs to be done," I forced myself to say.

"Babies, don't run those numbers on me," Feelgood said. "You honkies is all the same; y'all talk a better game than you play. You got a hole in your soul, so you goin' South to be with black folks so you can put a little soul in the hole. You think it's gonna be a 'rewardin' experience,' or some such jive. Listen, I've lived in both the North and the South, and you just don't know the score. You don't know how those peckerwoods think. I do. They haul you to jail, strip you, lay you on the cement floor, and ask you silly questions, and then they beat you and beat you until you're most dead. You think you're livin' in a democracy? Y'all dreamin'. This is a kill or be-killed country."

"I was told to expect violence," Esther said, "and I certainly do expect it, but I have no concept of violence—I've never known any."

"Well now, that makes you very fortunate, don't it?" Feelgood looked at all of us with bemusement. "Where have you folks been all your lives?"

"In schools," I answered for all of us with a guilty smile.

"How many black people in the South, do you think, don't know about violence?"

"None," I replied.

"That's right. And, babies, that's why y'all gonna need more than a summer to know what's happenin'. It wasn't my idea to bring in a bunch of honkies who don't know where it's at. Go down, Bob Moses, and such jive, that ain't my kinda tune, man. Do you know what it takes to understand what it means to be black?" Feelgood asked me directly.

"No."

"A life and a death—that's what."

Feelgood fell into a morose silence.

"All of us are apprehensive," Esther said. "Who wouldn't be? But we want to balance our fears against the good we think we can do. We want to hope for the best, but be prepared for the worst. Can't you give us specific examples of what we may be in for?"

"You're 'apprehensive'; you want 'specific examples.' Babies, y'all too much." Feelgood ran his falcon's gaze over the whole group, but his eyes lingered on Esther, as if he were trying to estimate the impression he was making on her. "I'll tell you what it's like to be in the 'hot box.' Will that be specific enough for you?"

"Yes."

"Me and Luvahn Brown got sent to the county farm for sittin' on the white side at the county courthouse in Jackson. When we got to the farm, they signed us in as 'Freedom Riders' and issued us striped uniforms, not the T-shirt and blue overalls the other prisoners was wearin'. We were put in the maximum security cell. The next morning the warden calls us out and tells us the rules. He says, 'When I tell you to do something, you do it. If I say grab a hoe, you get it. If I say grab a slang blade, you get it. You some of those smart niggers who tryin' to change things, but if you talk back to me, I'll take you behind the barn and give you a fist beatin' you won't forget. You see these other niggers here? They'll beat you, too, if I tell them. They're in here for decent crimes like bootleggin' and robbery.' He asked them if he should beat us, but they said they thought we'd be all right.

"Then they loaded us in a truck and put us to work clearin' a road. We were movin' logs, two men to a log, but the guard told me to move one by myself. I tried and I couldn't. 'You damn nigger,' he says, 'move that log.' He hit me with a leather strap across the face; then he says, 'Peewee, cut me a stick.' He come back with a stick about two inches thick and four feet long. He told Peewee and another prisoner to pull down my pants and hold my arms. Then he started wackin' me as hard as he could on my back and thighs. After he let me up, he pulled out his gun and pointed it at my face. 'Have you got anything to say to me, nigger?' he says, 'Cause I ain't done with you yet.'

"When we returned, he told the warden, 'I'd like to wrap my strap around this damn nigger's neck.' 'We got a place for smart niggers,' the warden says. 'Put him in the sweat box.' They took me to a hole in the ground, about nine feet by twelve feet, with a steel door and no window. 'What did I do?' I asked. They said, 'Nigger, just shut up, pull off your clothes, and get in.' It must have been a hundred and twenty degrees; the walls and ceiling dripped. It was pitch-black; the only time I saw a light was three times a day when they brought me bread and water. They left me in that slimy shit hole for over a week. If one of our lawyers hadn't found out where I was, I would've been a dead man. That's Mississippi for you, babies. They'll kill you for just nuthin'."

I stared at Feelgood, wondering if I could survive an ordeal like that. It was one thing to hear about atrocities on television, another to be told about them face-to-face.

"Do you think this Summer Project will make a difference?" I asked.

"If we really pulled off something big," Feelgood said with a sarcastic curl to his lip, "like if some of you babies was to die, that might do it, that might crack Mississippi wide open."

"I don't see why anyone has to die," Esther said, "to achieve something so basic as the right to vote."

"Babies," Feelgood said, "you don't see a lot of things, but you will."

I was lying in bed thinking about the harrowing events of the day and debating whether I should go or stay when Lenny showed up with Hal Zizner. He had been at the SNCC office in Atlanta and was furious at the FBI for not investigating the instant they learned that the three were missing.

"As far as I know," he said, "they still aren't on the case. And now it's too late."

"Why do you say that?"

I knew that the troubled look on Lenny's face mirrored my own.

"Because this morning the jailor's wife said the three had been arrested for speeding, fined twenty bucks, and released at six o'clock. But this afternoon we learned that they were released at ten and were last seen heading south on Route 19 toward Meridian."

"I thought they called the Philadelphia Jail late Sunday afternoon," I said.

"They did. That's one of the things that looks bad. You see the picture?"

"When does it get dark in Mississippi?" I asked.

"Between eight and nine."

"Why didn't they contact Meridian?" Lenny asked. "Aren't you allowed one phone call?"

"You are if they let you."

"So it was a setup," I said, finally seeing what Hal saw, "and the police were involved."

"Somebody tipped the cops off," Hal said. "The speeding charge was obviously trumped up. They held them until dark, took them to a concealed place, and killed them. They probably dumped the bodies in the Pearl River."

Hal's account, with its grim matter-of-factness, chilled my heart.

"Then there's no hope," I said.

"They never had a chance. When that church was burned, the FBI should have known something was up—the bastards."

Hal's anger undercut my resolve. I had assumed the FBI would provide federal protection; I hadn't realized that they simply didn't care.

"In Mississippi they're saying it's a hoax," Hal continued. "That our three guys are probably sipping Cuba Libres on Castro's patio in Havanna."

"What do we do now?" I asked.

"Now we've got to find the bodies. A bunch of us are driving down tonight to start searching. If we don't, they'll deny and deny and deny. You wouldn't believe how deluded those people are. You know the joke, 'What's got four eyes but can't see?' 'Mississippi.'"

"I wouldn't tell the other volunteers what I just told you," Hal added. "We don't want people to panic."

"Tom here is already nervous enough to be Anthony Perkins's understudy."

"I'm scared shitless," I admitted. "Do you know where Lenny and I are being sent? McComb."

"I won't kid you, McComb's rough," Hal said, "but I don't anticipate some kind of bloodbath. The power elite in Mississippi doesn't want violence; they're into the politics of 'let's pretend': Let's pretend there isn't any problem and there won't be one. It's the rednecks in the hick towns we've got to worry about."

"Aren't there a lot of them?" I asked.

"Enough. But if we can find the bodies and show the world what a hellhole Mississippi is, some of these crackers might have second thoughts. It's a terrible thing to say, but you two might be safer because those three guys are dead."

"I'm not sure I have the guts to go through with this," I said. "I'm scared of the high dive; how am I going to cope with Mississippi?"

"Listen, we're all afraid," Hal admitted, "but we can't let them kill the whole Summer Project. This is important. We can't back down now. Nobody is safe. You could be walking along a sidewalk in your home town and get killed by a flying hubcap. Once you understand that, you'll know what it means to put your body on the line. What do you want to do with your life: major in history or make history?"

I thought I'd rather take my chances with flying hubcaps, but Hal's mentioning of history brought me back to the reasons I had decided to go to Mississippi in the first place. Somehow, I had to find within myself the courage to be like Bob Moses.

3

I was congratulating myself on the return of my appetite at dinner Tuesday evening when Bob Moses came to the microphone with ominous news:

"Two Choctaw Indians spotted the station wagon about thirteen miles northwest of Philadelphia. It had been doused with gasoline and burned down to the frame and hidden off the highway near the Bogue Chitto Swamp. Some footprints were found leading away from the car, but there was no sign of the three boys. Robert Kennedy has invoked the Lindbergh Law, ordering the FBI to treat the disappearance as a kidnapping. Agents are now on the scene, and they plan to begin a full search tomorrow. We fear they may be too late."

My heart started pounding and a prickling sensation ran up my arms while the room broke into heated discussion. My unfocused fears had been replaced by specific terrors: a burned car, a fetid swamp.

"I thought they were last seen heading south," I said to Lenny.

"They were lying," Lenny responded glumly. "Remember what Hal said. They probably never got to head anywhere at all."

After dinner I joined our Freedom School group for a rambling discussion of our duties once we got to McComb. Whatever Feelgood's merits were as a project director, it was clear to me that organization was not one of them. He would skip from topic to topic and suddenly fall into a long silence that left me hanging. Unlike Moses, whose silences were always meditations, Feelgood would simply slip into a heavy funk. I sat beside Esther, breathing in the fragrance of dusky hair.

I fell into step with her after the session, and we began to walk and talk, eventually sitting together in a small, stone gazebo outside the chapel. She seemed to like the stories I told about growing up in Ohio and going to Hiram College. Her life had been remarkably different.

"I'm a red-diaper baby," she said. "My parents were leftists. And I mean *were*, at least in the case of my mother. It was a classic Lower East Side story—pushcart peddler meets sweatshop seamstress. When my mother married my father, she was a Trotskyite, totally committed to the working class, a corned-beef-and-cabbage person. Now her idea of lunch is champagne and oysters. She thinks Las Vegas is the most fabulous place on earth."

"I think it's a waste of electricity," I said, and Esther laughed in agreement.

I told her about growing up during the Mafia wars of the fifties, when Youngstown was called "Little Chicago" and gangland bombings and murders were common.

"When I was about ten, the Mafia shot a man on my street. One morning he stepped out his backdoor to go to work, and a sniper was waiting for him on the garage roof. I remember I ran down and looked at the house when I heard the news. The police and the ambulance had already come and gone, but I was curious, so I walked up the driveway. What I saw on the blacktop by the garage was a chalked outline of the body and a pool of blood. At that moment, a woman came out of the house (she didn't see me), connected up the garden hose as if she were going to water the flowers, and began to hose the blood down the drain in the center of the driveway."

"I suppose that's what it means to be a Mafia wife," Esther said.

"We probably shouldn't be talking about such gruesome stuff. I can't sleep as it is."

"We're all afraid. Now with those three guys missing, it's even harder to admit how afraid we really are."

"I know what you mean," I said. Somehow, acknowledging my

fear made it seem less terrible, and if Esther had the courage to go, I did too.

"I had a truly bizarre nightmare last night. It was so scary." Esther hesitated a moment. "I took a long kitchen knife and slashed two tires. Suddenly there was an ugly man there with bony hands who had a longer knife, and he slashed all four tires on our family Mercedes. I was furious, so I ran to my mother screaming, 'I only slashed two tires and he slashed four!' and I held up four fingers for emphasis. 'In this life,' my mother said in an absolutely calm and controlled voice, 'we must expect retribution.' At that moment I looked out the window and I saw the man slash his stomach open. . . . Then I woke up."

"I wonder what Freud would make of that."

"Oh God," Esther cried, "don't tell me. I hadn't even thought of it in those terms. It was just so terrifying!"

"How come your mom isn't political anymore?"

"Money. It's that simple. They made too much of it. She and my father used to do things, now they just discuss them. They think politics is a spectator sport; I think it's acting on your beliefs."

"What does your father do?"

"He's in advertising. You know that line for Playtex: *lasting stretch that won't wash out?* That's his. He still subscribes to the *I.F. Stone Weekly* and gets angry when he watches the evening news. He's big on cause and effect. If you do this, then that will happen, especially in terms of politics. My father still talks a good line, but what has he ever done? He thinks if he nods to the doorman, he's done his duty by the workingman."

"Do you think going to Mississippi will change things? Before I came here, I thought for sure it would, but the more I learn about how bad it is, the more doubts I have."

"I feel sure that going to Mississippi will change *me*. Someday I'd like to be a mother—I'm really curious to know what having a baby is like—but right now I want to give birth to my self—I want

Tom Morton

to be a new woman, a new direction, a start at something better. I want to become what I truly am. Feelgood's right about white people having a hole in their soul. People see their imperfections as holes, and they try to fill those holes with another person. But we need to make ourselves whole."

"What do you think about Feelgood?" I blurted out.

"Why do you ask?"

"I don't know; I saw him watching you."

"He's not the only one," Esther said, smiling over at me.

"Oh," I responded with a guilty laugh. "I guess the question is, 'Has anyone ever *not* told you that you're beautiful?'"

"Lots of people, but thanks. I don't see my body as so great. I just walk around in it. The only thing I like about my looks are my eyes."

"I wouldn't touch a thing."

"Oh, wouldn't you?" Esther broke into a throaty cackle.

"Feelgood has demons," she remarked, returning to my question. "He's been through a lot. All those SNCC guys have experienced incredible things. They are terrifically interesting, much more exciting than anybody I met in college. They aren't afraid to show their feelings, to laugh, cry, shout, sing. They don't just sit back and label life; they go out and confront it. That's what I want to do, too: I want to live with people who have solved some of life's simple problems. I've never felt so vitally alive as I have these past few days. This may sound crazy, but I think the fear adds to the experience."

I longed to kiss her and make that her next experience, but clearly her mind was elsewhere. We sat in silence for a while, watching fireflies flicker in the ravine. Then we stood up and hugged.

"You're a good listener," she said, smiling up at me. "I can tell that you're one of those people who remembers and mulls over everything they hear."

"Only if it's interesting."

"Well, don't think about things too much. Get some sleep."

4

After a night of tossing and turning to horrendous dreams—complete with poisonous snakes, quicksand swamps, and sadistic sheriffs—I welcomed James Lawson's topic for Wednesday morning: nonviolence. But his presentation left me cold. Although he was thoughtful and articulate, there was something aloof, pedantic, and off-putting about his manner. He was a mystical idealist who used abstract words as if they had absolute meanings. Listening to him, I was reminded of an anecdote Abe Ravitz, my American lit professor at Hiram, once told me: when Melville read one of Emerson's more vaporous essays, he felt impelled to scrawl in the margin "To one who has weathered Cape Horn as a common sailor, what stuff is all this!" Rather than being inspired by the philosophical underpinnings of nonviolence, I felt superior to its unrealistic expectations.

The early Christians in the catacombs may have kept their spirits clean, I thought, *but did the lions in the arena appreciate their accomplishment?* I didn't like the idea of nonviolence as a tactic to provoke white violence, shock the nation, and create a crisis only the federal government could resolve—that made us victims of the very mass culture I was in revolt against. Just because the media had become jaded and responded only to blood, did that mean that I had to bleed? Impulsively, I stood up and stated a part of my inner debate: "If putting my body on the line will make this a better world," I said, "I'm ready to do that. I just don't want my sacrifice to be in vain."

There was a long silence. Finally, from the back of the room, came Moses's slow, soothing voice. As usual, he had the last word:

"Politics without morality is chaos, and morality without politics is irrelevant. You must understand that nonviolence is essential to our program this summer. It is academic whether you embrace nonviolence philosophically or not. But if you are going to work in Mississippi with us, you must be prepared to accept the ground rules. Whatever your reservations may be in this, you can only act nonviolently in the Movement. If you can't accept this, please don't come with us. In the end, you see, everybody has to live together. In the end, Negroes and whites will share the land, and the less overlay of bitterness, the more possible an accommodation. I think nonviolence leaves the door open to reconciliation."

Hal had advised Lenny and me to go into town and buy some bib overalls and a denim jacket—the kind Bob Moses wore—to prepare us for Mississippi. He said the SNCC outfit wasn't just for show, but it also offered good protection if a cop took a notion to drag you down the street.

We all gathered on the grass behind one of the dorms to be instructed in security precautions, role-playing situations, and passive resistance. James Forman, the executive secretary of SNCC, was in charge. He calmly smoked his pipe as he issued multiple warnings about the dangers we faced. His instructions were daunting in their completeness, ranging from the normal precautions of locking doors and watching for suspicious cars to telling the men to shave their beards if they didn't want them pulled out hair by hair and the women not to wear earrings if they didn't want their earlobes torn.

Then we broke into small groups and acted out more complex scenarios. The SNCC staff played their roles in these situations to the hilt, falling instantly into character—from Klansman to sharecropper—and making the scene come unnervingly alive. For them, this was no mere exercise in stereotyping and melodrama. We volunteers, on the other hand, could only grope in the dark and try to imagine what we might do or say.

In one, Feelgood, as a jailor, grabbed me by the collar and shoved me into a cell with four SNCC guys playing rednecks.

"Got some company for you, fellas," he said. "One of those northern nigger-lovin' agitators. Treat him nice now."

"I'm certainly no troublemaker," I said, stumbling to establish rapport. "Don't you guys think Joe Namath is overpaid?"

Finally, we all assembled again on the lawn for instructions in passive resistance. I learned how to curl up like an unborn baby, using drawn-up knees to protect my vital parts, forearms to hide my face, and clasped hands to cover the nape of my neck. I followed directions, dropping to the ground and flopping on other volunteers for protection.

"Defend those family jewels," Feelgood shouted at me, slapping at my exposed areas with a piece of rubber hose he had brought along to test our mettle.

"I've only got two hands," I retorted.

"Swift, I don't think you can take it," Feelgood said, turning to Lenny.

"Look, I've suffered," Lenny replied. "Ask my dentist."

Forman then tacked a sign that read "COURTHOUSE" on a spreading oak tree and divided us in two groups. We determined "Niggers" had to march through a gantlet of angry "Rednecks" to reach the courthouse and have a chance to register. Emotions boiled up and over in a matter of seconds. Before I had taken five steps, I was smashed to the ground, kicked in the face, and smothered beneath a pile of writhing bodies. I shrieked with pain and cursed a blue streak as I tried to claw my way free.

"I'm hurt," someone cried. "I think my ankle's broken."

"Keep it up," Forman shouted. "Bundle together to cushion the blows."

After what seemed like an hour, we were ordered to untangle and pull ourselves back together. I had a sore lip, a torn T-shirt, and lots of grass stains. We all looked the worse for wear, but there were no serious injuries—just bruises, scratches, and one sprained ankle.

I was more than a little shocked by the experience. The speed with which jeers turned to blows was astonishing. I was shaken by my own pent-up fury; I had been swept by a rush of rage to hurt others before they hurt me. Our violent impulses were all too real, and yet we had withstood the onslaught. I looked at my fellow volunteers with new respect, as if we were raw recruits who had survived our first battle. I had yet to walk through the Valley of the Shadow of Death, but at least I had taken a first step.

The media people, cameras grinding, jumped at the chance to get some action shots for the six o'clock news. Afterwards, the CBS crew treated everybody to ice cream. At dinner I heard that a handful of volunteers had left. I was determined to stick it out. I looked around; the impending danger seemed to stimulate the hormones and spark the libido. In spite of the warnings we had received about interracial sex, people were pairing off and making out all over the place—on couches, in corners, on the grass, and down in the overgrown ravine.

"The bushes are shaking," Lenny noted as we walked across the campus back to our dorm.

I was still riding a rush of adrenaline from the afternoon. I looked around for Esther. How I would have loved to make some bushes shake with her!

Although we were supposed to meet with our project leaders after dinner, many of us played hooky to watch a CBS news special: "The Search in Mississippi." I squeezed into the crowded lounge just as Walter Cronkite announced that the nation's attention and concern was now focused on the state because of the disappearance of the three civil rights workers. Next came footage of the orientation session for the voter registration volunteers the week before. It was strange to watch the same SNCC staff saying many of the same things we had heard to another group like us. The camera zoomed in on one volunteer in particular: a reflective-looking young man with a boyish tousle of black hair, a delicate, well-defined mouth, and eyes at once dreamy and receptive—as if they interrogated, even slightly doubted, what the speaker said, reserving to the last the right to agree or disagree. I envied his repose. It was Andrew Goodman. He looked a lot like me.

They showed shots of Goodman's parents and Rita Schwerner. There was a distraught father pleading, "Please, David, come home; you don't know what you're doing." They even had interviews with a few volunteers; interviews that had been held the day before in the very room where we sat watching the program.

"I was misquoted," Lenny cried as the camera pictured him earnestly explaining why he wanted to spend his summer in Mississippi.

When Eastland was shown, claiming that all the darkies on his plantation were as happy as could be and didn't have a care in the world and when Governor Johnson called us "beatnik-type weirdos," we all shouted, "You're lying!" I relished Governor Johnson's slip of the tongue: "We have no racial fictions . . . I mean frictions, here." The room rocked with laughter. Finally Fannie Lou Hamer related how, when the owner of the plantation where she had worked for eighteen years said, "We don't need registered Negroes here," she had responded, "I didn't do it for you; I did it for me."

The program closed with a shot of us singing "We Shall Overcome." We stood up, joined hands, and began singing along with ourselves on the television.

"Let's hum the next verse," someone said. "Everyone hum softly."

As I hummed, I was moved by a black voice from the back of the room speaking with conviction: "You know what we're doing. . . . We're moving the world. We're here to bring all the people of Mississippi, all the peoples of this country, all the peoples of the world together. We're bringing a new revolution of love, so let's sing out together once again now, everybody hand in hand."

So I sang again, more fervently than before,

"Oh, Oh deep in my heart, I do believe,
We shall overcome some day."

I felt a warm glow as I walked out into the flower-scented summer evening. I wanted to find Esther and see if we could have another good talk like the one we'd had the other night. Then I saw her, arm-in-arm with Feelgood, heading down the path toward the lake.

Every evening we had dorm discussions about whether we should or shouldn't go and what the chances of getting hurt were. As I sang the songs and listened to the speakers, I certainly didn't become less afraid—if anything, I was more terrified—but something else emerged as well: a feeling of being a part of a united effort that truly mattered, so that personal doubts and misgivings diminished in comparison. By week's end I was at once scared to death and anxious to see what Mississippi was really like.

On Friday evening, James Forman talked to us first. The SNCC staff realized that this was their last chance to instruct us, so they wanted to make every word count.

"I'd like everybody to stand up," Forman said. "Put your arms around the person on each side of you and sing 'We'll Never Turn Back.'"

> *"We have hung our head and cried*
> *For those like Lee who died,*
> *Died for you and died for me,*
> *Died for the cause of equality,*
> *But we'll never turn back . . . "*

"The song you just sang is about Herbert Lee, who was killed for trying to help people register to vote. Louis Allen, who saw the murder, was shot down this past January. Medgar Evers was assassinated a year ago. Five other deaths in the last five months. I may be killed; you may be killed; the whole staff may go.

"We cried over you in the staff meeting because we love you and are afraid for you. We are grown men and women who have been beaten and shot at, and we cried for you. We want you to understand exactly what you are getting into. But one thing is sure: If anything happens to you, it will also happen to us. If you get beaten up, I'll be standing right behind you. We are going to be there with you, and you know we'll never turn back."

Then Bob Moses asked if any of us had read *The Lord of the Rings.*

"The hero, Frodo, obtains a powerful ring, which he knows he must destroy, yet as he carries it, he becomes corrupted by it, so that he is in danger of destroying not the ring but what is best in himself. When you spend your time fighting evil, you become preoccupied by it. It consumes your energy; you become part of the evil, and terribly weary. . . ."

He stared at the floor a long moment, and then, in a voice so soft he seemed to be whispering to himself: "The kids are dead."

He paused while the truth I knew but hated to admit sank in. He said he had known since Monday, but he had remained silent out of respect for Rita. He even said he hoped they found the bodies soon so that we would realize the danger we faced. I expected my heart at that moment to break into a thundering gallop, but I stayed surprisingly calm. Maybe I was better prepared to go to Mississippi than I realized.

"The responsibility for sending you into dangerous situations is mine," Moses continued. "I justify myself because I am taking the same risks; I ask no one to do what I would not do. Negroes who tried to gain their rights, nameless men, have already been killed in Mississippi. Herbert Lee, Louis Allen—people who trusted me— have already died. We want each one of you to stop and think, to face head-on the question: Are you willing to risk your life or not? Do you know what's important, really important, and are you ready to stand up for it? If the answer is no, we can say, 'Later, later, it's too dangerous now.'"

Could we? Could I? I believed that I had the courage to risk my life, and I knew for sure that I did not want to die. An undertone of pain in Moses's voice and a hint of inward agony in his eyes suggested that he almost wished we *would* say, "No, let's call it off; we don't want to go."

"Don't come to Mississippi this summer if you think you are bringing sweetness and light to the Negro. Only come if you understand, really understand, that his freedom and yours are one. All our strength comes from the local people. If they want sewing clubs or cooking classes, that's what we'll help them organize. It's their decision, not ours. Because they're the ones who will still be living there after we've gone.

"Now I want to say a few words to the Freedom School teachers: Please be patient with your students. Don't expect too much. Break off a little chunk of love and follow it. If you do nothing more than be friendly, if you don't teach them anything at all, that will still be something. When we bring people to register, they take a long time studying the test. And if they fail it, they take this to mean they should study it harder. They don't see it as a trick to steal their rights. Many of your students will be like that. But you must remember there is a difference between being slow and being stupid. The people you'll be working with aren't stupid. But they're slow. So very slow."

He stood lost in meditation, deliberating whether he had left something unsaid. Finally he mentioned that he wanted to meet with the volunteers assigned to the McComb and Natchez projects in the lounge, then he walked out the door. For a minute or two we sat in total silence; by now we knew enough not to clap. At last a lovely soprano voice lifted us all into song:

> *"They say that freedom is a constant struggle,*
> *They say that freedom is a constant struggle,*
> *They say that freedom is a constant struggle,*
> *Oh, Lord, we've struggled so long,*
> *We must be free, we must be free."*

I stood with my arms around Lenny and Esther and sang about how freedom was a constant crying, a constant dying, a struggle that had to go on. Next, as slow as a funeral dirge, came Bob Moses's favorite song:

> *"We are soldiers, in the Army,*
> *We have to fight, although we have to cry,*
> *We've got to hold up the freedom banner,*
> *We've got to hold it up until we die."*

Then I went to meet with Moses.

"We sat up through the night," Moses said as soon as we were assembled, "wondering what we should say to you volunteers. We wanted you to be scared—but not too scared. When no one had dropped out by Wednesday, I was worried. Now a few have left, but the rest of you have resolved to stick it out.

"As you know, the southwestern part of Mississippi is very dangerous. Already some homes have been bombed; vigilantes are drilling; automatic weapons and hand grenades have been stolen from an arms depot near Natchez. We have made a vow that we would not abandon the hardest areas, and so some SNCC field secretaries and a few volunteers will go to McComb and Natchez, but I have decided that the situation right now is simply too dangerous for the rest of you at this time. If a lot of people went now, they would face a high probability of being killed. Therefore, you will be dispersed to projects in the Delta where I think you will be safer. We will wait and see how the other volunteers are received. If conditions improve, you will be sent to your original assignments later in the summer."

As Moses read out our new destinations, some lines from *Three-Penny Opera* raced through my head: *"Re-priev-ed, Re-priev-ed, As the need is sorest, So the answer comes soonest."* I always thought they were purely ironic lines, but now I was taking them seriously. I felt a tremendous sense of relief, as if this last-minute reprieve were a confirmation of my heartfelt wish that I would not be harmed. My new project was in Tallahatchie, a relatively safe town in the heart of the Delta; Lenny would be in Greenville, the most liberal place in Mississippi. Of our group, only Esther was still going to McComb—no doubt at Feelgood's insistence. I told myself that if she stuck to teaching Freedom School and stayed within the black community, she would be safe too. But in spite of my fear, I still wished to be where she was.

"You spoke tonight of sacrifice," I said with surprise at the sound of my own words. "We are willing to go wherever you send us, no matter what the risks."

Esther glanced my way with what I took to be admiration.

"We understand that some of us may have to die," another volunteer added with passionate sincerity.

"Yes," Moses said softly, "people will always be expended." He looked at me, his eyes betrayed tremendous strain. "The question is . . . Are they ever expendable?"

After that we all walked outside where a group of volunteers were doing the hora. I watched Moses set the sheaf of papers he was carrying on the grass and, with solemn joy, join the circle of the dance.

Bob Moses

Liberty and McComb, Mississippi

September–November 1961

1

One Sunday in late September, John Doar came to McComb to see for himself what the situation was in southwestern Mississippi. In the week following my beating at the hands of Billy Jack Caston, several other SNCC workers had been beaten, including John Hardy, who was pistol-whipped by the registrar of Walthall County when he was inside the courthouse! That was so blatant a violation that Doar, on behalf of the federal government, had brought a suit, which, in spite of Judge Harold Cox's obstructionism, was making its way through the courts.

At first Doar couldn't take his eyes off the stitches in my scalp.

"The FBI report didn't say anything about cuts and abrasions," he said with genuine concern. "I didn't realize it was so serious."

"It could have been worse," I said.

We drove to Steptoe's farm, so that he could hear firsthand, in Steptoe's deliberate way, about the pattern of violence in Amite County.

"Have you ever tried to register yourself?" Doar asked.

"Oh, yes, several times," Steptoe said, "but they never let me fill out the form."

Steptoe told him that the only registered Negro in the county had a master's degree.

"You know, it isn't possible for all Negroes in this county to have master's degrees," Steptoe said. "I only know but one who has a master's degree, and that is my son. If it takes a master's degree to pass this test, he'll be the only Negro to redish in this county. The last time I tried to get Negroes to redish I had lots of trouble," he added.

"What kind of trouble?" Doar asked.

"Such as threats, such as jail, such as beatings."

"Have there been killings?"

"Oh, yes, they used to whup Negroes around here all the time," Steptoe said, his voice becoming slower, deeper, and more grieved. "They'd whup 'em most to death. Some they'd hang up in trees here; the bugs would get 'em. All's we found was bones."

"When was this?" Doar looked grim.

"Well, you know, that was five hundred years ago," Steptoe drawled. "That was way back there."

Doar stared in bafflement, unsure where the irony was.

"What about the people who are attending the voter registration school?" Doar asked. "Has anyone tried to intimidate them?"

"Oh, yes, there are always threats." Steptoe was as matter-of-fact as if he were merely stating that dogs bark at night. "E. H. Hurst told some people that if me and Herbert Lee didn't quit messin' with this civil rights business, he would kill us hisself."

I was startled to hear this; apparently Steptoe took the dangers so much for granted he hadn't bothered to tell me what Hurst had said. I had grown fond of Herbert Lee, a very quiet man who was always ready to drive me around the dusty back roads of the county to talk to people about registering. One evening he had me over to his home for supper to meet his wife and children. Apparently his kindness to me had not gone unnoticed.

"Who's this Hurst?" Doar asked.

"He lives across the road there," Steptoe said.

"He's a Mississippi state representative," I said. "He's also the father-in-law of Billy Jack Caston, the sheriff's cousin, the guy who hit me."

"Quite a cozy little town you have here," Doar remarked dryly.

"I've known those Hursts all my life," Steptoe continued. "They're all a mean piece of work. I once saw E. H.'s daddy knock a colored boy down, step on his head, and rub it in the dirt. Just because the kid was thirsty and cryin' for water. I whupped him once."

"E. H.?" I asked.

"No, his daddy."

"You did!" Steptoe's courage amazed me.

"Oh, yes," he said. "I was young then and feelin' my man, and he ordered me and my brother to head his cattle into the pens. Well, we was already tired from doin' our own, so we didn't do it. He jumps off his horse and comes at my brother and says, 'Nigger, next time I tell you to do something, you're gonna do it,' and he raises his cattle whip to strike him. But I steps between and says, 'Don't hit him, hit me, he's too small.' Well, he come at my head with the whip, but I took it away from him and he got whipped instead—maybe a little worse, 'cause as I was comin' down on his head I remembered what I saw him do to that little Negro child who just wanted a drink of water."

"Didn't anything happen to you?" Doar asked.

"Oh, yes," Steptoe said, "they tried. They sent and told my father to come on over to their place, but I told him, 'Dad, don't go over there; that's a trap he got set for you.' So my Dad didn't go. A few days later he come see my Dad and made 'tend he was sorry and said he was wrong."

"Are you taking any special precautions now?" Doar asked anxiously. Being Steptoe was a risky business.

"I maybe ought not to say this," Steptoe said. "If they get me I don't care, but we have our guns loaded, and they know this."

Steptoe lifted up a couch pillow to reveal a concealed pistol. Then he showed Doar a shotgun he kept behind the door.

"The sheriff has been up here," Steptoe added. "I asked him

what he want at my place. 'Just checkin',' he says. 'Just checkin'.' But I know he was checkin' whether he could hide hisself and find a way to bump me off, or kill someone else, whatnot."

"The sheriff?" Doar looked troubled.

"Oh, yes, here in this county every time a white man beats a Negro or kills a Negro, he gets promoted to higher office. Here in Amite County you don't know what might happen; you don't know what might take place. And you want somebody with you who is not afraid to tell what happened to you, if something happen to you. Because here in Amite County they're afraid to tell who did it; afraid to tell how it happened; 'cause they're afraid the same thing will happen to them."

After we left Steptoe's farm, Doar and I drove over to Herbert Lee's place to take an affidavit from him. The children were out back by the barn playing hide-and-seek. They cried, "Bob, Bob," when they saw us and ran up to see the new car Doar had rented in New Orleans. Their father wasn't home.

On the drive back to McComb, we were both deep in thought. Finally, Doar broke the silence.

"It's hard to believe," he said, his voice wavering, "that this is America."

2

A few days later I was in the Masonic Hall when the phone rang. It was Doc Anderson at the Negro funeral home in McComb.

"There's a body down here," he said somberly. "We'd like you to come over and see if you can identify it."

My heart sank with apprehension.

"It's a Negro male," he continued, "short, about fifty. Shot in the head."

"Where was he killed?" I asked, fearing that I already knew the answer.

"In Liberty."

The body, still in farm clothes, was stretched out on a cold metal table; a small dark hole was visible above the left ear.

It was Herbert Lee.

Lee had been shot at A. B. Westbrook's cotton gin early that morning. The body had been left uncovered where it fell. No one, black or white, in Liberty would touch it. Finally a hearse was summoned from McComb. The few blacks at the scene were too frightened to even say the dead man's name.

"Was it Hurst?"

"Why, yes!" Doc Anderson looked at me with perplexity and surprise. "It was self-defense. Seems Lee went berserk and attacked Hurst with a tire iron."

"Says who?"

"There's no point getting upset. Five people witnessed it. Three of them were Negroes. They all told the same story. Seems Lee owed Hurst some money. A coroner's jury has already acquitted him."

"Naturally."

I waited for nightfall, and then Curtis Bryant and I drove the pitch-black back roads of Amite County until I found someone brave enough to talk. Louis Allen, one of the three Negroes who had seen Hurst shoot Lee, was willing to tell the truth:

"I'd been haulin' logs in my truck that morning," Allen said, "but it broke down, so I was walkin' into town to get a fan belt when I come by the gin. I saw Herbert Lee drive in with a truckload of cotton. He was waitin' in line when Mr. Hurst nosed up behind him in an empty pickup, the blue one that belongs to Billy Jack Caston. I heard some yellin', an' I knew I ought to keep walkin', but I turned my head an' saw Mr. Hurst shoutin' at Herbert Lee. I was standin' off to the side by a telephone pole. I didn't think they could see me, but I could see them. I knew I shoulda kept goin', but I couldn't move. I saw it all.

"Hurst come over to Lee's truck, on the driver's side, an' was shoutin' about somethin'. He waved his arms in the air; then he pulled a pistol from his belt—I think it was a .38—an' pointed it at Lee.

"'I'm not foolin' with you this time,' Hurst yelled. 'I mean business.'

"'Put that gun down,' Herbert say, 'or I ain't talkin.'

"Hurst stuck that pistol back in his belt under his coat, an' Lee slid across the front seat an' got out on the passenger side. I think he wanted to keep somethin' solid between them an' talk to Hurst over the hood of his truck. But Hurst, he run 'round the front, out come that pistol again, an' he shoots Lee right in the head from a few feet away.

"I hurried on away from there as fast as I could, hopin' nobody seen me. But they come for me at the garage an' taken me to the courthouse. They had them a roomful of armed men, an' the Deputy Sheriff, Daniel Jones, he tole me that what they had was a clear case of self-defense. He said they found a weapon under Lee's body. 'If you just say that Herbert Lee had him a tire tool,' he said, 'there won't be no trouble.'"

To protect his family, Allen lied to the coroner's jury. He said that Lee had swung at Hurst with a tire iron and that the gun had gone off accidentally as Hurst was whacking Lee on the head. The jury decided it was a case of justifiable homicide, declaring that Hurst acted "in defense of his person while being attacked by the deceased with a deadly weapon . . . known as a tire tool."

"I didn't run," I saw Hurst boast to reporters, who must have noted that he was nearly a foot taller and at least fifty pounds heavier than the man who allegedly attacked him. "I got no rabbit in me." Hurst had known Lee since they were boys; he claimed that the dispute had nothing to do with civil rights but was over five hundred dollars. "That son of a bitch owed me," he said.

I called John Doar and told him what I had learned.

"Doc Anderson didn't find any powder burns," I reported.

"I'll have the FBI photograph the body and examine the entry wound," Doar replied. "If there were no powder burns, and this eyewitness you've found will change his testimony, we might have a case against Hurst."

The next day at the funeral, Mrs. Lee, shaking from grief and with reproach in her eyes, confronted me. "You killed my husband!" she wailed. "You killed my husband!" Her words cut me to the quick, but even harder to take was the fact that none of her nine children, lined up in the front row, would look me in the face. Even though Herbert Lee was my friend, and I had wanted only the best, I felt the sting of complicity in his death. I knew that martyrs in the Movement were inevitable, but why did it have to be this good man?

Several weeks later Louis Allen came to see Steptoe and told him, "My first testimony is worryin' me. Mr. Lee's dead. What should I do?"

"Well," Steptoe said, "you can tell Mr. Doar what you told Bob."

"I am," Allen said. "I'm gonna tell the truth."

"That's good. I believe you should."

I arranged for Allen to meet me in McComb.

"If I can be protected," he told me, "I'll let the hide fall with the hair an' tell what I saw."

I called John Doar. He said he didn't think they could guarantee protection or a conviction if Allen changed his testimony.

"What about the FBI investigation?"

"They botched it, Bob," Doar said with disgust. "By the time the Bureau in Washington had contacted the office in New Orleans and they reached their agent in Natchez, the body was already in the ground. I'm sorry."

"So am I."

When a grand jury was convened to look into the case, I had to advise Allen, for his own safety, to lie again. But the case still troubled him, and several months later he asked to talk to me a third time. We drove down to the FBI office in New Orleans, and he signed an affidavit that Hurst killed Lee "without provocation." The FBI didn't do anything about the murder of Herbert Lee, but somehow word reached Deputy Sheriff Jones about Allen's second thoughts and small rebellion. He was now a marked man in Liberty.

I was wracked with guilt over the death of Herbert Lee. If I had never come to Amite County, he would still be alive to enjoy his

Bob Moses

wife and children. Now black people in Liberty were afraid to even leave town, let alone confront the sheriff and the registrar at the courthouse. No one would come to the citizenship school. Steptoe was cleaning his guns in anticipation of an ambush. No Negro felt free in Liberty.

For me, the murder of Herbert Lee stood for all the indignities and atrocities unsung black people had suffered in the South for centuries. I vowed that his death would not be forgotten: by me, by SNCC, or by anyone else in the Movement. I also reluctantly decided to withdraw from Amite County for a time, but I made a promise to Steptoe before I left: "I'll be back."

3

During the weeks I spent in Liberty, SNCC workers had been arriving in McComb to initiate "direct action" (as if the response to voter registration wasn't direct enough!). The McComb high school students were eager to start sitting-in and picketing. Too young to register, they were frustrated and liked the idea of confrontation. Many of their parents, however, strongly disapproved of this new turn of events, especially when at the end of August three students—Isaac Lewis, Robert Talbert, and Brenda Travis— were arrested at the Greyhound bus terminal. Robert pleaded guilty and was fined two hundred dollars and given a suspended sentence. Isaac and Brenda, who said they weren't guilty, were fined four hundred dollars and were sent to the Magnolia Jail for eight months. The harsh penalties outraged the black community. They were particularly upset that alert, vivacious Brenda Travis, who was only fifteen and very well liked, should receive such punishment. Some people were angry that the judge would send a young girl to prison; others blamed SNCC for getting their children in trouble. Curtis Bryant held me personally responsible.

"The agreement was for three weeks," he told me, his already high-pitched voice rising higher as he became more upset, "and you were only to do voter registration. I cannot condone the use of children. That is contrary to NAACP guidelines."

"It's out of my hands," I said. "McComb is where the action is and SNCC wants to be here. Besides, the students want to protest and will, whether we're here or not."

"Can't you order them not to?"

"No. That's not the way SNCC operates. It's not my decision to make. In SNCC we 'go where the spirit say go, and do what the spirit say do.' Nobody gives orders to anybody."

"Well, that's no way to run an organization," Bryant said, shaking his head. "You've got to have procedure, guidelines, rules. In the NAACP we file vouchers for all money received and turn in detailed reports. Whenever we go into anything, we have our legal office tell us what we ought to do and what we ought *not* to do. This use of students is clearly beyond the boundary line. I'm afraid we'll have to disassociate ourselves to protect the integrity of our organization."

"We can't stop now," I pleaded. "This is no time for hesitation. We have to go ahead."

Seeing a chance to exploit our differences, Police Chief George Guy chose this moment to arrest Curtis Bryant—even though he had consistently opposed the demonstrations—for contributing to the delinquency of a minor. Ironically, this attempt to sabotage us failed. When Bryant got out on bail, he declared himself unequivocally on our side. "Where the students lead, we will follow," he told an NAACP rally.

The police also tried to entrap me on a trumped-up charge. I was down at South of the Border, a black restaurant in Burgland where the SNCC workers hung out. Alyene Quin, the manager, sensed trouble when she saw a patrol car pull up. She planted herself at the front door to stall them while I slipped out the back and ran up the alley to Nobles Brothers Cleaners. Ernest Nobles, quickly sizing up the situation, took my arm and stood me up inside a rack of hanging clothes where I couldn't be seen. When the police car came tearing after me, Ernest ran out and shouted to them, "He went out the front door, heading that way," and they sped off in the wrong direction. Once they were gone, he parked his pickup truck in the alley, hid me under a tarpaulin in back, and drove to Steptoe's farm where I would be safe.

After serving a month in jail, Brenda Travis was placed on probation and Ike Lewis was paroled. They asked Commodore Dewey Higgins, the conservative black principal who lorded it over Burgland High School, to be readmitted. He stated that because of their sit-in activities, they were expelled for the year. When the other students heard about this autocratic action, they stood up at midday chapel service and demanded an explanation; the principal refused to discuss the issue. A few students then took over the stage, fired up the others with freedom songs, and called upon everyone to walk out in protest. About a hundred of them left school and marched down to the SNCC office. We heard them singing *"Woke up this morning with my mind stayed on freedom"* as they came. They carried banners and signs and were ready to demonstrate downtown.

At first Chuck McDew and I tried to discourage them, but their spirit was so strong and contagious that we decided to join them. Bob Zellner, the only white SNCC worker in McComb, was determined to come too. We marched down Summit, through the heart of Burgland, and then took the viaduct under the railroad tracks to reach the white side of McComb. As we came up Main Street, an angry crowd began to gather, singling out Zellner for special abuse. Before long we were surrounded by a mob; they were in an ugly mood.

To show our peaceful intentions, the students knelt down one by one to pray on the steps of city hall. This was seen as an intolerable provocation; the police blew their whistles and began to arrest us. At the same time, the mob attacked, zeroing in on Zellner. A man in a sleeveless T-shirt went for his throat and another slugged him in the face. McDew and I threw our arms around him, trying to shield him with our bodies. To keep from being trampled to the ground, Zellner was hanging on to the iron railing for dear life. They pulled on his belt and beat on his hands in their effort to drag him out into the street. I saw one man grab him by the ears and try to gouge his eyes out with his thumbs. When Zellner threw up his hands to protect his face, he was immediately knocked down and kicked in the head until he lost consciousness. Only then did the police intervene, dragging us up the steps into city hall.

One hundred and nineteen of us were herded into the city jail. The mob gathered outside, milling around and shouting threats. When word of what had happened spread, the police began conducting guided tours for the curious "good citizens" of McComb. A contingent would enter the cell block, and invariably they would ask, "Where's Moses? Where's Moses?" until a student would point me out. They stared; I stared back—the Fiend at Bay.

"You don't believe in Jesus Christ, do you, you sonofabitch?" a man who said he was a minister snapped at me. "I'm going to personally see to it that you're in hell real soon."

"Say something in communist," a prim little blond said to McDew.

"Shiksa schlepp mensch shtick," he replied, looking completely serious.

We were brought upstairs one by one for a kind of kangaroo court. I warned the students to say they were under eighteen. If they could convince the court they were minors, they would probably be released. When my turn came, the air was thick with tension. To avoid having to say "Yes, sir" and "No, sir," I answered every question with a complete sentence. Fifteen of us were charged with breach of the peace and contributing to the delinquency of minors and taken to the Amite County Jail in Liberty.

"Why didn't you take us to the Pike County Jail in Magnolia?" I asked.

"This is a better place for y'all to think about what happened to Herbert Lee," the deputy said.

We were placed in the drunk tank, a solid concrete room, cold and damp, with nothing to sit or lie on but more concrete. In spite of the lack of heat, bad food, and no showers, spirits remained high in the cell; we sang freedom songs and told jokes. I made chess pieces out of matchsticks, with a cigarette butt as the queen and taught my cellmates how to play. Whoever captured the queen got to smoke the butt. After three days we were released on bond.

When the 114 students who had taken part in the march tried to return to school, the principal, under pressure from the white superintendent, refused to admit them unless they signed an agreement not to stage any more protests. The students refused, and walked out. This procedure went on for the next week. Each day the students would come to school; each day they would be ordered to sign the agreement; each day those who refused would walk out. The parents, meanwhile, were deeply divided on the issue: some whipped their children and told them to stay away from that mess; others resented the agreement, but wanted their children back in school; a few were urging their sons and daughters to keep up the pressure and shut the school down if necessary. Even the teachers, usually an impossibly conservative group, became involved. "I wish I was a student," one said, "I'd walk out too."

I was pleased to see the spirit of democracy spread as the students learned to stand up for their rights. They drafted a petition for fair treatment that urged "all our fellowmen to love rather than hate, to build rather than tear down, to bind our nation with love and justice without regard to race, color, and creed." Finally, the principal set a deadline of October 16 at three o'clock: any student who hadn't signed the agreement by then would be expelled. Fifty signed; sixty-four refused. That was the end of the McComb Walkout.

The SNCC staff set up a makeshift school for the expelled students: Nonviolent High. I taught math and English; Chuck McDew, history; and Dion Diamond, chemistry and physics. We met in the sanctuary of Saint Paul's Methodist Church and began each morning with freedom songs. The students were enthusiastic about learning—McDew, in particular, told them things about their country they never would have heard at Burgland High. They were also determined to continue direct action. We had long discussions about how to get their parents more involved. They even began an underground paper, *The Informer,* which called for a boycott of downtown stores. After a couple of weeks, an arrangement was made to transfer fifteen of the students to Campbell College in Jackson. That seemed to be a satisfactory solution at the time, but later I learned that several of the girls, away from home for the first time, became pregnant.

Brenda Travis was never readmitted to Burgland High or permitted to go to Campbell College. The judge declared her a delinquent for taking part in our demonstrations and sentenced her to the Oakley Training School at Raymond. One day we all piled into cars and tried to go visit her, but we were turned away at the gate by a squad of officers armed to the teeth.

On October 31, the fifteen of us who could be sentenced as adults were brought to trial. Judge Brumfield accused me of making "a clear, cold, calculated" attempt to violate the laws of Mississippi.

"You are bringing racial strife and rioting to a place that has only known racial harmony," he said.

"Kneeling on the steps of city hall is not my definition of insurrection."

"Robert," the judge replied, "haven't some of the people from your school been able to go down and register without violence in Pike County?"

"One of my 'people' is dead," I said, thinking that southerners are most exposed when they boast. "Others have been threatened, shot at, and beaten."

The judge sentenced eleven of us to four months in jail each. Bobby Talbert, Ike Lewis, Hollis Watkins, and Curtis Hayes, who had been arrested during the sit-ins, were given six months.

"Some of you are local residents," the judge said. "Some of you are outsiders. Those of you who are local residents are like sheep being led to the slaughter. If you continue to follow the advice of outside agitators, you *will* be like sheep and will be slaughtered."

We spent the next thirty-seven days at the Pike County Jail in Magnolia. We weren't allowed to work with the other prisoners for fear we would contaminate them. At first, visitors were permitted. The black community responded by bringing fried chicken and freshly baked pies. Then the visits were restricted to once a week, and the showers to twice a week. The meals were always the same: cold grits, sticky rice, watery gravy, dry bread, a congealed egg, and a slice of big town cake. We ate everything with a spoon and drank directly from a faucet, which drained down a hole in the cement floor.

By now we were pretty good at fighting boredom. Chuck McDew lectured on the history of black people in America. "If you think this jail is bad," McDew would say, "let me tell you about the slave ships." I gave the students pep talks based on Camus's philosophy of engagement. "Accept your personal freedom," I would say. "Dare to stand in a strong sun and cast a sharp shadow. Commit yourself to changing what needs to be changed so that this earth can be a satisfactory place for all people." Other times I would seek out a solitary corner and try to solve math problems in my head. Day by day we swapped stories, sang songs, and learned to support each other as a band of brothers.

All that November in jail I brooded about the Liberty and McComb campaign and what should be done next. With many of the most active students away in Jackson and with the black community divided and the white community hostile, we would have to move our base of operations. But where and how to begin?

I arrived at several conclusions: The established blacks—ministers, teachers, small businessmen—could not be counted on— they were too dependent on white favor and the status quo. Only those outside the power structure—small farmers, shop owners, but especially students—could be the seeds of change. I recalled what Amzie Moore and Steptoe had told me about how important the younger generation was as a vanguard to build a better world. The problem was that the teenagers, who lacked education and organizational skills, would have to be trained from scratch to attain the confidence and competence they needed to be effective.

In a letter smuggled out of jail I formulated a strategy:

"You dig yourself in and prepare to wage psychological warfare; you combat your own fears about beatings, shootings, and possible mob violence; you stymie by your own physical presence the anxious fear of the Negro community . . . that maybe you did *come only to boil and bubble and burst out of sight and sound. You organize, pound by pound, small bands of people who gradually focus in the eyes of Negroes and whites as people tied up in that mess; you create a small striking force capable of moving out when the time comes, which it must, whether we help it or not."* We in SNCC would be a small tremor in the center of the iceberg that was Mississippi—from a stone that the builders rejected.

Tom Morton
Freedom School

Tallahatchie, Mississippi

June 29–July 24, 1964

1

Every morning at five, a rooster outside my window sounded reveille. The first tortured notes from his raucous trumpet were greeted with howls of delight from the Hound Dog Five sprawled in the backyard. Their hullabaloo puzzled the rooster for a moment—he fretted on his fence post and made perturbed, guttural noises—but then, taking it as a groundswell of approval, he burst into an earsplitting rendition of a tomcat with its claw stuck in a light socket, Lucille Ball meets Jack the Ripper, and similar artistries—a display that inspired the whole company of barnyard impresarios to join their several voices in an ecstatic grand finale: "O Lonesome Me," fortissimo. The rooster, whose name was Joe, wasn't a bad bird normally. Cock of the walk, he strutted his stuff with his bloodred crown on high when he wasn't scratching the packed dirt, pecking kernels of corn, or doing his seignorial duty by his covey of clucking consorts. But each dawn I wanted to grab the rifle Eddie Mays kept by my bed and blast that strident bastard into eternal silence.

After a week in Mississippi I was learning to live with the heat and the fear. A year before I arrived there had been an attempt to firebomb the farmhouse where I was staying, and the Mays family still proudly pointed out a bullet hole in their living room as evidence of that encounter. Lucky for them, the bomb was a dud. And lucky for the Klansman who threw it that Ella Mays had unloaded Eddie's shotgun (worried that Buster, their seven-year-old grandson, might play with it) because Eddie had him in his sights. "Next time somebody come up in my yard and squat," Eddie vowed, "they gonna get wiped with buckshot." Since then the neighborhood had set up a self-defense system. The five or six black families that lived along that stretch of rutted country road had strategically enlarged its potholes and worked out a code whereby friendly cars could signal at night. Nevertheless, sitting on the porch in the dark, all of us would tense and fall into an uneasy silence whenever we heard the sound of tires spattering gravel and rocks whacking the underside of a chassis. Then the car would flash its lights, and we could relax and start talking again. The worst scares came when I was alone in my tiny room after everyone had gone to bed. It was too hot to sleep; my body was soaked with sweat; mosquitoes cruised in through the screenless window. Outside, a light breeze rattled the corn shucks; a mule snorted in its shed; crickets sang in the weeds; frogs croaked by the cow pond. If I pressed my ear to the wall, I could hear Jasmine, the Mays's teenage granddaughter, breathing in her sleep. Then I heard the unmistakable crunch of a footstep, and the dogs started to bark. Whoever it was took off running, with the dogs yowling in hot pursuit.

The blood pounded in my ears as I stood trembling at the window, straining to discern darker shapes in dark shadows. Bats swooping through the night seemed to herald the onset of some ultimate outer darkness. In spite of a full moon, I couldn't see anything. Somebody went crashing through the cornfield with the dogs yelping at his heels. Then it was quiet again. I took a deep breath. *We are not afraid.*

"Someone was prowling around last night," I informed Eddie the next morning.

"Hog."

"How could you tell?"

"They short, fat, got hooves," Jasmine added, putting a hand over her mouth to hide her smile.

"It sounded like a person to me. But when I looked out the window, I didn't see anybody."

"They short . . ."

"So I've heard."

"I bet that hog was lookin' for snakes," Buster said.

"You have a lot of snakes here?" I asked. Somehow the home-baked biscuit in my hand never made it to my mouth.

"Right smart," Eddie said. "We got some dandies."

"What kind?"

"What kind do you want? We got all kinds. Mostly moccasins and copperheads."

"Snakes like farms," Jasmine said.

"We keeps the ground clear around the house," Ella said.

"One lives in the outhouse," Buster announced.

"It don't live there," Ella corrected. "We just seen it a few times."

"One what?" My throat was so dry my voice cracked.

"A cottonmouth water moccasin," Jasmine said.

"How big is it?"

"I reckon that one will run you 'bout three or four feet," Eddie said.

"Now don't you go scarin' Mr. Morton . . ."

"Tom. You can call me Tom."

"Don't scare Mr. Tom," Ella continued. "That snake won't bother you if you don't bother him."

"I'm gonna kill it with a stick."

"Buster, you leave that snake be, you hear?" Ella looked at him hard to make sure he understood.

"Yes'm," Buster mumbled with lowered eyes.

There was a cottonmouth in the outhouse. A snake that moved like water and stung like fire. The place had been bad enough before, standing like a lone sentry box in the tall weeds at the edge of the backyard, with wasps and flies hovering around its splintery seat. The daily walks out there were an ordeal. One night, when a sudden fright wrenched me to the guts, I was in torment: *should I foul the bed or face the snake?* Finally, shame proved stronger than terror, and I made my hasty way to the jakes, trying not to imagine what might be slithering at my feet.

I soon learned the degrees of fear: the uncontrollable shakes; the cold sweats; the clattering teeth; even the "pucker factor," where your anus gets a notion to shrivel back to the amoeba state and migrate elsewhere. But I was also growing accustomed to barnyard noises: that metal clinking sound wasn't a redneck cocking his gun but the pony shaking its chain; that rustling sound wasn't stealthy footsteps but the cow munching grass. I had been accepted by the family and by the horde of mongrel dogs who prowled the neighborhood. At first they swarmed around me showing their fangs, so that I had to stop at the top of the street and shout for somebody to come quick and rescue me. But after a week I was part of the scenery—barely an eyelid twitched as I walked by.

Eddie and Ella Mays worked hard to make their house look respectable. Originally a three-room shack, over the years they had added two bedrooms, enlarged the kitchen, tar-papered the pineboard walls with fake brick, painted the trim white, and shingled over the tin roof. A porcelain commode, hunched in its crate like a giant toad, now occupied the corner where Eddie—in hopeful anticipation that one of the first fruits of voting rights would be water service—planned to build on a bathroom. Until that happy day, it was Buster's job every morning to load the pony with empty buckets and ride a mile to the nearest well. Before I came, I supposed I would find ready relief from the Mississippi heat beneath a cold shower. Instead, I took a pigeon splash in a zinc tub twice a week and learned to live with my sweat.

With water so scarce, it was hard to wash clothes. Trying my best not to be a burden, I had boiled a kettle of water on the stove and was rubbing my jeans on the scrub board when Jasmine came in, glanced at what I was doing, and put her hand over her mouth.

"What's so funny?"

"You doin' it wrong."

"I've got hot water, soap, dirty clothes. I'm scrubbing them. What's wrong with that?"

"You need two tubs, one to wash in and one for rinsin'; you don't scrub yo jeans until the last thing, 'cause they so dirty; and you usin' the smooth side of the board."

Jasmine went to the storage shed and came back with a large bucket that had a hand wringer attached, taught me how to use it, and told me which things I should wash first. When I was finished, both buckets were as dark as the Delta soil.

"How did you wash yo clothes at college?"

"I opened a little door with a round glass window, stuck them in, deposited my coin, and turned a dial."

"I used to dream 'bout how you'd come," Jasmine remarked offhandedly as we were hanging up my clothes to dry in the sun. "I thought it would be in a big new blue bus with *FREEDOM RIDER* painted in white letters on both sides."

"Actually it was an Edsel." She was talking about the civil rights workers in general, but it was pleasant to think that she meant me.

"You own a car?"

"Sort of. My dad gave me the family jalopy. I'm letting the voter registration people use it for canvassing. It's a wonder it hasn't already rattled apart on these country roads."

"See that car down there?" Jasmine pointed to a burned-out hulk at the edge of a cotton field. "That was a SNCC car."

"What happened?"

"Firebomb."

2

When I came to Mississippi, I imagined that the civil rights revolution would be everywhere in evidence. At any moment I expected to see hooded Klansmen brandishing bullwhips around a burning cross, or determined Negroes filling the streets with freedom songs as they marched to the courthouse to confront the sheriff. When I looked out my bedroom window and saw two long strands of rope dangling from the limb of a sturdy oak at the edge of the swamp, my first thought was of a lynching. I went to investigate and saw on the ground a small board, notched at both ends, which had once served as a child's swing. In truth, Mississippi looked pretty much like any other place—only flatter and hotter. There were farms and towns; the motels, drive-ins, and Dairy Queens were standard American. The gas station had a familiar pyramid of Penzoil cans between the regular and high-test pumps; pillars of spare tires lined the walls of the repair shop and a bright-red cooler of Coca-Cola, shaped like a mummy's coffin, stood by the door. Only a closer look revealed anything ominous: a pickup truck with a gun rack in the rear window and a bumper sticker that read: RESIST; and, along with the fan belts, fuel additives, and window cleaners, boxes of shotgun shells for sale.

Of course the farms weren't ordinary farms either. This was the Delta, that fertile crescent that began above Yazoo City and spread out over the northwestern corner of the state. Here, for eons, the Mississippi and its tributaries had been depositing the best dirt of the continent to form an alluvial soil deep and rich enough to produce crop after crop of cotton. When I first drove across the Delta on my way to Tallahatchie, I thought how easy it was to believe that the world was flat and ended at the levee. All I saw for mile after monotonous mile was a thin, straight road shimmering like a mirage of distant water in front of me and endless fields of cotton blurring by on both sides, the vast expanse broken only by the occasional weatherboard shack, tin roof flashing in the sun, looking bleak and stranded and ready to sink into that lush green sea of sameness. Inside the car or out, there was no escape from the steaming heat. A haze of dust hung over the land, sticking in the throat and coating the clammy skin the same rusty brown as the land. Slowly my sweat-stung eyes discerned yet another part of the picture: scattered far back among the rows, heads protected by caps, hats, and handkerchiefs from the relentless sun, black sharecroppers chopping cotton. It was then I realized that all those dark cruddy balls by the roadside, which looked like thousands of discarded Kleenex, were old puffs and snarls of cotton too.

The bean elevator of Tallahatchie, towering over the town like a medieval cathedral, was visible from miles away across the cotton fields. Remembering the warnings at orientation about the local police, I slowed down, keeping well under the speed limit. Nevertheless, as soon as I hit the outskirts, a big white car swooped down on me with its red light flashing and twirling. I pulled over. *Be still, my heart.*

A cop with a face as potholed as a Pennsylvania road asked to see my license and registration.

"You're a long way from home, buddy."

"Yes, sir. I guess I am."

"Down here for a vacation?"

"Sort of."

"Are you transportin' anything in your trunk?"

"Just my clothes, a sleeping bag, some books."

"You a big reader?"

"You might say that."

"Ever read *One Lonely Night?*"

He wiped the perspiration off his upper lip with the back of his hand while he waited for my answer.

"No."

"That's a good book."

"What's it about?"

"Scum like you," he drawled, showing his saliva-slick teeth. "Where are you takin' those books?"

"The Freedom House."

"The *what* house?"

"The Freedom House. It's a school."

"I know all about it. Get out of the car. Now!"

I got out of the car.

"Take your hand out of your pocket. Fast!"

I took my hand out.

"Boy, don't you know enough to keep your hands in sight?

You're lucky I didn't blow your head off. Do you know that?"

He glowered at me with a stop-me-if-you-can stare. I think he wanted to frisk me, but I probably looked too sweaty to touch.

"Who's this Ralph Morton?"

"That's my father."

"How come his name's on the registration?"

"It's his car. He gave it to me."

"Well, whose car is it?"

"It's mine."

"Can you prove it?"

"It was a gift. For college."

"What college?"

"Hiram."

"Hiram? What's that, a farm school?"

"No. It's liberal arts."

"I'll bet it is. Got any niggers there?"

"Maybe ten or twelve."

"So you think you know all about niggers now?"

"I didn't say that."

"But that's why you gutter-type people are down here, to tell us all about niggers."

"I'm just trying to help."

"Well I think you're the sorriest sonofabitch in the world, comin' all the way down here to Tallahatchie to live with the niggers," he said with sour-mouthed scorn. "Why don't you go back to Ohio where you belong? You got an inspection sticker on that car?"

"Yes, sir. Right there on the windshield."

"I mean a Mississippi sticker. You in Mississippi now."

"No. I don't have one. I got to Holly Springs yesterday, and I drove down here today. I haven't had time."

"Where did you stay in Holly Springs?"

"I don't know. It was night."

"I bet you don't know." His voice was as flat and dry as the Delta itself. "But you probably didn't have any trouble findin' some of that black poontang in the dark, did you?"

"Look, am I under arrest? If so, I'd like to know on what charges."

"No. *You* look. Get in the cruiser. I'm takin' you to the station."

"I have a right to know what I'm being charged with."

"Boy, you have the right to keep your damn mouth shut, or I'll shut it for you."

"What about my car?"

"That car can't be moved. The wrecker will get it. Open the trunk. I want to look at what you got in there."

"Not without a warrant."

"You'll get your damn search warrant later. Now give me the keys or I'll slap you down."

I gave him the keys and got in the cruiser. After all his worry that I might have a concealed weapon in my pocket, there I sat next to a pump-action shotgun. And so my first view of downtown Tallahatchie was from the backseat of a patrol car. We drove along Main Street to the police station, which was in a plywood annex to the courthouse. A sad black face looked at me from behind bars, and bloodhounds barked in their kennel.

"What's he charged with?" the bald man behind the booking desk asked.

"He's being held for investigation. Suspicion of transportin' deflammatory literature. Conspiracy to overthrow the state of Mississippi. Drivin' an illegal vehicle. Have him fill out a form and book him."

The cop walked into the courthouse, leaving me at the desk.

"Can I make a phone call?"

"I don't know nothing about it."

"What was that man's name?"

"You mean the deputy? Purvis Pratt."

"Could I see the sheriff?"

"Not till he gets here."

I filled out a form: name, age, address, etc.; had a picture taken—full front and profile; and was fingerprinted: each pinky rolled one way on an ink pad and the opposite way on paper, then four fingers pressed together, each one tapped in turn on top of the fingernail to insure a sharp impression. Deputy Pratt came back and waved in my face a hastily typed search warrant:

> *Whereas Purvis Pratt has this day made complaint on oath before the undersigned Justice of the Peace that printed material which advocates the overthrow of the Government of the State of Mississippi is being kept, stored, owned, controlled, or possessed by said Thomas Morton for the purpose of causing conduct which may lead to a breach of the peace, and whereas Purvis Pratt's belief is not feigned or malice against said Thomas Morton, but is founded on credible evidence, the said undersigned Justice of the Peace finds that probable cause for the issuance of a search warrant exists. Wherefore, we command that you proceed to diligently search the 1958 Ford Edsel now in the possession of the Tallahatchie Police Department for such printed material described above, that you seize the same, and that you arrest the above named person and bring him, and such printed material, before me. Herein fail not.*
>
> Witness my hand this 29th day of June, 1964.
> G. Buford Chappell
> Justice of the Peace

Deputy Pratt ordered me to follow him outside to where the tow truck had left my car. He opened the trunk and searched it for "deflammatory" literature. He pulled out the two boxes of books I had agreed to haul from Holly Springs and rummaged through my suitcase, knapsack, sleeping bag, and tennis gear.

"What kind of filth have you got in those boxes?"

"Just books people have donated for the Freedom Schools. I haven't looked at them."

"I'll bet you stole them."

He opened the boxes and began to inspect the books, pausing over certain titles and putting them in a separate little stack. Two men in street clothes came over and watched. One, with a camera, took various shots of me; the books; and Deputy Pratt, hot on the trail of subversion. The other stared at me with intense hatred.

In a few minutes we were joined by a tall, silver-haired man with a sheriff's badge prominently displayed on his chest.

"What have you found there, Purvis?"

"Look at the titles of these books, Sheriff. I had a hunch he was a commie, so I got me a warrant and damn if I wasn't right. Here's the proof."

The sheriff took a half-dozen books from Purvis and began to read the titles: *USA: The Permanent Revolution, The Seduction of the Innocent, Century of Struggle, Set This House on Fire, The Violent Bear It Away.*

He looked over at me with a slightly bemused smile.

"And these are your books?"

"Not exactly. I was just transporting them. I haven't read any of them, but I know the last two are novels by American authors. Southerners."

The sheriff opened the books one by one and began to examine the title page and the table of contents.

"Did you look inside these books, Purvis?"

"No, Sir. Those titles tell the whole story."

"Well, this book with *revolution* in the title was written by the editors of *Fortune* magazine, did you notice that?"

"No, Sir. I sure didn't."

"This one about *seduction* is an exposé of violent comic books. The one with *struggle* in the title is about American women in the nineteenth century. And those last two are novels, just like the man said. I don't think you've got much of a case here, Purvis."

"But he told me himself he was on his way to that 'Freedom House' they got over in niggertown."

"If he breaks the law, we'll put him in jail, but we can't arrest a man without sufficient cause. What else have you charged him with?"

"Drivin' an illegal vehicle. No bill of lading. Suspicion of stolen property. Improper registration. He don't have no inspection sticker; had to be towed."

Purvis was proud of his list.

The sheriff had a pained expression. Obviously he and Purvis didn't see eye to eye on the fine points of law enforcement.

"Well, I suppose the wrecker's got to be paid for," the sheriff said. "Charge him for a traffic violation and collect some money, but I don't want him in my jail, hear? Get him registered, give him an ID, and then bring him by."

My trial was swift.

"How do you plead?" the old judge asked, sticking his thumbs under his suspenders.

"I would like a lawyer."

"Pleads guilty. Twenty-five dollars. Next case."

I paid my fine and was escorted to the sheriff's office.

"Don't for a second think that because I ordered Purvis to drop subversion charges against you I'm in sympathy with what you're trying to do here. This is my town; I like it the way it is. And I don't want to see it changed. Are you a Christian?"

"I was brought up a Methodist."

"Didn't your folks teach you not to poke your nose in other people's business."

"They support what I do."

"What else do they support, the Communist Party?"

"They're Republicans."

"We've got some nigrah Republicans in this town. They vote. Some have held small federal offices. But then you wouldn't be interested in things like that; you think you already know the whole story."

"No, sir. I have a lot to learn."

"Then listen to me. After you've lived in niggertown for a while, after you've seen what those people are like on Saturday night—drinking and fighting and carrying on—you come see me and we'll have a nice little talk. But let me tell you this, as long as I am sheriff here, Tallahatchie is going to remain a law and order town. It is my duty to protect everyone, and that includes you and your friends. If you want me to do my duty, then you had better let me know what you are planning to do and when you are planning to do it."

"We're not planning demonstrations and things like that. I'm here to teach in a Freedom School. Other volunteers are working on voter registration."

"All you're working on is getting these young kids fired up, and they're gonna come pouring across the railroad tracks and cause me trouble. Don't you know you're playing with dynamite?"

"I know I'm in danger."

"This is Tallahatchie, not Philadelphia. If you cooperate with me, nobody is going to get hurt, no reporters will come snooping around, and the good people of this town will not see themselves humiliated and disgraced on the national news every evening. And when you get over to niggertown, you ask them about Sheriff Dan Wade and they'll tell you I'm a man of my word. I could tell you about all the colored friends I've got, and how well we get along, but you wouldn't believe that either."

"Like I said, I've got a lot to learn."

"That's right. If you were smart already, you'd have stayed in Ohio."

Deputy Pratt was waiting for me in the parking lot.

"Here's your keys. I didn't touch your motor."

"But you were tempted."

"I've got my eye on you, smart boy. I'm gonna know more about you than you know about yourself. We don't like outside agitators around here. . . . What are you grinnin' at?"

"It's just that whenever I hear the word *agitator,* I think of that whirligig gizmo on a washing machine, and, well, you know, that's inside not outside. . . . Never mind."

"I can be just as rough with you as you want me to be," he warned, bringing his pocky, irascible face close to mine. "If you don't want to turn up missin' like your nigger-lovin' friends in Philadelphia, you better watch your step. Because the next time I see you, may be the last time you see anything. If I was you, I'd hightail it over to the other side of the tracks where the rest of the niggers live and tell them to keep you out of sight. You in Tallahatchie now, and before long the sun will be goin' down. And if I don't get you, the niggers probably will, because they don't want you around here either. They told me so themselves."

3

From the courthouse I drove a few blocks due east to the train station and took the first street that crossed the tracks, noticing that the name changed from Chestnut to Bruce as soon as I was in "niggertown." I turned right on Revels, a dirt road that looked like a dry riverbed. Tallahatchie, I later learned, was laid out on a tilt, with the whites on higher ground and the blacks on lower. Although the present-day river was behind a bluff on the western boundary of the town, the old channel, now a wide bayou covered with green scum, sometimes overflowed during rain storms, flooding the black side of town, which had no drainage system. Revels was one of the streets south of Bruce that was periodically submerged, but not even the ravages of a flash flood could account for all the depressing sights.

Haphazard boxes hammered together of rough-hewn planks patched with scraps of tar paper, precariously propped on piles of rocks or stacks of brick, each shack finding its only apparent support by leaning on the others—those rows of dingy shanties listing this way and that epitomized all that was slipshod, tawdry, and askew. Jumbled together, windows boarded shut or blocked with cardboard, and with the sun beating down on their tin roofs, the heat inside must have been intolerable. No wonder so many people were outside, mostly old people clustered on rickety porches and barefoot children running in all directions. Where were the parents? Everyone looked either over sixty or under ten. After a few days in town I would be able to answer my own question: up North, under the earth, or in the fields chopping cotton.

Revels Street stopped at the bayou, so I took a left on an unnamed street (called, I learned, Jellyroll Alley), which was nothing but honky-tonks, hockshops, pool halls, and (I was to learn this too) whorehouses. I drove around the chuckholed streets until I found Bruce again, and then drove up the part of Revels Street that ran away from the bayou. Here the houses were in better shape, at least comparatively. Some were freshly painted, a handful were made of brick, a few tree-shaded cottages had well-kept yards and abundant flower gardens. Even the numerous weather-board shacks didn't look like they were on the verge of collapse. The Abiding Light Baptist Church was a plain cement-block building with a neon cross on the roof, but it sat in a lot with freshly cut grass and neatly trimmed shrubs.

The church was locked, but making contact was no problem. People gathered so quickly you would have thought I'd been ringing the go-to-meeting bell. If there was any hostility to my coming, that crowd certainly didn't show it. I solemnly shook dozens of warm hands, and every woman there asked me if I was hungry, would I like something to eat, when could I come to dinner. Giggling children huddled at my feet, eyes wide with excited curiosity. Jesus H. Christ in person couldn't have received a better welcome.

After a few days of working at the Freedom House, slapping together some shelves and sorting books while I talked to the stream of visitors, I realized that there were several black communities, all jammed together in incongruous proximity under the pressure of segregation and labeled "niggertown" by the whites. To the blacks, their side of town was known as Bruceville, which was subdivided into: "The Sanctified Quarter," home to the staunchest Pentecostals and Baptists; "DuBois Place," for the street where the few wealthy families lived; and "The Flats," the shabby part south of Bruce that ended at Jellyroll Alley. Most of the people also fit several rough categories: the terminally ill, the permanently drunk, the truly saved, the fully employed, and the kids. Or, to phrase it another way, the porch sitters, the big drinkers, the churchgoers, the cotton pickers, and the barefooters. The vast majority lived in poverty, and if they worked, it was as domestics, sharecroppers, or day laborers. There was a small middle class—store owners, school teachers, railroad workers—and a few families with money and property. The "Big Nigger" in town was one Midnight Grimes, undertaker, bootlegger, and preacher. His empire included several juke joints on Jellyroll Alley and a cotton plantation outside of town.

Before long most folks knew me by name, waved from their porches, invited me into their homes. The hospitality of the Abiding Light people never wavered.

When Ledell Simmons, the Tallahatchie project director, learned about my run-in with Deputy Pratt, he decided that it would be safer for me to stay at the Mays's farm, located across the bayou on a dead-end road a mile or so outside of town. He also convinced me to put my Edsel at the disposal of the voter registration workers.

"There's a footpath through the woods," he explained. "If you know the shortcut, it's real easy to walk to the Freedom House. But if you stay in town after dark, make sure you've got a ride back."

We then drove out to the Mays's home, where I was introduced to the family. I shook Eddie Mays's strong, calloused right hand, testimony to his lifetime of hard work. Buster peeked out at me from behind Ella's skirts until she pulled him forward.

"Say somethin' to the man," she commanded.

"I sure hope we get our freedom," Buster mumbled. "I sure do."

Jasmine smiled in the doorway, looking very pretty in a flower-print dress.

"We glad you come," she said. "You gonna teach in the Freedom School?"

"Yes, I am."

"What you gonna teach?"

"History, I think."

"I'm gonna be one of your students."

"Can I go too?" Buster asked.

"Do you like history?"

"I like history," Buster declared.

"Not the way they teach it here. We've got those crummy old books from the white school with a Confederate flag on the cover, and all they talk about is white man this and white man that."

"Well, we're going to study Negro history. Have you ever read the autobiography of Frederick Douglass? I'm going to start off with that one; I think you'll like it."

Jasmine smiled more broadly at that, and we all went into the house. I was to sleep in Buster's bed, while he took a cot in his grandparent's room. For the first few days everyone was wary and overapologetic, as we strenuously polished our manners and bent over backward not to get in each other's way. But before long I felt like a part of the family: Ella bossed me around like she did everybody else when she was in a bad mood, and she smothered me, as she did everybody else, with love and kindness the rest of the time. We still addressed each other rather formally (I called them "Mr. Mays" and "Mrs. Mays" and they called me "Mr. Tom"), but the atmosphere of the house was warm, close, and confiding, and good talk was considered the spice of life. Every evening we sat out on the porch and told stories; rather *they* told stories, while I listened and learned all I could about the trivial peculiarities and tragic fates of people, both black and white, in Tallahatchie.

4

Ella normally did the talking, while Eddie leaned back in his cane-bottomed rocking chair smoking his pipe, but on the subject of how they got their farm, he was the one who told the story. "That goes way back there," he said, and over several evenings he related a saga of how his ancestors had owned some land after Reconstruction, but then been forced into sharecropping for others. It wasn't until 1939, when the federal government stepped in, confiscated land, and sold it to small farmers, black and white, that he had been able to purchase the plot that fronted on the Tallahatchie.

Eddie had certainly done what he could with his hundred acres. In addition to his cotton and soybeans, he had a "truck patch" (where he grew corn, squash, sweet potatoes, and a variety of vegetables) as well as chickens, hogs, a pony, and a cow (all, by the way, with personal names). He even had a homemade tractor, which he had assembled with truck parts from the junkyard.

"I'd be doin' a lot better if these peckerwoods would give me half a chance. They hate it when a black man gets ahead. But at least I ain't croppin' for shares. Those folks are still doin' the same work the slaves done, and they still gettin' the same nuthin'."

"That's right," Ella said, "they still works them tight like they did in slavery days. These white folks around here has done a heap of wrong, an' they knows it."

"They'll take everythin' a man owns," Eddie said, "down to his last chicken or hog or ear of corn. They just plain takes it, that's all, and there ain't nuthin' folks can do 'cept scratch it out in the summer and strap it in the winter, like they always done. I tell you, it's hard. You gotta treat them like a silk hanky on a barbwire fence, and they treat you like mud on they shoe. But, you know, things ain't always the way you'd want them to be."

Eddie was also the one who explained to me the intricacies of the sharecropper system. Listening to him, I learned to talk crops, yield, tractors, credit, and foreclosure.

The problem for sharecroppers was how to survive for a whole year on the scanty and undependable wages paid for half a year's work. At the start of the growing season, the planter provided his croppers with a "furnish": basically a shack to live in, a designated plot of land to work, and credit at his store to buy food and supplies. Usually by the time the cotton was chopped, the sharecropper had little, if any, credit left. During cotton-picking time, however, if the harvest was abundant, everyone healthy, the market price high, and a sudden rainstorm didn't spoil things, sharecroppers could actually make some money. A picker received three dollars for every hundred pounds, and a good picker could bring in four hundred pounds a day. In addition, his children, starting at age nine, could pick one to two hundred pounds each. In this optimum situation, a family might clear over a thousand dollars.

Normally, of course, the outcome was much worse: the crop was poor, the market low, the children sick, and the weather too dry or wet. In that case, a family wouldn't break even; they'd be in debt to the planter and have nothing to live on until spring.

Eddie had a lot of sympathy for the sufferings of the sharecroppers, but he also didn't hesitate to criticize them for letting the system beat them and keep them down. "Some of those folks is they own worst enemy," he said. He told me a story about how when he was a boy the crops were good and prices were high. In such times, the planters always urged their tenants to buy luxury items—gold teeth, silk dresses, even cars—to ensure that they stayed in debt. Midnight Grimes, then a young man on the make, saw his main chance: he opened up the only Stutz Bearcat dealership in the Delta, sold the half-dozen cars he had on the lot in a month, and banked his profits. If anybody couldn't meet his payments, he repossessed the car and sold it again. When a car began to develop mechanical problems—and there's nothing like bumpy dirt roads and dust everywhere to put a car out of whack—he informed its owner that the nearest Stutz Bearcat repair shop was in Illinois. One by the one, the cars quit running and were left to rust beside the poor sharecropper's shack. Three of them were finally towed away and dumped in the swamp. "When the water's low," Eddie said, "you can still see their windshields pokin' out." Midnight Grimes, meanwhile, took the money he made from his venture in the car business and bought himself a plantation, where more than one once-proud owner of a Stutz Bearcat found seasonal employment.

5

Ella worked as a maid. Every morning at five she got up and fixed breakfast, then Eddie drove her into Bruceville where she joined a group of black maids to walk over to the white section of town. She fixed her white family's breakfast, made their beds, cleaned the house, did the washing, watched after their kids, and at noon prepared the main meal. After she had done the dishes, scrubbed the floors, and ironed, she returned to the farm, taking a path through the woods. In her absence, Jasmine was in charge of lunch, Buster, and the housework. At about five, Ella walked back into town, or Eddie drove her to Bruceville (white families didn't like to see their maids arrive by car), and she cooked the evening meal, did the dishes and any final chores, and either walked back home or accepted a ride, if offered. Her pay was twelve dollars a week.

The family she worked for owned one of the new red-brick, ranch-style homes along the small lake off Grove Road. Fortunately, this was a part of Tallahatchie close to the bayou, leaving her with a walk of about half a mile. In bad weather the path turned to mud, so she would have to take the long way round: across the tracks, through Bruceville, along Cain Ridge Road, and down to the end of Easy Street—a journey of nearly two miles. "When I get to heaven," I once heard Ella say, "I sure know the first thing I'm gonna do: sit down, take off my shoes, and rest a spell."

Years before Ella had worked for the Brandons, owners of the much-photographed Magnolia Hill, a porticoed antebellum mansion that occupied a small rise (anything above sea level in the Delta qualified as a "hill") on Magnolia Street. Family legend related that when word came to Mississippi that Lincoln was dead, a Yankee soldier, offended by piano music he heard coming from Magnolia Hill, marched in the front door and confronted Jenny Brandon, who continued to play in spite of his command to stop. The furious soldier promptly returned with a hammer and nails and nailed the keyboard shut, and so it had remained to the present day.

As a maid who talked daily with other maids, Ella knew all about the white side of town. Gossip for them was a kind of revenge. In a few weeks, I learned from her things that would have taken most outsiders years to discover. But first I had to learn to avoid direct questions. I was in the habit of initiating conversations as if I were exchanging resumés, whereas here it was bad manners to ask about background, qualifications, and accomplishments. The second day I was at the Mays's home, I noticed a photograph tacked to the wall of a very light-skinned woman with a graduation cap perched jauntily on top of her tumbling curls.

"Who's that?" I asked.

"Miscelia." Ella's answer was noncommittal.

"She looks a little bit like Jasmine."

Silence.

"Is she her mother?"

Silence.

At that point I had enough sense to drop the subject. About a week later, however, sitting out on the porch after Buster had gone to bed, the story of Ella's children came out:

"I had five in all," she said, "but only two lived to be grown. I named my daughter 'Miscelia' to make sure white folks addressed her like a lady. My son I called 'Douglass.' I never got no higher than sixth in school, but Miscelia, she always had her nose in a book (just like Jasmine), and we begun savin' up our money so she could go to college. Douglass never cared for much of anything except havin' a good time. He hated school and wouldn't go. All the womens liked him and he liked them. Didn't matter if they married or not, or white or colored, he they man. I knew he was headin' for trouble, but he wouldn't listen.

"When he was seventeen, he got a job as a yard boy, workin' for a white lady over in town. In the spring and early summer, when it rains a lot and the grass needs to be cut once a week, he'd show up twice a week. Then by August and September, when the sun's so hot the grass turns yellow and shrivels away, not a day don't go by but he's over there. Eddie tole him he was gonna get hisself kilt if he didn't watch out, but I guess he was born lucky. Because if it warn't for the war, he'd be dead now for sure. He got drafted, served in the Pacific, and afterwards moved to San Francisco. I don't know what he be doin' now; he don't write and it's too far to visit, but I'll tell you one thing—it sure ain't work."

Ella had a way of pursing her lips when she paused that suggested she was savoring her words before she spoke them.

"Miscelia was valedictorian of her little school, and she got a scholarship to go to Tuskegee. She didn't do so good there, but she come back with big ideas about what she wanted. She said she wasn't gonna be no farmer's wife and that the colored men around here don't know how to treat a woman. She'd gone to see that movie—*Spellbound*—and for weeks afterwards that was all she talked about. Then one day she told me Gilbert Brandon had the same kind eyes and pretty mouth of Gregory Peck and I knew we were in for trouble. She and Gilbert were about the same age and had known each other all they lives, because I used to bring the Brandon kids out to the farm on the afternoons so I could look after my own kids too. Course he started goin' to the white school, and she went to the colored, so they didn't see each other much.

"Miscelia was a good-lookin' woman. She knew she could have any man in town, but it was Gilbert she wanted and Gilbert she got. He'd come back from Ole Miss with a law degree, a sweet little wife, and twin babies—a boy and a girl. He had him an office over there on Court Square and was doin' right well. But all it took was Miscelia walkin' downtown one time in some clingy dress and he was hooked. He set her up in a house over on Sumner Street, facin' the railroad tracks, and bought her things she wanted: new shoes, fancy clothes, a radio, gold jewelry. I begged her to stop, but she said, 'I loves him, Mama, and he loves me; that's all that matters.' Course I knew that wasn't all that mattered, but they wouldn't listen to me, and they didn't care what the rest of the world thought, so it wasn't long before the whole town knew what was goin' on. Wasn't long neither before Miscelia was cryin' every night and gettin' sick every morning. When Jasmine was born, Gilbert didn't want no midwife; he had him a white doctor and a white nurse too. Some men in the Klan warned him he better quit this foolishness, but that booger stood up to them. His family, and his wife and her family, they pleaded with him to let her go (we tried to talk to Miscelia too). Finally they called it off, and Miscelia and her baby come to live with us.

"Miscelia stayed with us for about a year, but then she met a man she liked—Len Marks—and started livin' with him. We thought it was over with Gilbert Brandon, but it wasn't; she was still slippin' out to see him too. When Len found out, he beat her bad. He strop her down and rip most her clothes off right out in the street. She promised she wouldn't see Gilbert no more, but she was lyin'. She and Len fought a lot and drank a lot, and Gilbert, he didn't look too happy neither. The midwife come when Buster was born, but Len was somewhere off on a drunk. He done the best he could for Miscelia and the two kids, I reckon, but that little shack they had sure wasn't much. They just barely got by.

"I don't know how the fire started, but by the time Len and Gilbert got there, smoke was pourin' out the windows. The both of them went rushin' into the flames, but only Gilbert come back, with Jasmine and Buster in his arms. When they told him Miscelia was still inside, they had to hold him down to keep him from rushin' back. The whole town, black and white, had gathered by that time, so everybody, his wife and children, too, heard him sobbin' for Miscelia and cryin' out how much he loved her. Next mornin' the firemen found the bodies of Miscelia and Len, side by side, in the ashes. So I lost my precious baby, and a good man, too, and it hurts my heart to this day. Well, the white folks didn't care none about two dead niggers, but they was just scandalized by how Gilbert had carried on and made a spectacle of hisself, embarrassin' his wife like that in front of all they friends. No way he could live in Tallahatchie after that. He and his family moved out west some-wheres and nobody in town seems to know or care if they livin' or dead. So much done happen then I like to lose my mind. To this day, I think about it, I get depress. A pain in my chest. Here."

6

Not one black person I talked to showed the least surprise when, during the search for the missing civil rights workers, two black bodies, so badly decomposed they had torn in half, were found in the Old River. The victims, identified as Charles Moore and Henry Dee from Meadville in southwestern Mississippi, had probably been killed by the Klan, but once it was established that they were not the "right" (i.e., the "white") bodies, the news media dropped the story and the FBI dropped the case.

I thought of Bob Moses talking about all the nameless black men who had been killed when I heard tales around town of others who had died years ago: a man forced to jump into the Tallahatchie River at flood stage; a woman who had been murdered and buried in a shallow grave that the dogs dug up (strands of her hair hung on a barbwire fence as a warning); a man leading a mob on a wild chase through woods and swamp, stripping off his clothes as he ran, until he was finally cornered in an old sewer pipe that emptied into a creek—his bullet-riddled body tied with a plow line to the bumper of a truck and dragged through the streets of Drew. It seemed that everyone in the black community was related to or knew of someone who had been involved in foul play.

Although horror stories like these haunted the imagination, it was the petty manifestations of segregation that caused daily pain. Eddie and Ella intensely resented the fact that even though their lives were eminently respectable, they weren't treated with respect. They were never referred to as "Mr. and Mrs. Mays." No white man offered the right hand of fellowship to Eddie or opened a door and tipped his hat to Ella. Whites demonstrated their "higher civilization" by refusing to extend common courtesies. Ella had spent her life caring for their children and homes, yet she was forbidden to sit down at the dining table and had to enter by the backdoor. If Eddie went to market to sell a hog, he wasn't permitted to see the scales. White farmers met to discuss the cotton allotment, but black farmers had no say. At the few stores that served both races, Ella and Eddie would have to stand aside until all the white customers had been waited on. Buster didn't like being confined to the balcony at the movie theater, and Jasmine complained about the hand-me-down quality of the black schools. To make matters worse, the city fathers responded to the passage of the Civil Rights Bill by closing the public pool and deeding it over to the Kiwanis Club and by taking all the chairs out of the public library and the waiting room at the hospital!

Ella attributed this nitpicky vindictiveness to the fact that power in Tallahatchie was concentrated in the hands of the white middle

THE CHILDREN BOB MOSES LED

class, locally known as "strainers." "Those folks is always strainin' an' strivin' to get ahead," Eddie said. "They don't feel tall enough less they steppin' on somebody."

The local aristocrats had relinquished their authority long before. Now the scions of Brandons, Hamiltons, and comparable clans consoled themselves by restoring their mansions and boasting about their affairs. Ella, who had served as a maid at many of their parties, grew indignant about the way they caroused and carried on. The younger set gathered every evening at somebody's house, each man bringing his own wife and whiskey, but often sharing both before the night was over. The older folks met every Sunday afternoon in the garden of the reigning dowager and discoursed for hours about the grandeur of long-gone ancestors, exchanging tangled tales of lineage and land and planning for Old Home Week. Somehow they always managed to achieve consensus that the past was a better place where the better sort (ladies and gentlemen all!) enjoyed the undying devotion of loving mammies and faithful old-time family retainers. "Well they didn't retain me," Ella would add with disgust.

After my original run-in with the Tallahatchie police, I had made it a point to keep out of sight as much as I could. Every morning I would walk to the Freedom House, which was on Howard Street, a block away from the Abiding Light Baptist Church, and spend the day sorting books for the community center library, preparing for and then teaching my Freedom School classes, and generally talking with anybody who happened to be around. The Freedom House instantly became an all-purpose place for the people of Bruceville: day care, psychological counseling, family planning, neighborhood improvement, drinking problems, sewing club—you name it, we provided it, albeit on a very makeshift amateur basis. It was an education every day just to listen to the stories people told. I learned a lot about the black community and life in Mississippi, but I was curious, once I had my fear more or less under control, to see the white side of town. The funny thing was, the more I came to reject racial stereotypes and see blacks as individuals with the full range of human traits—good, bad, and indifferent—the more Mississippi whites became a blurred abstraction: the racist enemy. White faces put me on edge; scratchy voices grated on my nerves; pale skins struck me as anemic and unnatural. I don't know if my newfound self-reflexive racism was a factor or whether our personalities weren't quite in sync, but I had difficulty establishing close bonds with the other volunteers. We exchanged small talk and cooperated during the day, but in the evening they stayed in town while Jasmine and I, and sometimes Buster, walked back to the Mayses' farm. I rarely had a chance to sit back, relax (as much as that was possible in Mississippi), and have a drink with my coworkers. You'd think that the shared dangers would have made us all blood brothers for life, but I felt cut off from the other volunteers, and the whites in town were beginning to look like creatures from another planet.

I'd been in Tallahatchie more than a week when I finally worked up the courage to cross the tracks and walk downtown. The train station, with its gabled roof and fresh two-toned paint, had a quaint charm, but the dark windowless warehouses, stacked to the beams with great crated mysteries; the rusty watertower; and the drab row of gray wooden houses facing the tracks gave the freight yard a menacing air. In three blocks I came to Court Square where the massive red-brick, white-columned courthouse presided over the town. Out front, at parade rest, stood the regulation cast-iron Confederate soldier, cap crusted with pigeon droppings. I watched a fat man in Bermudas crank his camera and walk backward to get it all in. A gaggle of old-timers, who looked like they'd been holding the fort since the day Lee handed over his sword, occupied a long bench on the portico—an impregnable position from which they could chew and spit and comment.

It was Saturday afternoon and farmers had come in from the country to "make provisions" and to enjoy a break from the monotony of the cotton fields. The square was clogged with cars and pickup trucks, and the hardware, dry goods, grocery, and department stores were packed with customers. Blacks and whites seemed to intermingle easily, sometimes talking and laughing together. It was only on closer inspection that I saw how black men always averted their eyes from white women and avoided the center of the sidewalk. Every store in town also had a White Citizens Council sticker prominently displayed, as did several ostentatious Oldsmobiles filled with hard-eyed men who seemed to be on patrol.

I also began noticing the WHITE ONLY and COLORED signs, but in practice, segregation varied. One drugstore in town served everybody at the same counter and from the same soda fountain, but used different sets of glassware and reserved the booths for whites. Both races stood in the same line at the movie theater (matinee: *How the West Was Won;* late show: *The Carpetbaggers*), but then blacks would have to take their tickets to a side entrance, which led to the balcony (known as "The Monkey House"). Most of the retail stores on Chestnut Street, I had been told, were Jewish-owned and receptive to black customers, while the stores on Main Street valued caste over cash and were often rude to black shoppers, refusing to let them try things on and making them wait for service. I was astonished to discover some Chinese in town, who ran a steam laundry, a restaurant (which didn't serve Chinese food), and a few other small businesses. How strange to hear two small boys speaking Chinese with a Delta drawl!

At the post office I mumbled a request for stamps, without, I hoped, sounding too northern. I glanced at the most-wanted wall to make sure my mug shot wasn't on display. The local paper, *The Tallahatchie Tattler,* whose motto was Look to the Sunny Side, had published a photo of Deputy Purvis Pratt pointing a suspicious finger at two boxes of potentially subversive books found in you-know-whose trunk, but luckily only one sinister arm of the culprit was visible in the picture. Two stubble-chinned, lean-faced locals in cowboy hats were giving me the stare reserved for strangers in these here parts, but nobody spoke, and I left without incident.

I next went to the public library, which had indeed removed all its chairs, to look for books about the South. I wanted to study up so I could discuss Reconstruction with my Freedom School class. None of the southern historians I knew of—W. E. B. DuBois, C. Vann Woodward, or W. J. Cash—were anywhere to be found. Instead, they had *Moonlight Places and Merry Faces* by Agnes Whitestone Sprightly and Horace Snideville Fulknerson's moldy tomes: *Rambling Recollections of Early Days in Mississippi* and *The Negro; as he was; as he is; as he will be.* The librarian was one of those fidgety old biddies who become so nervous to see someone fondling her books you would have thought I was pawing her. The only other people using the library were genealogy buffs, huddled over a table piled with yellowed newspapers. Watching them, it occurred to me that the South's reputed sense of history was really a warped sense of time: not an act of memory but a failure to be contemporary. How easy to relive the past if you've never left it!

The building next to the library constituted a veritable culture center, encompassing a college of cosmetology, a charm school, an Arthur Murray dance studio, a stationery store, and an antique shop called the "Den of Antiquity." I couldn't resist browsing through the old books on display in a glass-fronted cabinet. The owner was a white-haired man with a pleasant pink face and an ironic smile. He sat in a rocking chair stroking a longhaired Siamese cat and smoking a cigarette.

"Come in, come in," he said, "but please forgive me if I don't get up. Pollux doesn't like to be disturbed."

The contented cat purred as the man blew occasional rings of smoke at the ceiling. I finally bought a copy of *Lanterns on the Levee* for five dollars.

"Oh, yes, I believe you'll like that," the man said. "Percy is our finest author."

"What about Faulkner?" I asked impulsively. "He won the Nobel Prize."

"Faulkner was no gentleman," the man stated firmly. "He spoke with a vulgar tongue and drank too much."

"Did you know him?"

"I had the dubious pleasure. A small, stiff man who would stand in a corner, chew on his pipe stem, and try to look superior. He was always four sheets to the wind and refused to discuss his work. I found him rude and remote. I once heard him exaggerate his exploits on the hunt. I believe his townspeople labeled him 'Count No-Account.'"

"I think he's a wonderful writer."

"Of course you would think that, Mr. Morton . . ."

"How do you know my name?"

"I believe I saw your photo in the paper."

I didn't challenge his answer; better to accept a lie than probe after an unpleasant truth.

"I did have a little run-in with Deputy Pratt."

"Well, you're not likely to find a very enlightened discussion of political science down at the local constabulary. If you want to know about Mississippi, you should talk to me."

"I *am* interested in history. What do you have on Reconstruction?"

"There wasn't anything constructive or reconstructive about it." The man remained seated, but he spoke as if he stood at ramrod attention. "A small clique of radical fanatics added insult to injury, sir. The war was bad enough, but the deliberate humiliation of a proud but defeated people was intolerable. We shall never forget or forgive. You'll find the whole sordid story in here."

He handed me a copy of *The Tragic Era* by Claude Bowers.

"How much is it?"

"I'll give it to you for free if you promise to read it."

"Oh, I'll read it all right. Thanks."

"Do you know what 'entropy' is?" he asked me with acute interest.

"Yes, I studied that in college."

"Well, your nigrah is entropic. He wants to sink back into the mud—that's the reason he's black. Young man, you don't know who you are or where you are. Why, right now you're standing knee-deep in quicksand and you don't even know it. I'd advise you to leave this place and go back where you came from."

"Thanks, but I plan to stay."

"Well, then, you come back and see us real soon now," he crooned as I walked out.

I wanted to enjoy my stroll up Magnolia Avenue, admiring the tall, moss-draped trees, the flowering shrubs, and the regal homes, but my mind kept flashing back to what I had just learned: I was already a marked man in Tallahatchie. My photo had been circulated among a small group of concerned citizens who, no doubt, were not all as mild-mannered as the owner of the antique shop. Nevertheless, I was determined not to be scared away. I tried to imagine myself as Spencer Tracy in *Bad Day at Black Rock*, but I completed my tour of the town as inconspicuously as possible.

As I walked down Church Street, I saw happy whites splashing in the recently acquired Kiwanis Club pool while unhappy black kids looked in through the chain-link fence; I saw black men mowing lawns while white men sat on porches; black women hanging laundry while white women watered flowers. Down the back alleys I even saw some black children playing, since in the older part of town, servants lived in shacks behind the house of the white family they worked for.

By the time I reached the suburban developments on the south side of town I felt I was no longer in Tallahatchie but in Anywhere, U.S.A. Here on streets laid out in geometric pattern and named for trees chopped down to clear the land, a limited repertoire of red-brick split-levels and ranch houses was replicated ad nauseam. A station wagon in the driveway; burgers on the backyard grill; a tricycle tipped over in the front yard. Those with aristocratic longings placed a plaster blackamoor hitching post by the walkway and nailed a brass replica of the national bird over the front door. This was the world I thought I had left behind in Ohio—a green ghetto where men performed the high-caste rituals of grass cutting, car washing, and charcoal lighting, while women gleaned wisdom from the soaps: as the world turns in the days of our lives we need a guiding light in our search for tomorrow because we have only one life to live. *Big deal,* I thought, *Hershey Kisses meets Hostess Twinky and they settle down to form a consumer unit with an exciting growth curve. Not this boy,* I thought. *Not ever.* Yet hip cynicism aside, I had to admit that Tallahatchie was a very pretty town. If I hadn't seen it from Ella and Eddie's point of view, I would have assumed that it was a nice place to live.

7

The next morning everyone woke up early and hustled and bustled about getting ready for church. Buster took a bath; Jasmine did her hair; Ella ironed clothes; Eddie and I washed the car. We were in for a whole day of religion: Sunday school, the regular service, an afternoon picnic, and a special children's service followed by a sundown lakeside baptism. Although Abiding Light Baptist in Tallahatchie was where the Mays family went for civil rights meetings, their regular church was Blessed Redeemer, located five miles out of town. The pastor was none other than Midnight Grimes, reputedly as talented at arousing a congregation as he was at arranging a deal. A pulpit impresario, his job was not to imitate Christ but to let loose with a real knock-down sermon. So long as he could deliver powerful emotions on Sunday, what he did the rest of the week was his own business. He had resisted the overtures of the SNCC workers at first, seeing them as a threat to his fiefdom. But he must have sensed that civil rights was here to stay, because he finally agreed to open his church.

"That man's ego knows no bounds," Ledell Simmons told me after negotiating with Reverend Grimes. "He thinks he's the next Martin Luther King."

The agreement was that Ledell and I would be allowed to discuss voter registration after the regular service was over. I was nervous; I hadn't spoken in church since high school.

As a teenager in Methodist Youth Fellowship I had undergone my own "conversion experience" one summer at church camp. The minister charged with saving my adolescent soul was an exotic creature undreamt of in our suburb—an Italian Methodist from Chicago! His prayers were intimate chats, as if he and Jesus were old friends. "Hello, Jesus," he'd say. "I'm down here at Lakeside with some kids I'd like you to meet. They're a terrific bunch, but I think they're looking for something that only you've got. I know you want to help them, Jesus. Shall I tell them the good news?" He was so smooth, and his voice so soothing, that my skin tingled. Afterward we each lit our one little candle and walked out under the stars to commune with the cosmos. There I heard the still, small voice of Jesus whispering on a breeze across Lake Erie, and I dedicated my life to his service.

My redemption lasted until I met the minister's daughter, a Natalie-Wood-type and a PK rebel, who led me one night out on the dock and, as waves lapped against the pilings, taught me beatitudes unmentioned by Matthew, Mark, Luke, and John.

"The one thing about the Bible that is literally true is that it is not literally true," I would assert during college bull sessions in which skepticism was the norm.

The essence of religion, I believed, was believing in something that wasn't so. It was a way not to *find* the truth, but to hide it. Hence, converts accepted blatant absurdities as articles of faith—resurrection, reincarnation, what-have-you—in order to deny the grim facts of death and decay. Whether Jesus was born of a virgin, walked on water, rose from the dead, and was the Son of God were, at best, obscure. What was clear was that people were ready to believe anything! And they always claimed the most certainty about that which was least likely. The only thing all the religious myths confirmed beyond doubt was that this old world *needed* redeeming.

Nevertheless, religion fascinated me. I joked about it constantly, toyed with its propositions, observed how people's beliefs shaped their behavior. "If God created the world in seven days," I theorized, "the key question is, What took him so long? But if there is no God, only the random arrangements of evolution, then the question is, How did it happen at all and why so quickly?" A course in comparative religions goaded me to ask blasphemous questions: "Did the Mound Builders pile dirt to get closer up to God or farther away from the mosquitoes?" "Did the stylites sit on top of their phallic pillars to castigate the flesh or to induce sexual fantasies?" A spiritual sophomore, I could neither believe, nor feel comfortable in my unbelief. At heart, I suppose, I was a typical American pragmatist who thought that what the world needed was not one great irrefutable premise in the sky, but a good working hypothesis here on earth. Still, even in my joking, the voice of Jesus haunted me. I would make up apocryphal quotes and solemnly whisper them to Lenny at unexpected times. My favorite was "When I die, paint chicken eggs many colors and hide them from your children."

Among the volunteers going to Mississippi, I noted many devout Christians and Jews who believed in the fatherhood of God, the brotherhood of man, and the need for social justice. But most of us came in spite of the church, not because of it; we saw ourselves as free thinkers who only wanted to do what was right. I was soon to learn, however, that for blacks in the South, religion was not a subject for idle speculation but an irrefutable force. Faith in Jesus was what gave a lot of people the courage to welcome the volunteers and stand up for freedom. That faith also accounted for why so many could live with compassion and dignity in the midst of an intolerable situation. They made my own skepticism look like mere posturing.

"What are you?" a black woman asked me during a service at Abiding Light Baptist Church.

"I'm an agnostic."

"Oh," she said, mulling that over, "do they immerse or sprinkle?"

Blessed Redeemer was a frail crackerbox affair dwarfed even further by a gigantic oak tree that spread its moss-draped arms across the parking lot. An overgrown graveyard, with timeworn tombstones tilted drunkenly in every direction, gave further testimony that this was the oldest church in the county. Midnight

Grimes had been preaching there since he was a boy, and perhaps it was nostalgia more than stinginess that kept him from spending a penny for repairs. A broom handle barred the back door and leaks from the roof streaked the side walls. Inside, there were frameless windows, a few rows of handmade park benches, and an unfinished plank floor. A potbellied, wood-burning stove provided heat in the winter. The only altar decoration was a crude portrait of Christ—your basic blond, blue-eyed Nordic Jew. There was no pulpit, only a thronelike chair with ornate gold trim and purple cushions set up front for the preacher. The choir stood for the whole service, calling out impromptu responses—"Well, all right!" "Yes, Lord!" "Yessuh! Preach it!" "Tell the truth!"—when they weren't singing and dancing.

The congregation, mainly women and children, was remarkably well dressed, even for Sunday, especially in light of how poor people were. I felt badly out of style in my blue jeans and work shirt. The women sported high-crowned hats embellished with fake flowers; the boys had been scrubbed to a shine; and the girls wore braided hair with fancy, bright-colored ribbons. Through a dust-crusted window I watched several teenagers smoking cigarettes and teasing each other. One couple wandered off, arm-in-arm, into the pine trees. Most of the men, including Eddie Mays, stayed outside, talking in the parking lot. Only a few white-haired old-timers in identical dark suits, which must have been stifling in the heat, came in for the service. Apparently, they were deacons, because they occupied a row of chairs up front. One immediately nodded off, while the others, when they weren't guffawing at the preacher's least witticism, sucked their teeth and stared morosely at the congregation. I sat on a splintery bench with Ella and Buster.

The choir consisted of Jasmine in a white dress, a dozen heavyset middle-aged women in white blouses and black skirts, one undersized man in a rumpled suit who kept his eyes on the ceiling and snapped his fingers as he sang, and a gaunt hat rack of a woman who somehow managed to dance beside the piano while she directed with one hand and played with the other.

Jasmine, the featured soloist, had remarkable range, from soul-shattering high notes down to low, throaty ones that conjured up stormy emotions and made her sound experienced beyond her years. I suppose she had taken some singing lessons, but hers was largely an untrained talent. She simply had it. She was like a young pitcher with a hopping fastball and a sharp-breaking curve who walked as many batters as he struck out, but you forgave all that for the sheer pleasure of watching him fire away. In one song, as the choir swayed, clapped their hands, and harmonized the refrain of *"Hush, hush,"* Jasmine came in with a lilting *"Somebody's callin' my name,"* and then *"Sounds like Jesus...,"* and finally, *"I'm so glad, trouble don't last always."* Better yet was *"Woke up this morning with my mind stayed on Jesus."* And when she sang "Amazing Grace" I thought my heart would burst. The whole congregation was stunned into silence except for one woman who kept moaning "O my!"

Midnight Grimes, a plump man who looked far younger than his sixty-plus years, strolled out and stood in front of us with a big smile on his face. His hair was slicked back, and he wore a satiny silver-gray suit with velvet lapels. The gloss on his shoes caught the light from the sixty-watt bulb hanging from the ceiling. His clothes made an impression on the congregation, and he knew it. He ran his eyes over us one by one.

"Ain't God been good to us," he cooed, still flashing his teeth. "Praise His name."

A few mumbled agreement.

"I said praise Him! Praise His name!"

A chorus of "Amens," "Thas right," and "Yes, Lord."

"He works in mysterious ways, His wonders to perform. . . . I never know what I'm gonna say until I'm standin' here in front of my blessed people, but I know the Lord knows what it's gonna be. He walks with me and he talks with me and he fills me with His Holy Spirit. I can feel Him workin' in me now. He has given me the call, and now I'm ready.

"You know God called to Moses out of the midst of a burnin' bush. He said, 'Moses! Moses!' and Moses said, 'Here I am.' And

God said, 'I have seen the afflictions of my people; I have heard their cry and I know their sorrows. I want you to bring forth my children and free them from oppression.'

"And Moses said, 'O my Lord, I am not eloquent. I am slow of speech and of a slow tongue.'

"And God said, 'You let me worry about that. I am that I am. I'll take care of yo mouth. I'll teach you what to say and do.'

"So Moses went to the pharaoh and told him he come from God with a simple message, 'Let my people go.'

"Course the pharaoh was a white man, so he didn't listen. And the Lord smote him and He smote him good. He turned his rivers to blood. He plagued him with frogs, lice, flies, locusts. He killed his cattle. He killed his firstborn child. But the man wouldn't listen. Just like a white man, he wouldn't listen. . . . But we're talkin' about Moses.

"See Moses didn't think he was ready. He hadn't been to college; he didn't have no degrees; he didn't know how to read and write. But the Lord said, 'Moses, I don't care if you been to Morehouse or the poorhouse; I don't care if you got a Ph.D. or no "D" at all. I want yo life.' 'But I don't speak good,' Moses said. 'That don't matter. I'll put the words in yo mouth. I'll tell you what to do. If you got somethin' you wanna say to me, say it with yo life.'"

At this point the preacher began to pace back and forth, intoning his sermon in a singsongy chant. His deep, gravelly voice built in volume and intensity, booming and breaking and landing on certain words with special emphasis. The text about Moses was left behind as he worked himself into such a frenzy he had to gasp for breath after each phrase. He pulled the largest silk handkerchief I had ever seen from his breast pocket to wipe his brow and wave in the air.

> *"God don't want just yo Sunday morning life.*
> *He want yo Saturday night life too.*
> *That's right! That's right!*
> *You know you can't ho with the hounds*
> *Without God sees you.*

He wants yo Monday-to-Friday life too.
He wants it all; He wants it all.
See God don't work on no shares;
God don't make no shady deals.
He don't say 'Well I'll take half
And let the Devil have the hinder part.'
That ain't the way God operates.
He wants it all;
He wants yo life.
He's got a land of milk and honey;
He's got a mansion in the sky
Just waitin' for you.
If you say it
With yo life."

As soon as the preacher started chanting, the congregation began responding in kind, calling out "Thas right," "Well," "Yessuh," and "Amen" at every pause. I could easily take the emotional pulse of the group by noting how rapidly the women fanned themselves and how vigorously they raised their voices to support what was said. Most of the time I watched Jasmine, who at first just swayed and nodded, but soon was clapping her hands and calling out her approval with the rest.

"You know the Devil is different.
He offers easy terms.
He say,
'No down payment;
Take as long as you wants to pay.'
Then a day come;
You hear a knock on the door;
You know who out there.
Thas right! Thas right! The Devil!
Come for his own.
You say, 'I needs mo' time.'
But the Devil say,

'I wouldn't lie to you.
I give you a whole lifetime to pay.
But it's over now.
You're off the scene.
I come for my own.
And if you had somethin'
You wanted to say to Jesus,
You're too late.
You'd just be beatin' yo gums for nuthin'.
You should have said it
With yo life.'"

Words alone were no longer enough for the spirited-up congregation. People began to wax ecstatic, tapping their feet and dancing in the aisles until I could feel the floor vibrate. The whole place began to shake and totter to the contrapuntal rhythms. One woman came and stood in front of another who was moaning and groaning and rocking back and forth in her seat. She bent over and sang to her in an effort either to calm her down or urge her on, I couldn't tell which.

"You know Jesus had troubles
Just like ours.
He didn't have no easy life.
You think those bossmen
Didn't give Him a hard time?
You know He had to work
For everything He got.
And in the end, they put
Their bloodhounds on Him.
They run Him down,
And they strung Him up.
They hung Him on high,
And they spread Him wide,
And they cut His side,

And they thought He was done for.
They'd shut His mouth at last.
But they was fooled you see
'Cause He'd already said it
With his life."

Reverend Grimes surpassed himself to act out the crucifixion: he trudged across the room with his handkerchief over his bent shoulder to simulate carrying the cross and then flung his arms out and gazed tragically into our eyes. At that, the woman sitting next to me jumped up, beat the air with her hands, and began to scream. Then she fell to the floor, twisting and turning in the throes of what seemed an epileptic fit. I reached down to help, but I was brushed aside by several women who immediately came to her aid. They obviously knew exactly what to do, holding her legs, arms, and head so she wouldn't hurt herself. One waved a shawl in front of her face while another picked up the woman's hat and made sure her dress stayed down. Grimes glanced over at her almost absent-mindedly and went on preaching.

"And what did Jesus say?
He said 'God is my Father;
All men are my brothers.
But I ain't no kin to the Devil.
Satan is a sweet-talker.
He got a butter-mouthed tongue;
He got a slippery shoe;
He got a fancy car.
But I took up the cross,
So you could wear the crown.
I gave up my life,
So you could be saved.
You may not have a telephone,
But you can call on me
At the midnight hour.

I'll always be there
To whisper in yo ear.
My message is easy:
You are not worthy,
But I love you anyway.
Only the despised few
Are comin' through.
The last shall be first.
I said that.
Thas what I said
With my life.'"

Several people were dancing; one woman with her hands pressed to her sides was hopping up and down in place; a young boy quickstepped around the room with amazing agility. Everyone was clapping and praising Jesus. I thought the sermon was over, but the preacher had only paused to catch his breath.

"What does Jesus want?
What you got!
Jesus wants what you got.
He wants it all.
The Devil will settle
For a little bit at a time.
But Jesus wants it all,
And He wants it now!
Say it with yo life.
Are you stuck in the muck?
Ask Jesus to help.
He'll pull you out;
He'll set you on solid rock.
Amazin' grace.
It sound so good.
It saved a wretch like me.
Praise His name!
Come on, Jesus,

And see about yo children!
Come on, Jesus,
And bring us joy!
You don't need no jukejoints;
You won't find it
In that bottle.
A slippin'-around life
Will only bring you down.
The only joy is Jesus.
Come on and call on Him!
Come on
And say it with yo life."

Grimes's voice was almost gone now, and he looked like he'd aged twenty years in the last ten minutes. One of the deacons tried to assist him back to his chair, but he shook off his arm, and suddenly stepped forward and, with a final rasping burst of energy, brought us all to our feet.

"Come on!
He's a friend of mine!
Come on!
He'll be a friend to you.
Come on! Come on! Come on!
Yeah Jesus!
Yeah Jesus! Yeah Jesus!
Jesus, Jesus, Jesus.
Jesus is the one!
Praise to my dyin' soul.
Jesus is the one!"

The choir came in on cue with "Do You Want a Good Religion?" while Reverend Grimes, his face drenched in sweat, finally accepted a deacon's assistance and slumped back in his chair. A woman wearing a turban brought him a purple towel to mop his brow and began to rub him down, massaging his back and chest. When the song was over, one of the old deacons stood up, shut his eyes so tight his whole face wrinkled, and murmured away at a long prayer I couldn't hear. After that, two deacons came forward with wicker baskets for the collection.

"Today is a special day," Reverend Grimes said in a hoarse voice, "and I want y'all to make a special effort to show your appreciation to the Lord. We got some Freedom Riders with us today and this week my youngest boy, Sterling, turns eighteen. Stand up, son."

Sterling Grimes was a tall, good-looking guy with droopy lizard eyes and a supercilious smile, dressed in a dapper, light-blue suit with gold buttons.

"You know I don't go in for newfangled things; I'm a lot for old times, gimme that old time religion. But today a young man who's lookin' to get married and wants to impress a woman has gotta have it in his pocket or he's outa luck. Woman don't marry for romance nowadays; they want finance. So today I want y'all to push hard and dig deep and come forward while we sing, 'cause I wanna raise fifty dollars. Here's a five spot to start it off."

Reverend Grimes snapped a crisp bill from his wallet and put it in the basket.

"Who's gonna match me? Anybody got five dollars to give? Come on up now."

Ella Mays and a few other wives of independent farmers came forward and presented their money. I went up with the one-dollar people.

"The white gentleman gave three dollars," one deacon announced loudly.

"All right, now the rest of y'all, come on up with whatever the Lord has blessed you with. Don't be shame, bring your quarters, bring your dimes. If you ain't got a dime, bring your nickels: we're all equal in His sight."

As soon as the last person had walked up front with quiet dignity, everyone watched expectantly while the deacons counted the collection and announced that it came to $47.50. We were then asked to kick in another quarter. When that was counted, we had $53.25, and so the call went out for dimes and nickels to see if we could get it evened off at $55.00, which was finally accomplished. I found the whole process of milking these poor people for their last pennies pretty shoddy, but the congregation didn't seem to feel that way; they followed the whole long drawn-out procedure with an ongoing commentary on who gave what.

Ledell didn't like it much either. He'd seen too many black preachers draining money from their people without giving anything concrete in return. "Some of these preachers act like Jesus' last words were 'Shear my sheep,'" he told me bitterly.

When Ledell was introduced, the preacher made it sound as if he—Midnight Grimes—had been at the forefront of the Movement from the start, and Ledell and I had just arrived to join his command.

"I want the whole world to know where I stand and what I demand," he said. "I won't let nobody turn me around. We welcome the people who are with us today. They don't know how it is down here. So we gonna work with them. And we grateful they have come. They had no morsel, so we fed them; they had no shelter, so we took them in."

"Don't you have any bread?" a woman next to me asked, looking very concerned.

While Reverend Grimes looked on with misgivings, Ledell did his best to shift the focus over to the things we hoped people would do to help us and to help themselves. He knew how to talk the talk, and he soon had their complete attention.

"Jesus didn't just pray," he said. "He walked what he talked. Religion should change your life right here on earth. You should see specific results. I'm talking about education for your children and better economic opportunities for you. I'm talking about good food, decent clothes, adequate housing, paved streets, and a political voice in your destiny. This is not a time to sit tight, but to step forward. We need you to go downtown and try to register. Because if you can't walk ten blocks to the courthouse, how are you gonna make it ten million miles to heaven?"

He was greeted with a chorus of "Ain't that the truth!" and "Thas right!" Ledell explained the Freedom Democratic Party and then he introduced me.

"I want to thank you for letting us join you today," I said in a shaky voice as I looked out at those expectant faces. "And I want to especially thank the Mays family for taking me in. Like the Good Samaritan, they know that loving your neighbor means helping anybody in need." As soon as I mentioned that parable, the congregation began to call out affirmations. The surge of confidence that brought was exhilarating. "If Jesus were alive today," I concluded with a flourish, "he would be doing exactly what Ledell Simmons and Bob Moses are doing, working for civil rights in Mississippi!"

Afterward everyone talked about what a good service it had been and came up and shook our hands and invited us to the picnic. The rest of the afternoon was an idyllic interlude in the midst of that summer's firestorm. People lingered around the church for an hour, joshing and passing the time, then we all piled in the available cars and drove out to a farm that had a small lake, where tables were heaped with fried chicken, potato salad, coleslaw, black-eyed peas, string beans, and watermelon. A roast pig was already turning on a spit at the barbecue pit. Unlike other church picnics I had been to, there were no planned activities: no sack races or softball games. The women passed babies from arm-to-arm as they spread out the meal and complimented each other on the delicious food; the men carried on the same low-key discussion, probably about crops and the weather, that had been going on during the church service. Most of the children stayed down by the lake where they skipped stones and tried to catch frogs. Teenage couples occasionally wandered off into the trees.

I spent much of the afternoon following Jasmine with my eyes. She stayed with the women and kept busy handing out plates, pouring drinks, and patting babies. Just when I had worked up my nerve to talk to her, Sterling Grimes came over and monopolized her attention, so I had to settle for urging mothers to send their children to the summer Freedom School.

In the late afternoon there was a revival service down by the lake, with all the songs and prayers directed specifically at the teenagers, still simmering from the afternoon sun or some recent sins. Midnight Grimes talked about how Jesus astonished the preachers with his spiritual wisdom when he was only twelve years old and how Jesus as a young man was baptized by John in the river Jordan.

As the choir sang *"I ran to the rock to hide my face; / Rock cried out no hiding place,"* he called on them by name to repent and receive the Lord, signaling out Jasmine for special attention.

"Jasmine, ain't you never been touched?" he cried, standing in front of her and looking searchingly into her eyes. "Don't you want to be a full-breasted member of the Blessed Redeemer? I want you to get down on yo knees and ask Jesus to touch you, to touch you today. I want you to accept Him now as yo personal savior."

Jasmine did as she was told, as did several others, while the choir sang and friends and relatives shouted encouragement. The new converts were promptly led away and brought back dressed in white robes. Midnight Grimes, standing waist-deep in the water, urged them, one by one, to come out to him and be baptized. The sun was sinking behind the trees and golden shafts of light made the ripples sparkle when Jasmine answered his call.

"The waters are a witness," Reverend Grimes intoned, reaching out for her. "Come to me in the name of Jesus. I baptize thee in the name of the Father, the Son, and the Holy Ghost."

He put his arm around her shoulders, clapped a hand over her nose and mouth, tipped her backward into the water, and then pulled her to him with a powerful hug that lasted, I felt, far too long. The cotton robe clung to her body as she waded out of the lake, and I could hear her sobbing. Ella was crying, too, as she stood on the shore holding wide a blanket to wrap her in.

"How do you feel, honey?" she asked as she tried to dry her off.

"I feel all glad inside," she said softly. "So glad, so glad."

My skin tingled; Jasmine looked radiant.

"Now may the grace of God that brought you safely here," Reverend Grimes called out in benediction, "lead you safely home."

8

Our Freedom School was a small frame house in Bruceville, which had been abandoned for several years. When I first saw its paneless windows and paintless walls, I thought we'd never be ready for the start of classes. But the whole staff set to work with scrub brushes and brooms; a house painter provided a roller; an electrician supplied light fixtures and radio tubes; a carpenter patched our leaky roof and fit frames on the windows; a plumber installed an indoor washroom; and hordes of children, when they weren't tramping in dirt, hauled out the trash and helped us paint. After a week, we had window screens trimmed in green, fresh white walls both inside and out, and old carpets covering the floors to protect bare feet from splinters. The classrooms were amply decorated with UNICEF and *National Geographic* maps of the United States and the world; UNESCO photos of Africa; SNCC freedom posters; prints by Miró, Homer, Hopper, and Gauguin. We had desks and chairs discarded by the public school, two battered typewriters, a radio, a record player, a tape recorder, and a freestanding blackboard complete with an eraser and a box of chalk. There was even a player piano, but no rolls. In the yard we strung up a volleyball net and laid out a baseball diamond in a nearby pasture, where runners mistook cow pies for bases. The final touch was a large sign over the front porch proclaiming the Tallahatchie Freedom School and picturing a white hand clasping a black one.

My main job was knocking together enough pinewood shelves to line one wall and sorting out the cardboard cartons of donated books. Most of the stuff was dusty junk: book club reprints and Reader's Digest condensations of thrilling plot-twisting, page-turning best-sellers; in sum, booklike experiences for leisure-class Americans to kill time by. There was an assortment of warped old textbooks and well-thumbed how-to books compiled in the belief that the simple truth could be made . . . well, simpler.

Amid this jumble I made a few personal finds: a first edition of Thomas Berger's *Reinhart in Love,* James Agee's *Let Us Now Praise Famous Men,* and a copy of *Lolita* with lipstick smudges on the dust jacket. I filled my shelves in descending order with good fiction (mostly nineteenth-century European classics and twentieth-century southern authors), high school fiction (Chip Hilton sports stories, Nancy Drew mysteries), and a respectable selection of children's books. Unfortunately, there was precious little in the way of American history and almost nothing about Negroes. When Jasmine and other eager students chose books with promising titles like *Black Beauty* or *Pride and Prejudice,* I had to explain and face their disappointment. A request for help produced another shipment of musty, moldy stuff from Holly Springs, but it also brought a wizened black man to our door with a box of pure gold: *Souls of Black Folk, The Facts of Reconstruction,* and a dozen other titles about black history. Immediately I began digging into the collection to prepare for my classes.

The better history books and novels were in great demand by a handful of serious readers, but in truth, the most popular items were the bra ads in the Sears catalogue—a big hit with the boys—and the Little Golden Books that a set of teenage girls poured over by the hour. The important thing, I suppose, was that they were reading something. After all, it wasn't many years before that I devoured a series of books about a twelve-year-old kid, the Huck Finn of the HUAC, who lived on a houseboat in Florida and spent his time combating pinko fellow travelers and Soviet agents.

In theory, our Freedom Schools were designed for only the most alert and motivated high school students. We would sit in a circle, like my college honors' seminar and, with no homework or report cards to distract us, discuss crucial issues. By the end of two three-week sessions, we would have developed a cadre of future leaders who knew the history of the Civil Rights Movement and wanted to stay in Mississippi in order to change things. On opening day, however, when prospective pupils from eight to eighty showed up, we had to scramble to make adjustments. Jasmine strolled in, holding Buster by the hand, and it took some fast talking for me to convince him to join a bunch of kids his own age. I had a dozen high school students as originally planned, but before long everyone was coming and going as they pleased. After a few days I spotted Buster beaming at me from the back of the room, sitting next to the old black man who had donated the box of books.

The first day of class all my students sat with their hands folded on top of their desks, too shy to look me in the eye. They listened intently to every word I said, but except for Jasmine, they answered even the simplest questions with only a safe "Thas right" or "Yassuh." Although they were approximately the same age, looks were deceiving: three grossly overweight girls who sat haunch to haunch in a row appeared to be in their thirties, while two short, skinny boys with similar elongated faces seemed better suited for grade school. Another gangling giant, knees higher than his desk, maybe belonged in the NBA. The rest, five girls and two boys, passed for typical high school students.

I could sense a repressed excitement simmering just below the surface. They were curious and eager to learn, but they were also wary of this white boy who might make unwelcome demands, hurt their feelings, and expose their shortcomings. At the same time, I was painfully aware of my own limitations as a teacher, especially in light of the expectations they probably brought to the Freedom School. I told them about myself and went around the room learning names and asking about future plans. Those covered a multitude of American Dream ambitions from Hollywood starlet to submarine commander (Jasmine wanted to be a teacher), but on one thing they were all agreed: as soon as they could, they planned to get out of Mississippi.

I made a pitch, received skeptically, for staying and working to improve their home state. Then I asked them to write a paragraph about how their high school compared with the white one in Tallahatchie. Everybody had something to say about that, but they struggled a long time, crumpling up page after page, until they could get it down on paper.

"Okay," I said after about half an hour of witnessing their effort, "who wants to read what they've written?"

No volunteers. Nervous silence. Finally a girl named Vanessa put her hand up.

She spoke hesitantly in a broken monotone, staring fiercely at her paper as if she were deciphering a lost language: "They thin' about school I don't like number. Lunchroom don't be clean at time; teacher be drink comin' to school; call student bad name; settin' in class readin' paper; don't teach nobody. They should not talk about student parent. They should not like one student better then other. They should not help only 'A' student. They should not whip girl on legs. Teacher should love all student."

"That Mr. Carson," one boy chipped in. "He mean. I seen him kiss girl behind school."

"Watch yo mouth, boy," a shapely girl, Hollywood-bound, with the apt name of Debbie Body, warned. "Who you talkin' 'bout?"

"She know who she is."

"You a lie!" Debbie shouted, springing from her seat with doubled fists.

I stepped forward to avert a confrontation.

"Do the teachers really whip girls on their legs?" I asked.

"They makes you bend over, touch yo toes, then they whips you on yo butt," another girl volunteered.

"They hits me on backa mah legs," Vanessa insisted.

The class then exchanged horror stories of teachers who used straps, belts, switches, and sticks to impose discipline. One girl told of being whipped in the first grade for not going to sleep during nap time, another was whipped during the past year for staying after class to ask a question. One boy stood up, lifted his T-shirt, and displayed the welts on his lower back.

"How they expect us to learn anything if they always switchin' us half to death?" one student demanded. "They always say, 'Sit down; shut up; do this; do that,' but they never tells us why or shows us how."

"Thas right," another added. "They passes you to the next grade with nothin' in yo head. Then you go to college and come back that same year and you made shame 'cause you don't know nothin'."

"Not everybody that way," Jasmine said. "Mr. Jones, Miss Rich, they good teachers."

"Yeah, but that Miss Rich, she so hard. She ain't never satisfied with what you done. She always say, 'Do it again. Colored people gotta be twice as good to go half as far as the white in this world.'"

"Shi-i," the young giant named "Tree" Norman complained. "What the point workin' so hard? You don't need no degree to pick cotton."

By this time whatever original shyness the students had was long gone. They all had strong opinions about their school and wanted to express them. For the next hour several voices were always talking at once, but from the seeming chaos and confusion a pretty clear picture developed of what the Julius Rosenwald School in Tallahatchie was like.

The building, dating from Brown versus Board of Education in 1954, was a relatively new brick structure comparable to the white school. But there the similarity ended. The school library consisted of a few incomplete sets of outdated encyclopedias and a dictionary, which the students never got a chance to consult anyway because the room was in constant use for classes. Physical education had been canceled because four classes met every period in the gym. The textbooks were battered hand-me-downs from the white school, likewise their sports uniforms and equipment. Chemistry lab consisted of a half-dozen beakers and a bottle of acid; astronomy was taught with a couple of tennis balls and a flashlight; advanced science used a book designed for the seventh grade. The homemaking classes had one stove and a few foot-peddled sewing machines. Unlike the white school, they had no geometry, trigonometry, foreign languages, art, driving lessons, nursing, speed typing, or shorthand.

"We needs new type write," one student stated, "the ones we got tore up."

"We needs new everything," another said. "We sits at those old raggedy desks, two, three lookin' at one crummy book. It hot. Got no air cool, no water cool, no lockers for our things; peoples steal."

Their school, everyone agreed, was a rat hole.

The students had no idea how many people lived in the United States, and when I asked them where Washington, D.C., was, ubiquity reigned until I pointed out the spot on the map.

"What's the farthest away you've ever traveled?"

"Memphis!" came the proud answer.

"Man, you never been to Memphis in yo life."

"Have too. I went shoppin' there last year with my mama."

"Yeah, was she buyin' or sellin'?"

"Least I got one."

"Let's leave the mamas out of this," I said firmly. "Tell me what you learned about black history in your school. What black leaders have you heard about?"

"George Washington Carver!" several shouted.

"What did he do?" I asked.

"Peanuts!" they shouted even louder and laughed.

"Who else?"

"Booker T. Washington," Debbie Body said with a wide smile.

"What did he do?"

"Met the president."

"Did you study slavery and the Civil War?" I asked.

"Yeah, we did," Jasmine said. "Only the textbook called it 'The War for Southern Independence.' The book said the South wanted to be free but the North wouldn't let them."

"So what was the war all about then?"

"States' rights, that's what the book say. What do you say?"

"I think the central issue was abolishing the evil of slavery."

Jasmine nodded her approval, and the rest of the class followed her lead, looking at me with renewed interest.

"Did you talk about Lincoln and the Emancipation Proclamation?"

One of the two pint-sized boys sitting in the back said he knew all about the "Master Payton Proctor Notion." That was when they "emaciated" the slaves.

"The word is *e-man-ci-pa-ted*. It means to set free. We'll talk about Lincoln and slavery in a few days. What about Reconstruction?"

"We skipped that part."

"How come?"

"Teacher say he not suppose to discuss that," Jasmine said. "He say we be 'taken a chance' to talk about that."

I didn't like the pattern I had fallen into of asking easy questions and correcting wrong answers, but it gave me a sense of what the students lacked: everything. How could we make activist leaders out of kids so in need of remedial work in basic skills? And I had decided what I would teach: Reconstruction.

"You prob'ly think we a bunch of dumbheads."

Jasmine hadn't spoken a word until we were alone on the pathway through the bayou that led back home.

"I was pretty floored by some of those answers."

"I know."

"Was it that obvious?"

"No. But I could tell. We all likes you 'cause you got a face that shows yo feelings. You got a nice smile and kind eyes."

"Thanks. Is that the general consensus, or just your opinion?"

Jasmine paused on the path, looked directly at me, and spoke with simple candor.

"I don't know that word—*consensus*—but it's what I think."

"Well, I certainly don't think you're a 'dumbhead.'"

"Some of us knew the answers to yo questions."

"Why didn't you speak up?"

"Didn't want to show nobody up."

"Do you get teased if you do well?"

"Oh, yeah. They be a lotta jealous-hearted nig . . . kids round here. They don't like the way I'm dress, the way I fix my hair, and how I always raises my hand in class. They call me 'a siddity bitch.' They say I think I'm smart. I hate them always puttin' people down. If you too dark, they gets on you about that; if you too light, same thing. They can be so cruel."

"What's that word—*siddity?* I don't know that."

"That mean uppity, tryin' to act like Miss Ann. They don't like nobody lookin' too good or gettin' too far out front."

"That *is* a nice dress you've got on."

"I made it myself. It's not like we rich. My grandma say lots a folk can't help bein' poor, but they ain't no excuse bein' dirty."

In fact, Jasmine and Ella spent a part of every evening sewing and scrubbing. I felt a twinge of remorse when I thought of my own messy room.

"You said today you wanted to be a teacher," I remarked. "So do I."

"What you want to teach?"

"History."

"What school you go to?"

"Hiram College. I graduated this year."

"You got a degree! My that must feel nice to be all done with school!"

"Not quite. I'm going to Case Western Reserve University in the fall."

"Man, you must be rich."

"Not really. My folks are teachers. I couldn't afford to go to graduate school if I didn't have a scholarship."

"They go to college too?"

"Oberlin. My father's a junior-high principal, and my mother teaches English at Youngstown University."

"I want to teach English. I like to write poetry and read novels. How many books you read?"

"I'd guess maybe a thousand."

"Naw," Jasmine objected, glancing up at me to see if I was joking.

"It's true. I used to read novels on the sly at school and several summers I worked at a fishing lake where I had lots of free time."

"What kinda job is that, workin' at a fishin' lake? Can't people fish for free?"

"There was an old black guy with his face all wrinkled like a walnut who came by the office to ask if he could gig for carp. I always let him, but anybody who went out in a boat had to buy a permit."

"I wish I lived up North," Jasmine said.

"Why do you want to leave Mississippi?"

"I'm tired of this jive town. They ain't nothin' to do."

"What do your grandparents say?"

"Grandma say I should stay. She say we got kin and our own land here, and that's a lot. But I don't wanna marry no farmer. Farmin' is too hard. I wanna be a teacher and read a book a day like you doin'. I tole her, 'Grandma, don't fool yoself. As soon as I graduate, I'm gone.'"

"But just think, if black people could vote, they'd control the whole state! Why not stay here and teach? The schools need good teachers."

"Some ain't so bad. Mr. Jones, my math teacher, he helps me all the time. He say I'm comin' along fine. Others is just pitiful. That one I had last year, she couldn't even do her multiplication tables. And she be shame to admit it. These teachers is afraid. They scared to show they care. A hug never hurt nobody, but they always yellin' 'bout discipline."

"Where do you want to go to college?"

"I don't know. Tuskegee maybe. I got a year to decide."

"How old are you?"

"Sixteen."

"I thought you were older."

"Everybody say I don't act my age. When I turned ten, that was somethin' big. That took both my hands. I was a ten-finger person.

But sixteen don't feel no different than fifteen, though I knows I'm gettin' on to bein' a grown woman."

"Sterling Grimes thinks so."

"Why you say that?"

Jasmine gave me a lingering look then turned her head to one side.

"I saw him flirting with you at the picnic."

"He always be messin' with me, but I don't pay him no mind. I don't wanna marry me no preacher man."

"Are you going with anybody?"

"No. How come you want to know?"

Jasmine glanced at me out of the corner of her eye and smiled.

"I'm just curious, that's all," I said, trying to sound casual, but a catch in my throat gave me away.

"The boys around here don't respect a girl. They don't treat her right. They just want a good time. Grandma say they ain't to be trusted."

"Are your grandparents real strict?"

"Yeah. They don't want me datin' the boys round here," Jasmine admitted in a playful tone devoid of resentment. "Grandpa say most of them is no-good dogs. He got those boys afraid to come out to the house."

"What about your grandmother?"

"She all the time warnin' me about men. She say I gotta keep my knees together, my mouth shut, and my purse to myself. To hear her talk you'd think all a boy hafta do is touch you to get you pregnant. If that was true, I'd be pregnant now." Jasmine began to laugh to herself.

"What's so funny?"

"You mens, always grabbin'."

"I didn't do anything. I'm just sitting here."

I folded my arms across my chest for emphasis.

"Not you. You sweet. But the other day I was in the store and Mr. Harper, a neighbor down the road, he there too. He always liked to pat me on the head when I was little, but that day he kept bumpin' into me. I say, 'Excuse me,' thinkin' maybe it was my fault. Then I realize what he be doin'.'"

"I guess he'd rather pat you someplace else now."

"I wish he'd just leave me be. You wanna hear a joke?"

"Sure."

"It funny, but I be embarrass some to tell it."

"Go ahead. I like jokes."

I couldn't take my eyes off Jasmine's animated face as she warmed to her story:

"This girl is goin' out on her first date and she ask her mama what to do. Mama say, 'Chile, if that boy ask to hold yo hand, you let him. If he want to put his arm around you, that okay too. You can even kiss him on the mouth. But don't you *ever* let him lie on top of you, girl, or you'll get pregnant, hear?' 'Yes, Mama.' So they goes out on a date and when they alone the boy say, 'Can I hold yo hand?' Girl say, 'Yes.' Boy say, 'Do you mind if I put my arm around you?' Girl say, 'Thas all right.' Boy say, 'I sure would like to kiss you.' So they kiss. Then the boy say, 'Oh, I love you so much. Let's take off our clothes and I'll lie on top of you.' Girl say, 'Oh, no. You can't do that. My mama warned me about that. She said if I *ever* let a boy lie on top of me, I'd get pregnant.' Boy think about that awhile, then he say, 'What if you lie on top of me?' Girl say, 'Mama didn't say nuthin' 'bout that. I suppose it be okay then.' So that what they done. Next day the girl come up to one of her girl-friend at school, point out the boy, and whisper in her ear, 'See that boy over there? He pregnant.'"

We both laughed, but then there was an awkward pause as we gazed at each other. I felt an urge to kiss her, but a warning was sounding inside me that I was slipping into exactly the situation I had been cautioned about during orientation. Getting involved with Jasmine would be sheer folly.

"Gots to be headin' back," Jasmine said with an alluring re-luctance in her voice. "Grandma gonna be mad if I ain't there to help."

We didn't say a word on the walk home, but after dinner

everybody sat out on the porch and talked and talked. As dusk fell, the crickets began to sing. And as we watched the moon rise through the trees, Jasmine and I found a lot more to laugh about.

9

I asked Ledell Simmons to come to my Freedom School class one day to talk about Africa. He had spent a year there as part of an exchange program, and I knew from our staff meetings that he could be an inspiring speaker. He had been a graduate student at Columbia University before he dropped out to work for SNCC. The students leaned forward in their seats and listened to him with rapt attention.

"If you don't know where you've come from," Ledell said, "you don't know who you are. And if you don't know who you are, you don't know where you're going. And if you don't know where you're going, you're already there. Now the white man has conspired to keep you from knowing how wonderful you are. Their weapon has been words. They have deliberately used words to denigrate black people. A black cow gives no milk; a black hen lays no eggs; Africa is a dark continent. And when a cake is white and light and fluffy, what do they call it?"

"Angel food," the class responded.

"That's right. And they call their country a 'nation,' but what do they call a group of Indians in America or black people in Africa?"

"A tribe."

"Yeah. And they call their leader a 'king,' but what do they call a king in Africa?"

"A chief."

The class was relaxing into the rhythm of Ledell's questions and eager to take part in the discussion.

"And their king wears a crown, but what does the African king wear?"

"Feathers?"

"Sometimes. You're sorta right. He wears a 'headdress.' What's the word we're taught for women who know all about roots and herbs?"

"Witch."

"And what do we do to witches?"

"Burn them."

"So you see how words can mess with your mind and bias your thinking. When I became aware of these things, I wanted to know more about myself and I began to think about Africa. Countee Cullen, a black poet, asked, 'What is Africa to me?" Well, I wanted to find out, so I went. I don't know what it was," Ledell stated, his nostrils flaring with sudden intensity, "but it gripped me so; it was an uncanny experience for me. When I first went to Africa, I kept saying, 'I know this place. I've smelled it. I've been here.' Africa. Africa! How do we bring Africa with us to America, and how do we hold it in who we are?

"Every race begins their history with a moment of glory. The whites start out with Greece—'the glory that was Greece.' That's all right for them, but we go back even farther. Of all the Seven Wonders of the Ancient World, which one is still standing?"

"The Pyramids," Jasmine answered.

"That's right. And who built the Pyramids?"

"The Egyptians."

"Only who were the Egyptians? To hear the white man tell it, Egypt isn't even in Africa, but that just doesn't go with the eyeball. Look at the map on the wall. There's Egypt."

The students smiled when they spotted Egypt in the upper, right-hand corner of Africa.

"We're the ones who built the Pyramids. We Africans. But the white man has tried to hide that fact from us. And the Egyptian Empire lasted three thousand years. Many times longer than the Roman Empire. Look at this picture. Do you know what that is?"

"The Sphinx," Jasmine said.

"That's right. Hey, you're pretty smart. How come you already know this stuff?"

"I don't know it all, but I seen that picture in a book."

"Can y'all tell me what's wrong with this face?"

"Got no nose," the class yelled.

"Now why is that, I wonder. Looks like somebody took a pickax and chopped that nose clean off. Why would they do that?"

"Maybe he was mad."

"Could be. Only why would he be mad? What did that ole Sphinx ever do to him?"

The class exchanged furtive glances to see if anybody knew.

"Look at the lips on the Sphinx. What kind of lips do you see?"

"They thick."

"Who else has thick lips?"

That was good for some disparaging remarks about who had the fattest lips, but the point was made: the mouth on the Sphinx looked African.

"So why did somebody chop off the Sphinx's nose?"

"To hide its African face," Jasmine said.

I contemplated Jasmine's lovely features where two continents mingled.

"That's right. It's the same with most of those old statues; they chopped off the nose to hide the African face. And what else did they chop off?"

Ledell held up a picture of a classical Greek statue.

"Oh, man, I bet that hurt," one of the boys howled.

"That's what whitey has done to us, you see. He has robbed us of our face, our potency, and our history. But we should never be ashamed of our African heritage. We should accept this legacy gladly and proudly pass it on. Even now, it is all around us. It is in the rhythms of our bodies and the words we speak. You know that word *tote,* as in 'tote that bale'? That's from the Bantu *tota,* to lift or carry. What do you call this?"

Ledell held up a picture.

Some of the students shouted "turtle," but others insisted it was a "cooter."

"That's good. *Cooter* is a Bantu word too. Some people eat cooter, you know, although we don't admit it.

"See, freedom is not a simple thing. You can take the chains off a man's wrists and ankles and put them around his mind. Our freedom is not in the Constitution; it is in the human sacrifices we are willing to make. *We* have to do it. It is in our hands. You young women: don't get married until you know who you are. You young men: boys make babies; men take care of them. In order to *be* a man you have to *see* a man. You don't have to look for evil; it will find you. But sometimes you have to look for good. Look for a strong black man you can admire—someone like Bob Moses—and try to live like him. Remember: the drums of Africa are in your blood and the hope of our people is in your hands."

The students gathered around Ledell with excited questions. I had been looking forward to another lively discussion with Jasmine on the way home, only this time we argued about the speech. She took offense that I found anything to criticize.

"Look, he's an amazing speaker, but I wonder about some of his facts and interpretations," I said, sounding very much like a history major headed for graduate school.

"That the best speech I ever heard in my whole life, and you wanna find fault with it? What's *wrong* with you?"

Jasmine gaped at me in bafflement.

"Like that business of the Sphinx's nose and the Greek statues," I asserted. "Probably the weather—the wind and rain—eroded that nose away and fanatical early Christians systematically emasculated pagan art. But it wasn't a white conspiracy."

"Systematically *what*?"

I explained.

"How you know it was the wind and rain. You wasn't there, was you?"

"No. But probably that's what happened."

"Uh huh," Jasmine said with heavy irony. "And those early Christians, weren't they white?"

"Yes, but . . ."

"Uh huh. What else you got to criticize?"

"Well, that business about the middle passage and slavery, I think he said fifty million people died and he made the slave quarters sound worse than a Nazi concentration camp."

"You gonna tell me you was there countin' all them bodies they threw to the sharks?"

"Of course not, but fifty million is way too high. When the slave trade was abolished there were several million slaves in the United States. The slave ships *were* hideous, but probably a few million is a more accurate estimate of the deaths."

"A *few* million!" Jasmine gave me a scathing glance. "What does it matter the exact number! The man was makin' a point."

"I know, but it seems to me you undercut rather than reinforce your point when you play fast and loose with the facts."

"What facts? You the one playin' fast an' loose with all them fancy words. You just tellin' me something you read in a book."

"I suppose I am, but some books are more reliable than others. Like from what I've read, most slave owners didn't starve their slaves or work them to death. Otherwise the slave population wouldn't have increased so much after the slave trade ended."

"Now what you tryin' to say, white boy? That slavery wasn't so bad?"

Jasmine's voice rose with scorn and her eyes flashed at me in anger.

"No, not at all," I pleaded, throwing my hands up in anguish. "Please, I'm not trying to say that. Slavery was terrible, but I think we should try to be accurate about exactly how and why it was terrible. Any system involving millions of people is bound to be very complex. Some masters were kind, some were cruel, and all the degrees in between. And regardless of how they were treated, not one slave was *free*. I agree that slavery was evil; I just think we need to try to understand what actually happened in history."

"You actin' just like the white man Ledell talkin' 'bout. You want it all neat and clean so you can store it away in yo intellect for the winter. Well, history ain't facts, it feelin's. I feel in my heart that what Ledell sayin' be true. What he say is touchin' my life. *We* built them pyramids; *we* died because of slavery; and it's up to *us* to fight for our freedom. That's what important."

"I agree with that, and I thought Ledell gave a great talk, but..."

"You know what else I think?"

Her eyes were still flashing, but not with anger.

"What?"

"Think you're jealous, white boy," Jasmine said with a sassy smile.

She had me there.

10

Asking questions was at the heart of my course. Because I knew that the black school stressed manners and memorization, I wanted a wide-open, no-holds-barred discussion in which everyone was free to disagree. We would probe instead of parrot, debating whatever struck our fancy or hit a nerve. The students were quick to find the confidence to speak up. They loved to argue and exchange opinions, but whether they listened to and learned from each other is something else. They responded immediately to the fact that I took them seriously, but they had difficulty taking themselves seriously. If only they could see how precious their lives were and achieve mutual respect!

Stunted and backward academically, they were sophisticated and wise beyond their years in other areas. With regard to racial matters, they had already learned all the rationalizations and expected responses, which they could use to hide rather than express their true feelings. At first they resented me for bringing up so many touchy topics, but after a while we worked past that and they could express genuine emotions, sharing the hurt, envy, and rage they felt about their situation.

My favorite moments were those in which our discussions got off on unexpected tangents. Once I asked what was the best way to ensure that the roads on the black side of town were paved.

"We could kidnap the mayor's daughter," one student volunteered. "Hold her hostage."

"Yeah, but where you gonna hide a white girl?"

There were a plethora of suggestions. They had obviously given the subject of hiding places a lot of thought. Then the discussion degenerated into a debate as to whether the whites would be too stupid to find her or some black person would be dumb enough to tell them. So much for paved roads.

Some of the students had been drilled pretty thoroughly on the accepted rationalizations for white supremacy. One argued that there ought to be a strict literacy test as a part of registration, because only the educated should vote.

"Absolutely!" I said expansively. "Since I am not only the handsomest man in the world, but also the smartest, I think that only I should vote. Don't you agree?"

"No."

"Man crazy."

"You not *that* smart."

"What about handsome?" I caught Jasmine's eye.

"You don't wanna hear the answer to that one," she said, smiling.

"Before the Civil War," I continued in a more serious vein, "what was the biggest evil in this country?"

"Slavery!" the class shouted.

"If only college graduates in the South could have voted on whether to abolish slavery before the Civil War, how would they have voted?"

That stumped them for a minute, but then the answer came.

"They woulda voted to keep slavery."

"If only illiterate blacks were allowed to vote on the issue," I added, "how would they have voted?"

"Get rid of it!" the class shouted in unison.

"Who was right?"

"The slaves."

"With no education."

"Thas right."

"How come? Why were they wiser on the issue than the well-educated whites?"

"'Cause they knew what slavery was like."

"That's right. And the uneducated slaves would never have voted to fight a war in defense of slavery either. So you see, if slaves were allowed to vote, there wouldn't have been any slavery or any Civil War. In a democracy, it is essential that everybody—each man and woman, poor and rich, black and white—have a say if our system is to serve everybody's needs. That's why we say 'One Man—One Vote.'"

"What about women?" Jasmine asked playfully.

"By all means women," I said. "'One Woman—One Vote' sounds good to me too."

"Laws ain't gonna change nuthin," one student protested. "My teacher this morning say, 'You can't legislate morality'."

"You know, the irony is they say you can't pass laws that help people be good, but then whites turn around and pass laws that make it unlawful to welcome the needy into our homes as Jesus commanded. It is illegal to give a black person lodging for the night in southern hotels or food at southern restaurants. And what if a white person actually fell in love with a black person? The penalty for that in Mississippi is ten years in prison."

Most of the class looked bored at that point, but Jasmine frowned with concern.

"How come they so mean, passin' all them laws against us?" she asked.

"You tell me."

"I think they afraid," Jasmine said. "If we really was as low down and bad as they say, they wouldn't hafta pass no laws to hold us down, we'd just naturally stay at the bottom. They wouldn't hafta pass no laws against anybody lovin' us if we was just naturally unlovable. They got all these laws to keep us in 'in our place,' 'cause they know this *ain't* our place."

She stared intensely at me to gauge my reaction while the rest of the class nodded their heads in agreement.

Jasmine, I thought, was the opposite of unlovable.

11

I opened the next class with a brief lecture on Reconstruction. I tried to get the class to imagine that far-off time when the only radicals—a small group of idealistic reformers who believed in multiracial democracy—were, of all things, Republicans. These Radical Republicans in Congress, seeing President Andrew Johnson sabotage legislation on behalf of blacks, took Reconstruction policy into their own hands. They divided the South into military districts until each of the former Confederate states had a new constitution that respected the political rights of blacks as well as whites.

"You see, after the war, the South required radical change, but only a few leaders understood the complexity of the changes required. Even most abolitionists saw slavery as a moral sin to be purged, not as an economic system to be replaced. Very little thought had been given to Reconstruction, and the country was deeply divided about what needed to be done."

Most of the students looked a little baffled whenever I took off on one of my flights of professorial rhetoric, my voice going up an uncomfortable octave as I became more sincere, but role-playing was always a big hit. My class wanted to be given their characters and start playacting right away; they were impatient with my long-winded explanation of the myths of Reconstruction and who the carpetbaggers, scalawags, and black leaders really were. They wanted to jump right in and ad-lib as we went along.

"Okay, Adlena, your name is James Alcorn."

"Am I a white man?" She looked perturbed as she glanced from side to side to measure the reaction of the rest of the class. "I don't wanna be no white man."

"Just for today, okay?"

"If you can't do it, I can," Alfron volunteered.

"Who says I can't do it?" Adlena insisted. "I'll be that white man."

"Good. You're a scalawag. You're a planter who doesn't want to see the old Mississippi leaders back in power. Why not?"

"Don't know."

"Of course you do, Mr. Alcorn. What was wrong with those old leaders? What did they do to Mississippi?"

"They lost the war."

"How do you feel about that?"

Adlena fidgeted in her seat and made a sour face.

"Sad."

"How come?"

"Lost my slaves."

"Why does that make you sad?"

"'Cause now I gotta work harder. I ain't got nobody to pick my cotton."

"Good. But you're willing to cooperate with the North, while most of your white neighbors aren't. Why?"

"Got no choice. They won the war."

"Yeah, so you see yourself as a realist. You're willing to face facts. The war is over; reform is inevitable. What do you gain by working with the North?"

"Maybe I can get some help."

"You think that if you join forces with the North you can gain assistance and influence." I walked back and forth as I spoke, keeping one eye on Jasmine, who seemed to be enjoying the class. "You don't want the old fanatical leaders with their insane defense of slavery and states' rights back in power, but neither do you want to see the North change the South beyond recognition. So you're willing to support moderate reforms.

"Ernestine, your name is Adelbert Ames. You're a carpetbagger. You're from the North, middle-class, well educated, a veteran of the war and a person who has some capital to invest in the South.

You are also a sincere reformer who believes that all U.S. citizens should be treated equally. What do you want to see in the South?"

"I wants to see everybody treated right."

"Good. You have the support of the Republicans in Congress. They're the ones that backed the thirteenth, fourteenth, and fifteenth amendments making black people citizens with equal protection under the law and entitled to vote."

I wrote the amendments on the blackboard and explained their provisions.

"You, as a carpetbagger, support those amendments. But who do you want the freedmen to vote for?"

"Me," she said proudly.

"You're a pretty smart carpetbagger. A lot of them, because they did support equal rights, won the votes of black people and so were elected.

"Okay, Mr. Ames, now you're in office. What are you going to do?"

"Gonna give peoples land."

"Well, as we were saying, they tried that. But what went wrong? Mr. Alcorn, what do you think about giving black people land?"

"Not mine."

"What if it's somebody else's land?"

"Maybe. But not too much."

"Why not?"

"I wants people to work my land."

"You see, that's a good reason to be involved in Reconstruction, so you can protect your own interests. What do you think of the freedmen being citizens and voting?"

"I don't mind."

"Why not?"

"They my friends. Maybe they vote for me."

"I can see we have a pretty sharp scalawag here. You are willing for the freedmen to have political rights, in part because you think that as a planter with a reputation for honesty and fairness you can be their leader. What do the freedmen think about all this?"

"He white. What do he know about bein' black? We wants our own leaders."

"That's right. Okay, Alfron, your name is John Lynch. You will become speaker of the house of the Mississippi legislature. Napoleon, you're Hiram Revels. You will be appointed to the U.S. Senate. Willie, you're Blanche Bruce. You will be elected to the U.S. Senate too. You guys are black leaders. What do you want?"

I could see by the class's excited reaction that none of them knew black men from Mississippi had ever held such important political offices.

"We wants land."

"Good, that should have happened but it didn't. What else do you want?"

"Schools."

"I don't want schools," Willie asserted. "Schools is boring."

"Are you bored now?"

"Not today."

"What good are schools anyway?"

"Learn to read and write."

"Get jobs."

"Don't have to pick cotton."

"Yeah. All those things. But who's going to pay for the schools? Before the war, only wealthy whites went to school, and now you want to have schools for everybody. That's expensive."

"Make the rich folks pay."

"Who are the rich folks?"

"The planters."

"They *were* the rich folks, but are they rich now?"

"Sure is."

"No they ain't."

A debate followed over how bad off the planters were after the war.

"So we're agreed—somebody has to pay for the schools, but

there isn't much cash on hand. What's the fairest way to raise the money?"

"Take up a collection."

"Get it from the bank."

"Make people pay accordin' to what they got. That the best way."

"So you raise taxes. Are you black leaders agreed? Let's poll our delegation."

Their decision: tax the rich.

"Mr. Alcorn. What do you think about more taxes?"

"I don't like it. It my money."

"Mr. Ames. What's your opinion?"

"I been to school, so everybody else gotta go. I supports it."

"That's sort of what happened. Although actually Mr. Alcorn supported schools, too, provided they were segregated. Alcorn University is named after him, and, Mr. Revels, you were the first president of Alcorn. After the war there was no federal plan to aid the South, so the only way to pay for recovery was to raise taxes, but most people, black or white, didn't have any money. Jasmine, your name is Beauregard E. Redeemer. You fought for the Confederacy and are proud of it and you're damn mad that you lost the war *and* your slaves. What do you feel about all these carpetbaggers, scalawags, and freedmen taking over?"

"I don't like it none. I wants things the way they was before."

"So what are you going to do about it?"

"I'm gonna resist."

"All by yourself?"

"No, sir! I'm gonna call all my frens and we gonna resist together."

Jasmine, giving herself to the role, spoke with convincing defiance.

"Okay, Perley, Lulabell, Debbie, Tree, y'all are Beauregard's friends. Go over in that corner and plan your strategy. And you scalawags, carpetbaggers, and freemen go over in that other corner and plan yours."

In the free-for-all that followed, chronology was scrambled and history twisted, but the battle lines of Reconstruction were drawn with surprising clarity. Beauregard E. Redeemer and company were resolved to get their beloved Mississippi back by violence if necessary. Messieurs Alcorn, Ames, Lynch, Revels, and Bruce had all kinds of difficulty agreeing on a unified strategy. In fact, Alcorn and Ames began pulling each other's hair, and nearly came to blows over who was the most militant.

"You see how hard it was for the reformers and the freedmen to work together?" I concluded. "As I said yesterday, I think that if the federal government, from the president on down, had been united behind a strong and just policy, the time for radical change was right after the war. But since that wasn't the case, it's hard to know what was possible. At least they tried to establish a standard of justice and they showed that biracial democracy, if given half a chance, could work. Had they succeeded back then, we wouldn't need a Civil Rights Movement today. That's why it's so important to understand what happened."

12

Jasmine and I didn't talk much on our way home from the Freedom School. I don't remember who first veered off, at a place marked by a Coke cooler riddled with bullet holes, down a side path that meandered through a patch of pine forest spreading out beside the bayou. It was a hazy, humid day, with the kind of burning sun that compels people to do compulsive things. As we walked by the bank and looked out at the old cypress trees knee-deep in sluggish water, frogs stopped croaking love songs and plopped beneath the pea-green surface. Pestering flies buzzed round our heads and eluded our slapping hands. A large, red-crested woodpecker, tapping at a dead trunk, cocked its ear to detect bugs beneath the bark, then resumed drilling. We sat down on a fern-covered fallen log and listened for a while to what the birds had to say.

"I loves the way birds sing," Jasmine announced joyfully. "Seems like they happy every day just bein' here. I feels like they know they only got one life and that's enough. Wonder how many songs they know."

"Three: 'I'm Hungry,' 'I'm Horny,' and 'Somebody's Coming.'"

"I'm serious," Jasmine said laughing. "Birds sing beautiful."

"Birds are okay, but you're better. Where did you learn to sing?"

"My grandma taught me. When I was small, she sang to me every night. Then when I got a little older, I learned her favorite songs and sang them to her. That reminds me of a strange dream I had last night. There was a pretty house on a hill that kept changin' seasons—first it was spring, suddenly it was winter, then it was summer, then all the leaves changed color and dropped to the ground. At the bottom of the hill my mother was sleepin' under a mound of earth, and on top of the hill a beautiful tree was growin' beside the house and an old woman—I think it was my grandma—was wavin' to me and pointin' at the tree and the birds in the branches. Then in a flash all the birds burst into flame and I woke up."

"What do you think it means?" Jasmine's dream reminded me of Esther's, only hers was filled with terror and this one seemed to contain some kind of affirmation.

"I don't know. Just that my grandma is very important to me, 'cause my mother is dead."

"Maybe it's your grandmother, teaching you how to sing the mystery of the seasons."

"That a nice way to say it. I likes to listen to you talk."

"I'd rather listen to you sing. Who's your favorite singer?"

"Aretha Franklin. Who's yours?"

"Bob Dylan."

Jasmine looked at me as if I'd just announced my favorite drink was sand.

"I don't like white music much; it's too slow. All these copycat white singers take black music and bleach it out. I hate that. They don't seem to know the difference between movin' yo mouth and singin'."

"Do you ever feel—you know, because of your father—part white?"

I had never before alluded to Jasmine's parents.

"I may be light-skinned, but I don't feel like I'm white. Use to bother me. Once when I was little I went to my grandma and cried 'cause of my color, but she say, 'You are a very lucky child. Just think of all the time God took to blend His paints and paint you.' That made it all right. When I was older, my grandma say, 'Anybody a little bit black is all the way Negro.' Well, that fine with me. I likes who I am. I considers myself a very important girl, and I plans to 'mount to somethin' and for my life to turn out happy. Some of my frens calls me a 'goody-goody' and say I have 'big notions' but I wants to be a teacher and marry me a tall, handsome brown man, who will love me and treat me with respect, and have two children—a girl and a boy."

"You've got it all mapped out."

Jasmine glanced at me, then shyly turned her head aside. She reached over and broke a long twig from a nearby branch and began peeling off the bark, laying bare the white glossy shaft of sapwood.

"Feel how smooth," she said. "Isn't that nice?"

As I touched the glistening stem, Jasmine ran her fingers lightly up my arm.

"Yo skin so smooth! This place on the inside soft as a baby. I love smooth things. When I was a girl, I slept with a polished stone under my pillow, and all night with my fingers I felt how cool and smooth it was."

I took one of Jasmine's long, shapely hands in mine, turned her pink palm to the light, and kissed the pale blue lifeline pulsing at her wrist.

For a long time the only sound was our breathing.

"You shouldn't oughta done that," Jasmine said, but she didn't withdraw her hand from mine.

I looked directly into Jasmine's eyes. "It's just that I like you a lot."

"I know."

"How do you feel about that?"

"I have mix emotions. I likes the way you treat me."

Hesitating, my heart racing, I lifted my hands to her face.

We kissed lightly, and then more fully, before pulling back to gaze at each other.

"You're beautiful," I said, my lips still tingling.

"You're pretty nice for a white boy yourself."

Jasmine smiled at her own remark and began running her fingers through my hair.

"I like your hair too," I said. "Especially when you wear ribbons in it."

"You like the way I have it now?"

"Yes. What do you call that style?"

"Cornrows, I calls it. Maybe it's got another name."

"I also like it when you have that big bang over your forehead and curls at the side."

"That take a long time with a hot comb."

"A what comb?"

"Now ain't you somethin' else! Ain't you never heard of that?"

"No."

"Well let me tell you it is a pain. You touch yo head with that hot comb and it can burn yo scalp real bad."

"I'll kiss it and make it well."

"You crazy thing!" Jasmine laughed, pushing me away. "Get yo mouth outa my hair!"

For a suspended moment neither of us spoke, then a snarling chain saw from the far side of the swamp cut the silence.

"I wish we could stay here forever," I said.

"You know we takin' a big chance bein' here this long." Jasmine glanced around warily.

I don't think either of us had given any thought to the danger we were in. Suddenly a surge of guilt dampened my desire. *What if we were caught?* I was doing exactly what we had been warned about during orientation. Jasmine was only a girl; had I taken unfair advantage of her? It certainly didn't feel that way, but how would it look to others? I heard the faint disapproval of their voices as I watched my hand reach for hers. Looking searchingly into her face, I said softly, "I really do love you. If anything should happen, I'll do the right thing."

"If somethin' happen," Jasmine retorted sharply, "I'll tell *you* what the right thing is. That's the problem; you white folks act like you own the world. You think everybody got to adjust to you."

"I didn't mean it that way."

"It don't make no matter," Jasmine replied with shining eyes. "It just sort of hurt my pride, you know."

"I'm sorry."

"It ain't you. I feel confuse, that's all."

I felt a slight chill as silver strands and tatters of Spanish moss gently fluttered in the first breeze of evening. A pine cone fell like a wooden blossom at my feet.

"I guess we really should go before anyone sees us."

"Why can't they leave us be?" Jasmine sighed, fixing me with a lingering gaze, and the sough of the wind in the trees seemed to echo her complaint.

"We'll have to be careful," I said, feeling the clammy mists of the bayou creeping into me. "We're already late. Will your grand-mother be upset?"

"Oh, grandma!" Jasmine cried in alarm. "I promised her I'd help her iron up some clothes this afternoon. She gonna be mad."

"What will you tell her?"

"I'll think of somethin'."

"How do I look?" I asked as I brushed the leaves and briars from my blue jeans.

Jasmine gently combed my hair with her fingers.

"Like you ain't been up to no good," she said with a frown.

As dusk fell, the mosquitoes appeared in full force to work the night shift. We had to walk slowly to be sure we didn't lose the path. By the time we got home it was already dark. Ella was wait-ing on the porch. And so was Bob Moses.

Bob Moses

Ruleville and Greenwood, Mississippi

January 1962–June 1963

1

When we were released from jail in December, we left McComb and moved to Jackson to work with the students at Campbell College and Tougaloo. We wanted to try a direct-action campaign, but the "jail no bail" idea just didn't take hold. Instead, we decided to run black candidates for Congress in the Democratic primary in June. That was how I became unofficial campaign manager for the Reverend Robert L. T. Smith, a Jackson grocer and preacher, who not only had the guts to run but the gall to proclaim, "We can't lose." Of course the opposite was the case: since most Negroes couldn't register, the racist incumbent, John Bell Williams, was a shoo-in. But Smith's campaign provided an excellent format to publicize and localize the issues. Because the Third Congressional District included Liberty and McComb, I felt I hadn't completely abandoned Steptoe and the others. The highlight of the campaign was when the FCC, pressured behind the scenes by Eleanor Roosevelt, ruled that Smith was entitled to equal time on the Jackson television stations. In a city that systematically blacked out all national news about the Civil Rights Movement and gave their own racist twist to what was happening in Mississippi, the appearance of a black man giving a political speech on TV was a revelation. Smith's campaign became the talk of the black community. I began to think, *Why can't Negroes form their own political party? What better way to articulate our needs and provide a direct means of action?*

Meanwhile, SNCC had been in contact with the Kennedy administration about receiving funding for a massive voter registration project. Although Amzie Moore and I had drawn up our original proposal *before* Kennedy was elected, John Doar and the Justice Department had made, I thought, a good-faith effort to support what we were trying to do in Liberty and McComb. Now, Attorney General Robert Kennedy was hinting that if a way could be found to allay the suspicions of white liberals and soothe the envy of Roy Wilkins, money would be made available to us. We set up an umbrella organization—The Council of Federated Organizations (COFO)—to coordinate our activities. Aaron Henry of the NAACP was named president; I was to be director of registration; David Dennis of CORE, assistant director. COFO gave the black people of Mississippi the reassurance of a united front while enabling SNCC, which provided most of the shock troops, to receive money without arousing the jealousy of the other civil rights organizations. Of course the Kennedy administration assumed that the people we registered would vote Democrat in 1964. Our understanding, in turn, was that if we in SNCC put our lives at risk by working for voter registration, the federal government would provide us with protection.

By the spring of 1962, Amzie Moore was ready to support a voter registration campaign in the Delta. Our locally recruited staff would concentrate on midsized towns with large black populations: Greenville, Greenwood, Cleveland, Hattiesburg, Clarksdale, Indianola, and Holly Springs. After a week of orientation at Myles Horton's Highlander Folk School in Tennessee, the SNCC staff spread out over Mississippi to begin summer operations. I moved to our headquarters at Amzie Moore's house in Cleveland.

The work was day-to-day drudgery, punctuated by moments of

sheer terror. Upon arrival in a town, the SNCC worker would be seen as an outsider and a threat. But once he found someone who would take him in, then he could begin, doing what the people did, winning their trust, and making it clear he was working for them. The fear was intense; paranoia, in that situation, was a form of sanity. Everyone knew that their homes, jobs, even their lives were in jeopardy if they were seen with a "Freedom Rider." Some thought the SNCC workers were either hopelessly crazy or impossibly brave. We had to show them we were human, with the same fears they had, but we were neither paralyzed nor apathetic; if we could act, so could they.

Slowly the people's resistance gave way. A minister would open his church so that town meetings could be held, voting schools started; a barber, an undertaker, a maid, a sharecropper would take that long walk to the courthouse, knowing they faced a possible beating and probable humiliation. But the idea of freedom was in the air, a thread to knit the black community together until the time came when they were ready to take to the streets, go to jail, do whatever was necessary. In this way, not only individuals, but whole communities, gained a new sense of identity.

Some towns, like Greenville, under the moderating influence of Hodding Carter's newspaper, were relatively easy and Negroes registered there without incident, but most were hard and mean. Greenwood, in particular, was hell.

When Sam Block arrived in Greenwood, people said he would just get somebody killed and then leave; few were willing to talk to him, let alone try to register. One day the sheriff spat in his face and told him to pack his bags and get out of town.

"You pack," Sam replied. "I'm here to stay."

The next night, Sam received a phone call: "Get out of town, nigger. If you don't, we're gonna kill you."

A week later he had to leap behind a telephone pole to keep from being run over by a truck. A few days after that, he was badly beaten. Sam still didn't leave.

One night in mid-August he called me.

"Cars are circling the office," he said in a hushed voice. "Men are milling around outside with guns and chains. Me, Guyot, and Brown are holed up here. I think they're planning to come in after us."

"Have you called the police?"

"Are you kidding? The cops are right out there with them."

"Get out if you can," I said. "I'm on my way."

I called John Doar at his home in Washington, then Willie Peacock and I raced the forty miles to Greenwood. We arrived at about two in the morning. The office was over a black-owned store on Avenue I. The door had been smashed off its hinges. No one was inside. A table and some chairs were tipped over, the drawers ripped out of the file cabinet; papers were scattered all over the floor. I saw no sign of blood.

"What do we do now?" Willie asked.

I pulled out the couch, spread a blanket, flipped on the fan, and lay down.

"Let's get some sleep," I said.

Willie looked at me with wide eyes.

"You're sleepin' here?"

"Where else?"

The next morning I felt a hand shaking me awake. It was Sam, who told me what had happened. They had waited, crouching in fear in the office, until they heard footsteps on the stairs and chains rattling. Then they pushed up the window, scrambled across the roof to the cafe next door, shinnied down a TV antenna, and ran to the home of a friendly minister.

"They stole our files," Sam said, kicking disgustedly at the jumble of stray papers.

A few days later the police told Sam's landlord that they were going to charge him with bigamy—unless he got "those educated niggers" out of his building. After he was evicted, Sam spent the next several nights sleeping in the backseat of a junked car. Five months passed before he found a suitable office.

Charles McLaurin, thirty miles away in Ruleville, was having an equally hard time. Sunflower County was an area where blacks slaved as sharecroppers and lived in poverty, while a few whites grew rich, including Senator James Eastland, whose cotton plantation covered thousands of acres. Ruleville, a typical small Delta town due north of Indianola, was a hotbed of bigotry where the Citizen's Council was very strong. Charlie canvassed the town by day, a dangerous enough job, but at night the risks escalated: he stole onto the plantations, riding a mule or driving with no lights to elude the guards; behind drawn curtains and with only a candle on the floor for light, he would tell the people that the vote was the key to changing things.

When the mayor of Ruleville learned that some Negroes had tried to register, he announced that anybody who wasn't satisfied would get a one-way ticket out of town. In late August I was arrested in Ruleville for passing out leaflets. The next day, as we were busing some people to the Indianola Courthouse, the police stopped us again. The charge: driving too yellow a bus. The intrepid authorities had thwarted our nefarious plot to impersonate a school bus!

"We gonna see how tight we can make it," the driver was warned. "Gonna be rougher than you think."

The local paper published the names of those who tried to register, thus insuring reprisals: sharecroppers were turned away from the fields; workers, or their kin, were systematically fired.

"We gonna let you go," the mayor told a garbage collector, "your wife's been attending that school."

One harmless old black man was ordered by his employer to go to Indianola and take back his registration form.

"What have I did wrong?" he asked.

"Get your name off that book."

"I wants to satisfy you," he said.

That same day he went to the courthouse, asked for his form, and wrote, "I, B. T. Wall, withdraw."

All those firings made our work harder. One, however, made it easier. Mississippi never made a bigger mistake than trying to intimidate Fannie Lou Hamer. The evening after she had gone to Indianola to register, she was sitting inside her weather-board shack on the B. D. Marlowe plantation when she heard voices outside.

"Pap," Marlowe said to her husband, "your wife's gone and done a damn fool thing. She's in big trouble."

Mrs. Hamer went to the door.

"Fannie Lou," Marlowe said, "did you register?"

"Yes, I did."

"Why did you do it?" he cried. "Mississippi isn't ready for that kind of foolishness. They gonna worry hell out of me now."

"Mr. Dee," she said, "I didn't do it for you. I did it for me."

He told her to get off the plantation, where she had picked cotton and been a timekeeper for eighteen years, and never come back.

She left, but she didn't disappear. She moved to Ruleville—defying death threats, shots fired at her home, and a terrible beating in the Winona Jail—to become one of the best local leaders we ever found. She spoke and sang with passionate intensity, straight from the heart. Listening to her could lift you right out of your shoes.

Several weeks after Fannie Lou Hamer was forced off her plantation, Amzie Moore and I were in Ruleville talking to some people on the sidewalk about registering when I saw a man beckoning to me from the cab of a red and white pickup truck. He had a hard, sunburned farmer's face, but he seemed friendly enough.

"Are you the folks gettin' people to register?"

"Yes," Amzie said, "we are."

"Well, I've got a plantation out there." He waved his hand toward the northeast. "I want you to come on out and register my people."

"Okay," I said, taking his offer seriously. "We'll come out."

"I've got a shotgun waitin' for you," he snapped back. "Double-barrel."

He shook his fist and tore off. I made a note of his license number.

"As long as I've been in Mississippi," I said to Amzie, "somehow I never get used to all the hate."

"Seems like white folks got a surplus, and they need a place to dump it."

In Jackson a week later, I received a call from Charles Cobb, in Ruleville. He talked so fast I couldn't catch a word.

"Calm down, Charlie," I said softly. "Tell me what happened."

"I was over at Joe McDonald's house when I heard gunfire. I went outside and somebody shouted that night riders had just shot up the Sisson's home. I sprinted up the street, rushed in the door and . . ." His voice was choked with anguish. "My God, Bob, I slipped in the blood! Two girls from Jackson State were hit."

"How bad is it?"

"One got shot in the neck and head. She's in critical condition."

"Where are you?"

"I'm at the police station."

"What for?"

"Attempted murder."

"Oh, man," I said, squeezing the phone in frustration.

"Yeah. I was at the hospital when the mayor comes in. First thing he says is, 'Bob Moses is the cause of all this.' Then he sees me. 'I think you shot up those houses on purpose,' he says. 'Y'all need violence to get publicity.' Then he ordered the sheriff to arrest me."

"Don't worry, Charlie," I said. "We're on our way."

Four of us left Jackson at two in the morning in a battered Chevy with a motor that quit if the speed dropped below thirty. We were dead tired, nobody could stay awake for long, so we had to switch drivers without stopping. Just outside Belzoni we all fell asleep, and the car left the road at the first sharp curve; we smacked through a fence and jolted to a halt in the middle of a cotton field.

We didn't get to Ruleville until the next morning. The one girl had been taken off the critical list and the police were prepared to drop the charges against Charlie, but the shootings had the black community so upset that we decided to leave Ruleville and concentrate on Greenwood.

The next night at a press conference, President Kennedy was asked what he thought about the shootings in Ruleville.

"I commend those who are making the effort to register every citizen," he said. "They deserve the protection of the United States government."

2

In October, to retaliate for our voter registration drive, the Board of Supervisors cut off the federal food program in Sunflower and Leflore County. Over twenty thousand people, sixteen thousand in the Greenwood area alone, needed that food to see them through until the next cotton season started. Without federal surplus milk, rice, beans, and flour, their situation was desperate. Winters in the Delta are cold and wet; the icy wind stabs through the cotton clothes and the uninsulated shacks and chills to the bone. People huddle around woodstoves and kerosene heaters, warming one side at a time. They tack newspapers in layers on their walls and stuff them under their clothes, but still they shiver and shake and fall sick. Just because black people wanted their civil rights, the local white authorities were willing to add to this misery by causing a famine.

In November, a baby died of starvation.

Dick Gregory helped us organize a nationwide appeal. He himself chartered a plane and flew down from Chicago with several tons of supplies. Ivanhoe Donaldson drove truck after truck of foodstuffs from Michigan to Doc Henry's place in Clarksdale. One time the police arrested him for "trafficking in narcotics." (His cargo included aspirin bottles inside first-aid kits.) Another time, a cop stuck a gun in his face and said, "You and the other goddamned Moses niggers around here ain't gonna git nuthin' but a bullet in the head!"

He cocked the hammer, but his partner intervened.

"You can't kill that nigger here," he said.

Hundreds of poor sharecroppers came in from the countryside to line up at the Wesley Chapel. As we distributed the free cheese and blankets, we talked to them about how precarious their lives were. There was a connection, we pointed out, between their present hunger and the political situation—without the vote, things would stay the same. We didn't turn anyone away, but we certainly preferred to feed people who had the courage to try to register. Before long, we had as many as a hundred going down to the courthouse together.

This show of support made some whites resort to violence.

The trouble started on February 20 when four Negro businesses—Jackson's Garage, George's Cafe, Porter's Pressing Shop, and the Esquire Club—were firebombed. When Sam Block suggested to the police that it might be more than coincidental that all four were located near the SNCC office, he was charged with "circulating statements calculated to create a breach of the peace." That was the seventh time Sam had been arrested in Greenwood. While he spent the weekend in jail, the black community recalled his tenacious support of their rights and rallied to his defense. One hundred people showed up at city hall to protest his trial. The judge offered to suspend his sentence if Sam would agree to leave town.

"Judge, I ain't gonna do none of that," Sam said.

He received six months in jail and a five hundred dollar fine.

Over two hundred attended a mass rally that night; you could feel the people stirring and getting ready to take a stand. The next day there was a long line at the courthouse to register. We were finally creating the tremor in the center of the Mississippi iceberg I had been hoping for. Greenwood's time had come.

A week later, Randolph Blackwell, the field director of the voting project, drove up to the SNCC office in Greenwood to see how we were doing. Actually, he had been sent down to investigate. He was pleased by the number of people trying to register, but few passed the test. Also, he was very upset that I had spent money for food and clothes.

"What else could I do?" I asked Blackwell. "People around here are starving."

"But entries like that could cost us our tax-exempt status, Bob. If you're going to spend voting funds to feed people, at least don't write it down."

After a while, Willie Peacock came in and told us he had noticed three white men sitting in a '62 Buick across the road beside the charred remains of what had been George's Cafe. They were still there at dusk, as we were preparing to leave. I sent a teenager out to spot their tag number.

"No plates," he reported.

Night was falling and we knew we were exposed. Blackwell tried to leave, but the Buick trailed him down the street, so he returned to the SNCC office.

Hoping that there was safety in numbers, Jimmy Travis and I got in Blackwell's car and the three of us drove to a nearby gas station to fill the tank and eat some sandwiches.

The Buick parked down the road, waiting.

"I better drive," Jimmy said. "If they starts chasin' us, I knows these back roads."

We tried to slip out the back of the station. For once I was happy the black side of town didn't have any street lights. Jimmy did his best to shake them, stealing through that maze of dirt roads with only his parking lights; then he swung out onto Route 82 headed toward Greenville. Suddenly the Buick zoomed past, speeding in the opposite direction. They slammed on their brakes and spun around, bearing down on us with their high beams. Jimmy slowed to thirty-five to see if they would pass. They stayed behind, letting the other cars pass instead, until it was just us and them on the dark road. Then they made their move. Jimmy tightened his grip on the wheel, and we braced for the worst. The Buick surged forward and swerved out beside us. I glanced over and saw three men in sunglasses. I heard the roar of rapid gunfire and the crash of shattered glass.

"Pull over!" Blackwell shouted. "Hit the brakes!"

"I've been shot," Jimmy cried out, and slumped in his seat.

I held on to Jimmy with one arm, reached for the steering wheel with the other, and stretched for the brake with my toe. The car zigzagged down the road and skidded to a stop.

I saw blood oozing from the back of Jimmy's neck and soaking his shoulder. I was sure that he was dead, but then he began to moan. Blackwell pressed his shirt to Jimmy's wounds and we eased him into the backseat. I drove to the nearest town—Itta Bena. We couldn't find a doctor there, so we rushed back to Greenwood.

"Hold still," I told Jimmy. "Don't move."

The doctor in Greenwood took one look at Jimmy and said his condition was very grave; a delicate operation was required.

"No white man in Greenwood is gonna cut on me," Jimmy insisted between clenched teeth. "Take me to Jackson."

The next morning in Jackson a bullet was removed from near the base of Jimmy's skull. Because it was only a fraction of an inch from his spinal cord, they had to operate without anesthetic for fear of damaging his nervous system. The surgeon said that had the window glass not slowed the bullet's impact, he would have been killed.

Blackwell and I counted a dozen bullet holes in the side of the car.

"Machine gun," Blackwell said. "You know who those were meant for?"

"I know."

"This is the work of the Klan," he added. "You're high on their list."

"I've heard the rumors."

"They aren't rumors anymore, Bob. What are you going to do?"

"We can't back down," I said, "without destroying everything we've accomplished."

That night, after a long debate, SNCC unanimously decided to gather all available staff in Greenwood and redouble our efforts.

"Leflore County," I announced, "has just elected itself as the testing ground for democracy."

It was a hard test.

Bob Moses

The next week Sam Block and three others were sitting in a car beside the SNCC office when a shotgun blast blew out the car's front window. Two weeks later the office itself was burned to the ground, and a few days after that, shotgun pellets shredded the front door of the Dewey Greene home. All the Greene children were active in the movement: Dewey Greene Jr. wanted to follow in James Meredith's footsteps at Ole Miss, and one daughter, Freddie, was considered the nicest girl in Greenwood. The community was especially outraged that anyone would shoot at her. An angry crowd gathered at Wesley Chapel and a spontaneous march of protest to the courthouse began. At city hall the police were waiting for us in their yellow riot helmets; one held a growling German shepherd on a taut leash. I grew up in the city; dogs make me edgy; but I kept walking.

"I would like to see Chief Lary," I said to the line of clenched-jawed cops.

"You can talk to me," the mayor said, stepping forward. "It's the 'Kennedy Twins' that put you up to this, isn't it?"

Just then the attack dog lunged for my leg, sinking his teeth in my jeans and tearing them from cuff to thigh. People started screaming and running in all directions. The police waded into the crowd and arrested all the SNCC staff they could find. Ten of us were taken to the station and charged with disorderly conduct.

The following day the people marched again, adding our arrest to their list of grievances. The police turned out in force, bringing more dogs. Angry whites lined the curbs. As the marchers came closer, the dogs strained at their leashes and showed their fangs; the mob started to chant, "Sic 'em! Sic 'em!" Suddenly a squad of cops with dogs charged at the demonstrators, causing instant panic. In the melee, the Reverend D. L. Tucker of Wesley Chapel was badly bitten on the calf. Reporters on the scene saw it all. By morning, people across the country knew about Greenwood.

When we were brought before the judge for our preliminary hearing, eight of us refused bail and went to jail to protest the trumped-up charges.

During the days, we kept up our spirits by singing, *"Do you want your freedom, / Are you ready to go to jail?"* and every night before we turned out the lights we sang "Keep Your Eyes on the Prize," adding our own second stanza:

> *"We have served our time in jail*
> *With no money to go our bail.*
> *Keep your eyes on the prize, hold on.*
> *Hold on, hold on,*
> *Keep your eyes on the prize, hold on."*

In truth, the Greenwood demonstrations were headed for stalemate. Because the federal government wouldn't step forward to protect people from being arrested, and we couldn't raise the funds to bail them out, and the registrar wasn't about to accept them as qualified voters, more and more black people in Greenwood began to ask, "What's the use?"

The only hope on the horizon was the fact that John Doar and the Justice Department had sought a restraining order that demanded our immediate release and a cessation of interference with Negroes attempting to exercise their constitutional rights. At a press conference, President Kennedy even spoke in favor of the Justice Department's suit, stating that the denial of rights to black people in Greenwood was "evident." Two weeks later we were released. We marched arm in arm out of prison singing *"This little light of mine, / I'm gonna let it shine"* to the cheers of waiting friends, well-wishers, and reporters. For the moment, I was jubilant. Then, when I learned the terms of our reprieve, I became bitter and depressed.

The Justice Department had settled for a compromise that secured our release in return for a vague promise by local leaders that they would permit Negroes to register safely. In effect, our fate was placed at the whim of officials elected specifically to keep black people down. We were free, but the crucial point had been lost: we could not count on the federal government to protect us *before* violence took place. We needed help on-the-spot, not after-the-fact. Had the Justice Department stuck by its guns, establishing a strong federal presence and enforcing the law of the land, lives could have been saved. Their decision to *re*-act, rather than act, meant that it was still open season on civil rights workers in Mississippi.

I was deeply upset by the federal government's willingness to compromise their moral position in the interests of political expediency. John Doar had good intentions, but he, like the other Kennedy people, was a troubleshooter who thought that all problems could be mediated, talked away, smoothed over, litigated. Yet, by letting the Dixiecrats control the southern courts, Kennedy guaranteed that litigation would be an impossibly tedious process.

"I was overruled," Doar told me regretfully. "Burke Marshall didn't think we could win the suit, so we took what we could get."

"It wasn't enough," I said. "You've left us out on a limb. That's not a position any Negro in Mississippi wants to be in."

3

Over Easter weekend SNCC held a retreat in Atlanta at Gammon Seminary where I presented my analysis of the Greenwood situation. The local blacks, I said, were being pulled in two directions: we wanted them to assert their rights; the whites didn't. SNCC was also under pressure: the Justice Department wanted us to cool it, the Citizens Council wanted us out of town, and the Klan wanted us dead. Our food drive had brought hundreds to the Movement, but most people were still apathetic; we would need thousands to seize power in Leflore County. Even if our voter registration drive was successful and the test administered fairly, a majority of blacks would still fail the literacy requirement. Either that would have to be eliminated, or the quality of Negro schools would have to be drastically improved. Both options required emphatic federal action. Although most Mississippi Negroes didn't know how to read or write, they did know who their friends were, and they knew their own needs. If they could, they would vote in their best interests—which is what democracy is all about.

Because blacks heavily outnumbered whites in the Delta, they were seen as a threat to be suppressed at all costs. Only a showdown could force federal intervention and the requisite changes. Unless change came soon, however, all could still be lost, since automation, agribusinesses, and intimidation were driving Negroes from the South at an accelerating rate. We might win the battle in Greenwood only to find that our people had moved to Chicago and Detroit. Another danger would be to achieve power in the Delta with middle-class black politicians who were content with the status quo. What we wanted were local leaders who represented the masses and understood that only radical change could improve their situation. SNCC needed a two-pronged strategy: foster indigenous leaders through community organizing and stage protests to capture national attention and compel federal intervention.

My idea of an authentic local leader was Hartman Turnbow. Like Steptoe, he was an independent farmer who owned seventy acres of land near Tchula, in Holmes County. John Ball from SNCC went to Turnbow's church in the Mileston community and organized a voter registration school. When a group of fourteen were ready, he and Sam Block drove them to the Lexington Courthouse. Deputy sheriff Smith was standing at the door.

"March forward," Sam said.

"None of that goddamned forward stuff here," the sheriff replied, putting one hand on his blackjack and the other on his pistol.

Hartman stepped forward. "Mr. Smith, we only come to redish."

The deputy sheriff ordered them to gather under a tree on the north side of the courthouse.

"All right, now," he said. "Who's first?"

Everyone exchanged nervous glances.

"Me, Hartman Turnbow, will be first."

So Hartman was directed inside. After hours of delay, he was finally permitted to fill out the form. The next day the local paper listed all the people who had attempted to register, identifying Hartman as "an integration leader."

A month later his home was firebombed.

I went over in the morning to inspect the damage. A couch, burned to the springs, was in the front yard; most of the windows of the house were broken; the living-room walls were smoke-blackened; the smell of smoldering wood lingered in the air.

Hartman, his wife, and his pretty sixteen-year-old daughter had been asleep when the firebombs exploded. Hartman jumped up, grabbed his old Remington .22 and slipped outside. When they saw him coming, one man ran, but another opened fire with a .45 automatic rifle. While Hartman and the man exchanged shots, a third man was blasting away at the front of the house. Then the attackers drove off.

When I first heard about the firebombing, I contacted John Doar; as Hartman and I were assessing the situation, an FBI agent arrived from Memphis. We showed him the bullet holes in the living room. He was prying the slugs out of the clapboard when Deputy Sheriff Smith finally drove up. Turnbow told the deputy what happened, showing him three quart beer cans smelling of gasoline and the obvious indications of a gun fight. Smith ignored all the evidence and arrested me instead for "impeding an official investigation" because I had been taking pictures of the house. Then he charged both Hartman and me with arson.

"Arsony?" Hartman cried out, "but this is my place!"

"You done it yourselves," he said, "just to get our niggers all excited."

"Why, I ain't never owned a .45 in my life," Hartman insisted. "Them's .45 bullets and .45 holes, and I never owned nary'un."

The FBI man watched, took notes, made no comment.

Later that month I flew to Washington to tell Hartman Turnbow's story to a congressional subcommittee investigating voter intimidation. Our arson case, I pointed out, would be tried by a racist judge, who probably would reject the Justice Department's injunction on our behalf, thus making it clear to local blacks and whites alike that the sheriff could get away with whatever he wanted. In fact, that was the purpose of many of the civil rights arrests: the charges were designed to be as arbitrary and absurd as possible to demonstrate the pervasive and inescapable rule of the white power structure. The message was—We can get you any time we want, for whatever we want, and there's nothing in the world you can do about it. In the Delta, where blacks outnumbered whites two to one and everybody owned a gun, it was very dangerous to let justice be mocked. Black people were not about to let their homes be firebombed on a regular basis; Turnbow and the other independent black farmers were committed to armed self-defense. It wouldn't take much for a full-scale war to break out. I hated to play the violence card, but the threat was real, and violence was what the country responded to. I closed by reiterating my position that Negroes should either be allowed to register outright, or a massive literacy program, federally financed but run by local people, should be established immediately.

"The people of Mississippi want to learn," I said. "They want to vote. They feel that for once they have a chance to better their condition."

Again the federal government averted its eyes and sat on its hands and so the arrests and beatings continued. In the spring, national attention switched from Greenwood to Birmingham, where Bull Connor's police dogs were unleashed on little children.

Medgar Evers, the head of the Mississippi NAACP, launched a series of demonstrations in Jackson in favor of a modicum of dialogue, desegregation, and common courtesy. The mayor seemed to be amenable to negotiations, but then he reneged on his agreements and began arresting people en masse. The state fairgrounds were converted into a concentration camp surrounded by a chain-link fence. Demonstrators by the hundreds were hauled there in garbage trucks, separated by sex, and herded into the animal stockades. The sanitary conditions were deplorable and there were random beatings. Concurrently, the mayor was proclaiming Jackson the closest place to heaven on earth.

Evers made a speech in response.

"Freedom has never been free," he said, after citing the city's egregious inequalities and indicating what needed to be done. "I love my children," he added in a seeming afterthought. "I love my wife with all my heart. But I would die, and die gladly, if that would make a better life for them."

Meanwhile, the cumulative impact of events in Greenwood, Birmingham, and Jackson were having an effect on President Kennedy. On June 11, he made an urgent televised appeal to the nation and announced he was sponsoring a Civil Rights Bill.

"We are confronted primarily with a moral issue," he said. "It is as old as the Scriptures and as clear as the American Constitution. The heart of the question is whether all Americans are to be afforded equal rights and equal opportunities. . . . We preach freedom around the world, and we mean it. And we cherish our freedom here at home. But are we to say to the world—and much more importantly, to each other—that this is the land of the free, except for Negroes? that we have no second-class citizens, except for Negroes? that we have no class or caste system, no ghettos, no master race, except with respect to Negroes?"

That night, after Kennedy's speech, a sniper, hidden behind a clump of honeysuckle in an overgrown vacant lot across the street, was waiting for Medgar Evers to come home. When he stepped out of his car, the man raised a 30.06 Enfield deer rifle to his right eye, adjusted the telescopic sight, and shot him in the back. At the sound of gunfire, Mrs. Evers and the children, coached for this dread contingency, fell to the floor. Then, hoping against hope, Mrs. Evers switched on the front light and opened the door. Evers lay face down at her feet in a pool of blood, the house key clutched in his outstretched hand. "Please, Daddy, please," the children cried, "get up!" An hour later he was pronounced dead at the hospital. His last words were, "Turn me loose!"

The assassination of Medgar Evers caught the country's attention. President Kennedy saw to it that he was buried in Arlington National Cemetery with appropriate ceremony. Unlike Herbert

Lee and the other unsung black men who had been killed, Evers was connected to the larger society. As state leader of the NAACP, his name was known. Because of his death, the nation's eyes were now focused on Mississippi.

Tom Morton
Voter Registration

McComb, Mississippi

July 24–August 20, 1964

1

When the bomb went off, I was sleeping in the front room of the McComb Freedom House. I awoke to a clunk, the screech of tires, and then the blast: in rapid-fire succession three thunderclaps turned the world to noise and reduced my surroundings to smithereens. I found myself sprawled on the pinewood floor, pinned beneath an overturned couch. Shattered glass and chunks of plaster crashed around me; mattress stuffing floated in the dust-filled air like snowflakes. My ears pounded and my body shook convulsively. Gripping a shred of sheet like a helpless child, I felt sure that the next thing to explode would be my heart. With smoke-stung eyes, I looked through a gaping hole directly into the next room where Feelgood and Esther, naked as jaybirds, clung to each other on what was left of the bed. Their eyes met mine with an expression more of surprise than terror. My vision blurred; I raised my right hand to wipe away what I thought was sweat; it was blood. The next thing I remember I was leaning against a car whose horn wouldn't stop honking.

Who parked a car in the living room? Why was my hand so hot? Everything was smoke and confusion. People were screaming and running. A burst gas line at the side of the house shot flames at the sky. The paint on the car began to blister. I put my hand in my mouth and stared at the mangled house. The hole in the wall would have been big enough to drive a truck through if the roof hadn't collapsed. A man covered with blood staggered toward me. I pulled off my T-shirt to clean his face. It was Lenny. He looked like he'd lost a scratching match with a passel of alley cats.

"Where are you hurt, Lenny?"

"What?" His eyes refused to focus.

"Where are you hurt?"

"Hurt? I'm not hurt."

"You're bleeding."

"You're the one that's bleeding, man."

A black woman wearing a turban came with a wet towel and washed us off. Another woman held a flashlight while she took some tweezers from her purse and extracted a small sliver of glass from above my eyebrow. I felt some stinging on my skin and my head was ringing. Lenny had a bruise on his forehead and splinters in his hands. He was a little deaf in one ear.

Feelgood had been hit by a spray of flying glass from a shattered window and had a nasty gash on his thigh and lacerations on his back and arms. Esther, who had only superficial cuts, begged him to go to the hospital. He refused, insisting instead on addressing the angry crowd that poured in from the neighborhood. By the light of the torched gas line, I could see tears glistening in people's eyes.

"You see how hard they tryin' to stop us?" he shouted over the gathered faces. "But we ain't scared and we ain't gonna be stopped. Even if they kill all of us, they gonna be more to take our place."

Squad cars came charging up the street. Their flashers and sirens pierced the night. The police pushed the crowd away from the house and unwound yellow ribbons to seal off the crime scene. One of the first officers to arrive peered at the three-walled wreck and remarked to his smirking buddy, "Looks like termites to me."

It was dawn by the time the FBI arrived. The agents in their matching white shirts and brown jackets poked around in the flower beds, fished through the rubble, and scooped with a miniature shovel a bagful of soil from a small crater in the driveway. They found a two-inch section of plumber's pipe with a strand of black electrical tape still sticking to it.

In the morning light the extent of the damage was apparent. The blast had destroyed the thin wooden wall facing the street and ripped through the roof. The corner of the house near the gas line was blackened with smoke. The concussion had burst windows in nearby houses. Inside, the place was in shambles: jagged cracks in the walls, floorboards torn up, debris everywhere. We found long slivers of glass driven like knives into the remnants of Feelgood's mattress and the couch that had shielded me. Everything was coated with a layer of plaster shards and dust; the odor of cordite fumes permeated the air. Luckily, our typewriters, mimeograph machine, phonograph, and expensive radio equipment were in the back room and undamaged.

After we completed our inspection, Feelgood led those who still lingered in a solemn march three times around the house. No one said anything, but I took it as a ritual to ensure that lightning wouldn't strike twice.

2

Lenny had been as surprised as I was to learn that Bob Moses wanted him to go to McComb. On the drive down the day before, I told Lenny all about my experiences in Tallahatchie. He was happy to get out of Greenville, an Uncle Tom town where nobody was willing to step forward and push for important changes. Civility ruled, at the expense of progress. Still, the town had its compensations. The volunteers, provided they weren't recognized as such, could treat themselves to great steaks at Doe's Eat Place and, when the heat built up, take a dip in Hodding Carter's swimming pool.

Apparently Feelgood had asked specifically for us. Since the start of the summer, the Klan, by a logic that escaped me, had been burning crosses and torching rural black churches near McComb to demonstrate their devotion to Christian principles. But Bob Moses thought that if we were careful in Burgland and only collected signatures for the convention challenge, we would be safe. At the time, my chief concern was leaving Jasmine, not the dangers I faced, but who was I to tell Bob Moses no?

When Lenny and I arrived at the Freedom House, a black woman named Gayl Norris met us at the door. With undisguised scorn in her voice she noted that the rest of the staff were out drinking at the McComb Club. We spread our sleeping bags on two couches in the living room and soon fell asleep, so our first look at the staff was in the chaotic aftermath of the bombing.

Actually, there were two Freedom Houses: one at 702 Wall Street and the other just around the corner on Denwiddie Avenue. In theory, the house on Wall Street was the main office where the men slept and the other was for the women. In practice, most people hung out at the place on Wall Street since that was where the action was.

Gayl, I soon learned, was the exception. When she wasn't teaching Freedom School or attending staff meetings, she usually kept to herself in the other house. She was short and compact with a face as plain as a potato and a deep crease on her forehead that gave her a look of perpetual sorrow, but she carried herself with such an innate sense of dignity that everyone usually deferred to her. She obviously didn't think much of the two black girls on the staff—Leetonia Fulton and Wachula Tracy. As a matter of fact, she rarely approved of anybody. She and Feelgood were often at odds; she didn't get along with Esther; and the other black men— Lance Malone, Jason Irving, and Marcus Carver—stayed out of her way. The new recruits—Lenny, myself, a blonde girl named Misty Brooks, and a black guy who had just arrived from New York named Amontillado Poe—she placed on skeptical probation until we proved ourselves.

Monty Poe was a slightly built, intense, narrow-faced man with a dead white scar on his dark left cheek. A permanently spooked look in his glittering, protuberant eyes reminded me of one of those small tropical animals that come out only at night. In the morning light after the bombing he looked at the four white faces standing in front of the Freedom House, turned to Feelgood, and asked, "What are these honkies doin' down here, man? I thought this was gonna be a black thing."

Feelgood simply shrugged, nodded toward the disaster area that had been our Freedom House, and said, "Babies, we got work to do."

For several days we worked together, patching the hole in the wall, repairing the furniture, sweeping and mopping, painting and scrubbing. That spirit of cooperation, however, was not to last. At our next meeting, some of the latent hostilities—the spites, gripes, resentments, and suspicions—began to surface. With all the racist forces arrayed against us, we should have drawn together and not allowed our mutual antagonisms to harm us. Instead, we often found ourselves at the mercy of all the petty irritations of inter-staff strife. The beloved community, it seemed, was capable of generating all the rivalries and animosities of a traveling repertoire company.

"Babies, they gonna be some changes made," Feelgood announced. "From now on, Monty is gonna head up the Freedom School."

Most of us were sprawled out on the living-room floor, and it was almost as if we collectively stirred with discontent.

"What about Esther?" Gayl asked in a perturbed voice. "Isn't that her job?"

"Not anymore. Esther is gonna start workin' on voter registration."

"But wouldn't Gayl be the better choice?" Esther insisted. "She's been working hard with the kids all summer."

"It's not for you to say."

"Can't we at least discuss it?"

"This is my decision; it's not for debate."

"But I still think Gayl . . ."

Esther stopped in midsentence, flushed with annoyance.

"How can you say Monty can't do the job?" Feelgood growled. "You don't even know him."

"That's the point," Leetonia broke in, "we don't know what Monty can do, but we know Gayl."

"Gayl doesn't have a degree."

"Only because she dropped out of Fisk to join the Movement," Leetonia added.

"Monty's a graduate of Howard University."

"Did you know each other before?" I blurted out.

"What does that have to do with it?"

"I mean, you went to Howard too!"

"That right?" Poe gave Feelgood a sidewise glance.

Feelgood seemed uncomfortable. Esther looked down at her hands and said nothing.

"Esther has a degree too," I said. "So do Lenny and I."

"But what do you know about the nitty-gritty of black experience?" Poe demanded. "What do you have to teach the black masses?"

"I didn't say I wanted the job. I was just pointing out that we have degrees too."

"Yeah, honkies got all the degrees," Poe admitted with a wry grin, "but that don't make you qualified, you dig?"

"Can't we drop this?" Gayl interjected. "We have other important things to discuss."

"Like what?" Feelgood demanded. "Are you settin' the agenda?"

"Like who authorized your taking the project car to New Orleans?"

"Who says I took it?"

"We do."

"Who's 'we'?"

"The group."

"So I stand convicted?"

"It's no secret, man," Lance stated.

"We just want to know on whose authority," Gayl said.

"Nobody but me, babies. I needed a break."

"We all need a break," Lance affirmed, "but for three days

we didn't have a car here to take people down to the courthouse."

"So you just took off on your own?" Gayl asked.

"Only he didn't go on his own," Lance said.

"Oh. Was someone with you?" Gayl arched her eyebrows.

"I went with him," Esther admitted in a voice that carried an undertone of irritation.

"How nice for you!" Gayl compressed her lips in a tight line.

"It's just that we have a transportation problem, man," Lance continued. "We need to know if that car is the project's car or the project director's car."

"We don't have a transportation problem," Gayl argued. "We have a people problem. We need to set up some guidelines concerning the use of the car."

"I can't be handled like a puppy on a string," Feelgood said morosely. "If I want to drive that car, I'll drive it."

"But we've wrecked two cars already," Gayl said. "We can't have the one car left being used for dates."

"Who are you, woman, to tell me what I can or can't do?"

"But that's what we're getting at. Who decides? Do you decide or do we decide?"

"Yeah, I thought we were supposed to discuss everything and come to a group decision," I said, concerned that my car would be wrecked next.

"We're discussin' things now," Feelgood replied.

"But who decides?" I insisted, feeling increasingly irritated by Feelgood's offhand manner.

"I do!" Feelgood shouted. "We discuss things and then I decide, that's my job."

"Does that mean what we say doesn't count?" Gayl inquired sarcastically.

"That means you got to do what I say."

"Can't we change the subject?" Esther suggested, trying to avoid trouble between Feelgood and Gayl. "Now that the house is fixed up, I think we need a plan to keep it clean."

"Are you sayin' we ain't clean?" Wachula demanded.

"Of course not," Esther replied. "I'm simply saying that before the bomb hit, the house was in terrible shape. I'm not accusing anyone. It's a mess we all made."

"We always have been pretty sloppy," Leetonia admitted.

"What it comes down to is somebody's got to do the shit work," Feelgood said.

"Why don't we just look after ourselves?" Lance said.

"We've tried that," Esther replied. "Nobody cooks; nobody cleans; things pile up."

"Why don't we take turns?" I suggested.

"Naw," Feelgood insisted. "I'll settle this. From now on, Misty and Wachula are responsible."

"For what? All of it?" Wachula objected.

"For whatever. You two clean the crapper, wash the dishes, mop the floors, and do the laundry."

"That'll take all day," Wachula complained.

"I can help," Esther volunteered.

"No," Feelgood said. "You'll be too busy with voter registration."

"I didn't come down here to be a maid," Misty said.

"It's your guilt trip, baby, not mine."

"That's cold," Lance said.

"For how long?" Misty demanded.

"Until I say different."

"That's not fair," I said, "and you know it."

Feelgood stared at me and, without blinking, turned to the girls. "Do it, babies, I got more important things to think about."

"So that's your job," Gayl interjected, "to do the thinking?"

"That's right. I have to think about what's best for all of us."

"Does that mean that we don't think?" I asked.

"That means I'm the project director," Feelgood said in a commanding voice. "Monty heads the Freedom School. Wachula and Misty clean the Freedom House. And tomorrow I take Lenny, Tom, and Esther canvassin'. Meeting adjourned."

"Is he always like this?" I asked Esther as we walked out on the lawn.

"He's just moody, that's all."

She must have seen the doubt in my eyes.

"He's tired. He's been through a lot. You don't know how much. We're all tired. There's no letup to this work. The tension never quits. That's why I thought a few days in New Orleans might do us both good."

"Was it your idea?"

"God, I needed a break! Feelgood knew a place near Jackson Square where interracial couples could go. New Orleans isn't like the rest of the Deep South. The races have been mixing there for hundreds of years."

"Are all the staff meetings like that one?"

"It can get a lot worse," she said, wincing. "I dread Saturday nights when all the men get drunk. I can't handle the abuse. No matter what I do, my motives are suspect. Just wait, you'll see."

Esther seemed preoccupied and remote, a different person from the vital woman I'd met the previous month. I still felt drawn to her, and strangely responsible for her, too, and yet I knew that there was nothing I could do.

3

Canvassing was hard, boring, heartbreaking work. Every morning we would walk our "beat," the part of McComb our team was responsible for, going from house to house to explain about the Freedom Democratic Party and the convention challenge, ask people to fill out a Freedom Form, and urge them to register to vote. The sun blazed down and at almost every door I came face-to-face with fear, apathy, ignorance. How do you persuade people that voting is worth the risk of their livelihood if not their lives? If I were in their situation, I knew I'd think twice before I signed anything or promised to go down to the courthouse.

Bob Moses had decided to concentrate on freedom registration so that we could present hundreds of thousands of signatures at Atlantic City. I considered that an "overly optimistic assessment" (my motto, "Go with what you've got"), but I was more than willing to sit on porches, discuss issues, and get as many forms filled out as possible. The sad truth was that most people within reach of our projects had already been contacted and only fifty thousand signatures had been gathered. What remained were slim pickings.

Feelgood went along on our first outing to show us the tricks of the trade. He pointed out a house where the woman had given him the runaround a few days earlier.

"I know she's home," he announced, "but when she sees me she's gonna hide."

Feelgood told Lenny, Esther, and me to conceal ourselves behind a nearby shed, then he went striding up to the woman's front door, singing "O Freedom." He pounded forcefully and then stepped back with his hands on his hips.

No answer.

He made a show of throwing his hands in the air and marching off as if resigned to defeat. Before long we saw him sneaking up an alley and positioning himself behind a large tree near the woman's porch. A minute later the woman opened her door, stepped outside, and scanned the street in both directions. Just as she was about to go inside, Feelgood began singing "O Freedom" again.

"Is that you?" the woman called. "I been workin' in my garden and must not of heard you."

"I can dig it," Feelgood said, stepping out where he could be seen. He waved for us to come over.

Seeing three white people heading for her house, the woman was more nervous than ever, but she was also under pressure to be on her best behavior.

"Now I know you just a little bit afraid," Feelgood told her after he had introduced us, "but you gotta step out to see the light."

"Well, I'm with you one hundred percent," the woman insisted.

Feelgood nodded seriously, as if he'd never heard that one

before. "But you gotta come out. If you don't, who else is gonna come out? You know, nobody else can register for you. Nobody else can sign this Freedom Form. You gotta do it yourself. You gotta see the light."

The woman looked as though she'd rather be a mole burrowing in her garden, but we had her trapped.

Before she knew what hit her, Feelgood helped her fill out a Freedom Form. He also made her promise to show up for Freedom Day at the Magnolia Courthouse August 15. When we left, she looked more stunned than pleased, but Feelgood, a big smile on his face, was singing "O Freedom" loud enough for the whole street to hear.

"You gotta get down to the natural-born fact with these folks," he told us. "Preach freedom and they will follow."

Then we were on our own.

Esther and I usually worked one side of the street, while Lenny and Lance, an easygoing local black guy from up near Brookhaven, worked the other. After the first hour or so, the day went slowly. The tedium, the tension, the monotony of repeating our spiel over and over wore us down. By evening we were so streaked with sweaty dirt you would have thought we shoveled coal in a mine shaft. And the Freedom House had only one shower, which was usually out of order. The human nose, I learned, can become accustomed to almost any odor. Even on days when we were freshly scrubbed and closely shaven, the local whites referred to us as "filthy bearded beatniks." It wasn't surprising that some of us came to scorn the spic-and-span, clean-cut look as a capitulation to the enemy.

Often, as I walked the rutted roads of Burgland, I thought of Jasmine and wondered what she was doing and whether she missed me as much as I missed her. I had felt a hollowness since I left her that made much of what I was doing vaguely unreal.

Esther and I always knew who was at home: whole families sat out on their porches, catching whatever breeze was available, talking to passersby, and waiting for their lives to begin or end. It was a leisurely world, and it had to be approached in a leisurely way.

"How are you doing?" I'd say.

"Doin' fine. How you doin'?"

"Pretty good. A little tired. Mind if we rest a minute."

"No, course not. Come on and sit a spell."

We would take a seat on the steps, thus ensuring that we were looking up at them rather than the other way around.

"It's awfully hot, isn't it?"

"Sho is."

"I think this is the hottest day yet."

"Could be. You want a drink a water?"

"Thanks, I'd appreciate it."

The tepid water was served in a communal tin cup and tasted rusty. I tried not to think if it might be from a contaminated well.

"My name is Tom Morton and this is Esther Rappaport." We would reach out to shake hands; if they accepted the handshake and then introduced themselves, we were in luck. If they wouldn't shake, tell their names, or look us in the eye, we were in for a long afternoon. "We work for the Congress of Federated Organizations."

"You the COFO folks."

"We're down here for the summer to help people register to vote."

"That so."

"Are you a registered voter?" I would ask, trying to establish eye contact.

"Nawsuh."

"Have you ever tried to register?"

"Nawsuh."

"Would you like to vote?"

"Well, I wouldn't know 'bout that."

"What about you, Ma'am?"

"We don't mess with it. That's white folks' business."

"Voting is everybody's business. You pay taxes, don't you?"

"I reckon we do."

"Well, if you could vote, you'd have some say in how those tax dollars were spent."

They looked at me with suspicion, wondering if I were truly trying to help.

"The politicians would come and ask what *you* wanted so they could win your vote. You see?" Esther explained.

"They'd treat you with respect," I added. "You'd be able to demand blacktopped roads, sidewalks, streetlights, a sewer system, garbage pickup, and better police protection."

I shouldn't have thrown in the last phrase, which around there was an oxymoron. In the black community, when the patrol car went by, people tensed up and stopped talking.

"Now is the time to decide. We are making a big push this summer and we need everyone's support. We could come by to pick you up tomorrow."

"I'd like to help you, but I just don't get out much. You see I took a fall about a year ago and hurt my hip."

"No problem. We'll drive you door to door."

"But I don't think I can walk at all."

"My friends and I can lift that chair you're sitting in right now and carry you to the truck and up into the courthouse. You'll never have to take a step."

I waved my arm in the direction of Lenny and Lance across the street.

"I wouldn't want to put you to all that trouble."

"Oh, it's no trouble. That's what we're here for."

"But don't you gotta get ready for that test? I hear it's hard."

"It's not that bad. I have a copy right here. See, you just fill out these two pages. The only tricky part is interpreting the constitution."

"Oh, I don't think I could do that."

"The important thing is to try. Then, even if you don't pass, we have evidence that you wanted to vote. See, we hope to get the rules changed and the registration process simplified."

Admittedly, this was the confusing part. From the point of view of the legal case we were trying to make, the more people who failed their registration tests the better, because then we could prove that the registrar discriminated on a wholesale basis. Our challenge to the regular Democratic Party at the convention in Atlantic City was even more complex. The step-by-step procedure of precinct, county, and district meetings; state conventions; delegates and alternates; and parallel structures left people baffled. They had difficulty understanding how this elaborate strategy hinged on getting them to sign their name to a simple nine-question form that, strangely enough, didn't even mention the Mississippi Freedom Democratic Party.

After an hour of talking, two people agreed to go down to the courthouse. But the next morning when the truck stopped to pick them up, nobody was home. We would have to come back another time to tell them about Freedom Day.

Canvassing became a battle of wills. People were afraid and didn't want to take any unnecessary chances. At the same time, they mostly knew that what we were doing was for their own good. I sometimes felt like a doctor administering castor oil: "This tastes bitter, but you'll feel better in the morning."

I soon became a connoisseur of excuses. "I'm too old" or "I'm too sick" were the most common. If age was the excuse, I would ask how old the person was and then mention the names of people older than they who had already registered and signed a Freedom Form. If that didn't work, I would urge them to stand up for the sake of the young people. In the case of sickness—and the truth was that many people were in bad health—I would inquire about the problem and talk about the blind, crippled, and seriously ill who had already been to the courthouse. Everyone was afraid, so I would admit that we were afraid, too, but that the best way to find courage was to take action. The curious thing was, I never felt braver than when I was cajoling frightened black people to show some guts. When I was alone, it was a different story.

With those who were ashamed—the educated, because they hadn't registered, and the uneducated, because they couldn't read the test or fill out the form—I would argue that late was better than never and that now was the time to be counted. For those who were worried about losing jobs or welfare, I could honestly report that in McComb not many people had been fired. The more who went, I would argue, the less likely reprisals were, since the economy depended on black labor. When someone said they were busy, I would offer to help them with their chores and then take them down to the courthouse. In this way, I mopped a kitchen floor, washed a stack of dishes, shelled a basket of beans, chopped weeds in a garden, and got four more people to register.

Only the schoolteachers in their brick houses were immune to my entreaties; they were terrified their contracts would not be renewed. One woman at least had the nerve to go ask her superintendent if she could register, but he advised her strongly to wait. The fact that none of their teachers were registered voters was a lesson in civics not lost on the students. They began to plan a school boycott to force their teachers to set a better example.

I had a repertoire of replies for all the standard excuses, but the more unusual ones left me speechless: the woman who said she couldn't sign because she didn't have a name; the man who claimed his wife didn't believe in it; the woman who couldn't find her glasses; and the one who didn't have a second to spare because she was waiting for an important phone call—which never came. There were plenty of Uncle Toms and Nervous Nellies who didn't want nothin' to do with it, because they were very well satisfied, and besides "My white peoples told us not to fool with y'all, and we don't want to hurt they feelin's." One woman's eyes pleaded with me: "Please don't let me get involved with this. Please get off my porch before somebody sees." Another came around the side of her house toting a shotgun and shouting, "Get away from here with that freedom mess or I'll blow yo head off."

Esther became upset with those who would summon Jehovah, Jesus, and a multitude of the heavenly host to justify their caution. One woman said politics was un-Christian. Another, that she couldn't sign because she had promised God not to.

"Why would you do that?" Esther asked with exasperation.

"Because He want me for His own."

"But don't you think he wants your help to see that his work is done on this earth?"

"Oh, no, honey. He do everythin' in His own time and in His own way. He don't need no help from me."

"God helps those who help themselves," Esther insisted.

"I have help myself to His blessin'."

"But there are some things that God can't do. God can't fill out a Freedom Form. You have to do that."

"God can do whatever He want."

"Don't you want a better life for your children?"

"I reckon God sees after 'em. They in His hands."

"Well, why doesn't he do something about that?" Esther gestured toward a ditch running with raw sewage where some children were playing. "Why doesn't he do something about all this poverty? Why doesn't he feed his hungry people?"

"Y'all hongry? I gots some streak meat an' beans."

I could barely repress a smile at her good-hearted offer.

"No, I'm not hungry," Esther cried. "I just want to scream, that's all."

The woman looked at her with puzzled sympathy. I then made my pitch, talking about Moses and the Promised Land and how the Israelites risked everything to follow their leader, coming around at last to Bob Moses and the need to march down to the courthouse.

"I loves to hear those Bible stories," the woman said with a warm approval for God's unfolding plan. "They the best ones."

"The Jews fought for their freedom," Esther said.

"I puts my trust in the Lord."

"I wish you'd put a little more trust in registering to vote."

"I'll pray on it."

Esther angrily crossed her name off our list and we headed for the next house.

That same day an old man with a shock of gray hair hobbled off his porch and down to his gate to greet us. His face was a map of pain, but his voice was lively.

"You're freedom," he said.

"I suppose we are."

"Well, come on in and tell me 'bout that."

We introduced ourselves. He shook our hands solemnly, with the limp grip characteristic of old black men in the South. Inside, he insisted that I take his rocking chair by the fireplace; Esther sat on a couch covered with a faded quilt. The man was obviously very poor, but everything was neat. Photos of children in graduation garb were lined up along the mantle. We kept offering to surrender our seats, which were the only ones in the room, but he remained standing.

"Those my grans," he said, pointing proudly to the photos.

Then a boy about six came into the room.

"This my gran too," the old man said, placing his hand on the boy's head. "He lives with me since his mother passed."

I asked the man if he was a registered voter.

"No, suh. I never did believe in puttin' myself in the way of that." He tilted his head and looked askance, as if I had just asked him to step in front of a fast train—which, in a sense, I had. "Now I'm too old. I'm gettin' ready to die."

"How long have you lived here?" Esther asked.

"All my life in Pike County. Eighty-some years."

"And you've never voted?"

"No, suh. I ain't never been mixed up in it."

"Do you still work?"

"I gardens a bit when I kin git it, but I can't do much. I only got one good eye."

"Do you make enough to live on?"

"I gits by. What I needs, folks provides."

"Are you on welfare?"

"I tried for that. I went to see the welfare, but I was turn down. I did not receive it," he said with slow formality.

"And now you think you'd like to vote?"

"Well, I wonder if I should. I knows what y'all doin' is right, but I believe I am not qualify."

"Why is that?"

"Well, I can't fill it!"

I watched Esther studying the man with frank curiosity, impressed by his openness and honesty.

"I can fill it out for you," I said. "This is a form. Shall we do it?"

"Yassuh, I'm ready."

I walked him through the questions and then gave him the pen and showed him where to sign. He slowly printed his initials in large block letters.

"Now I can vote," he said with dignity.

"Can I vote too?" the boy asked eagerly.

"Not yet," the old man said. "You too young."

"But I can make an X."

"You goin' to school. You gonna learn to read and write."

"I'm afraid you really can't vote yet," I reluctantly explained. "This form is just part of our convention challenge. In order to vote, you have to register."

"I ain't redish?"

"No. You have to go to the courthouse and register with the circuit clerk. Would you like to do that?"

"I've come this far. I ain't turnin' back. When do we go?"

"We can take you right now. We have a car down the street."

"Wait till I gets proper. I wants to be presentable."

He stepped into the bedroom and returned wearing a white, freshly starched shirt and clean denims held up by suspenders. He put on a dark jacket that must have been impossibly hot in that weather and a straw hat; we waited quietly until the car came. At the courthouse I helped him up the steps, but we were stopped at the registrar's door.

"What do you want?" a milky-eyed man with a receding chin asked.

The old man spoke up without hesitating. "I come to see the circus clerk."

"You want to register?"

"Yassuh, I wants to redish."

"Go on in there and take a seat, but this scalawag's got to wait in the hall."

"I'm not a scalawag. I'm a carpetbagger from Ohio."

"You're white trash from hell as far as I'm concerned. Stay in the hall."

The old man was in the room for a long time. Every once in a while he would ask the registrar to fill a part of the form out for him. The registrar, in a considerably kinder voice than he had used with me, told him he couldn't tell him the answers, although in fact I think he did give him some assistance. After an hour or so he came out.

"My eye give out," he said, but he didn't sound discouraged.

"He couldn't complete it?" I asked the registrar.

"No, but I told him he can come back tomorrow."

"You did!"

"He can pick up where he left off."

"Thank you, suh," the old man said, hat in hand.

"That's all right, uncle. I'm just doin' my job."

"I feels straighter now," the old man told me as we left. "I'm gonna vote."

I didn't have the heart to tell him that, in spite of the consideration he was shown, it was not likely that the registrar would approve his application.

"What do you want to vote for?"

"Well, I wants to improve things. It's not enough to scrape by, you gotta make this world a better place."

"You'll need to vote for the best person."

"Who's that?"

"Whoever you think is best. You get to choose."

"Well, I believe I will," the old man said. "I believe I will."

There were at least as many people like him who stood up and took the risk of registering as there were those who stayed back and made excuses. We spent a lot of time complaining about the apathetic and afraid, but the real miracle of the summer was how many common people showed uncommon courage.

One day I knocked on a screen door and a voice came from the back bedroom.

"Wait out there, honey. I'se all disdressed."

I waited on the porch, admiring the potted plants, which, on closer inspection, proved to be exactly that: flowers growing in old porcelain chamber pots.

"You can come on in now," the woman said. "I've been waitin' for you."

She was almost as wide as she was tall.

"How do you do, Ma'am. My name is Tom Morton, and I'm with COFO."

"Well, my name is Mary Allen, and I'm a fat Democrat."

She laughed loudly, a celebration of flesh, and looked at me intently.

As soon as I started my "sales talk," she began nodding and saying "That's true" to everything. There was no need to continue. She was one of the few registered blacks in Pike County and was very well versed on what was happening. For some reason she had waited until we contacted her, but she knew all about the Summer Project and was quick with helpful suggestions. She volunteered to be a block captain; I gave her a stack of Freedom Forms, and she began putting in her days as a full-time canvasser. Her energy and persistence paid quick dividends: in two weeks she had been to all the Freedom Democratic Party meetings and had been elected as a delegate to the state convention in Jackson.

She was the kind of natural leader we were always looking for but so rarely found. Although I got credit for recruiting her, in truth all I did was knock on her door.

4

In the aftermath of the bombing, the Freedom House was like an outpatient clinic for nervous disorders. We thought we were going to die and so we lived with thin-skinned intensity day by day. The discovery of the bodies of Mickey, Andy, and Jim in an earthen dam outside Philadelphia in early August did nothing to calm our fears. Because Mississippi had gone to such lengths to deny the truth, there was a certain satisfaction in having their murders confirmed, but the grim facts were an all-too-vivid reminder of the dangers we all faced. Apparently they had been shot at close range and Jim Chaney had been beaten, although the bodies were so badly decomposed it was hard to say for sure. Nobody was arrested, but we had no doubt who did it—the cops and the Klan. The Schwerners wanted their son buried beside Jim, but Mississippi said that was against the law, and so the funerals of Mickey and Andy were in New York and Jim's was in his hometown of Meridian.

After that, everyone was even more irritable and on edge; tempers frayed to the breaking point. My gut felt as taut as a guitar string and I suffered from skull-splitting migraines. Some nights I woke up in a cold sweat with my face twisted in a grimace. My skin itched as if bugs were crawling on it. I was so high-strung I couldn't stand still; even when I sat down, my leg kept bouncing. At dinner my knee hit the underside of the table so much Lenny said we might as well have been at a séance. Everyone had their share of symptoms: some complained of constipation or diarrhea; others got drunk every night or guzzled milk by the quart for their ulcers; I once saw Marcus and Jason sniffing glue.

Although I wrote twice to Jasmine, I had received no reply, a fact that only added to my anxieties. At night I would try to picture her face and recall kissing her soft lips. Sometimes the images would come to me so vividly I would shiver with desire and hug my pillow in despair. I also brooded about Esther. I think she liked canvassing with me, and we enjoyed some good talks as we walked from house to house, but Feelgood was never far away and come evening he always monopolized her time.

Meanwhile, staff tensions had become a major problem.

Misty was one of those irrepressible optimists who made life miserable for the rest of us; she was always saying or doing something to rub Esther the wrong way. Instead of preparing her lesson plans, she slept in; she combed her hair compulsively to achieve just the right curl and pouted that her hands were swelling. She flirted with any number of guys who hung out at the house. They went for her pale, Clearasil skin, her freckled face and straw-colored hair, her Cupid's bow mouth, the way she posed and postured, smiled and looked sad. What kept her relatively safe was the fact that she had so many suitors she was rarely alone with any one of them. When Esther warned her about leading men on, she blinked her big blue eyes and the advice bounced off their serene surface.

One day Misty asked Marcus Carver to drive her to a small grocery store across the railroad tracks on the white side of town because no store in Burgland carried her favorite brand of "cigs." He did, was seen doing it, and was promptly fired from his job at a local gas station. From then on he ceased to function as an effective member of the staff. Slack-lipped and sullen, sapless and depressed, he started drinking before noon until he was completely wasted. When I came back from canvassing in the evening, I tried to avoid the vacant look of defeat in his wine-clouded eyes.

In addition to the constant stream of out-of-state visitors—ministers, lawyers, reporters, parents, and politicians—who had come down to see the endangered COFO in its unnatural habitat, an incredible assortment of local people hung out at the Freedom House and impeded our operations: winos begged for money to buy one more brown-bagged bottle of cheap sweet wine; kids, so famished for acceptance they would do anything to get it, woke us up in the morning, were under our feet all day, and had to be forced to go home in the evening; assorted adults, assuming that we Freedom Riders had the power to be their right-hand white man, wanted us to fill out their welfare forms, see their parole officer, or talk to the man they planted cotton for. As usual, the staff couldn't agree on how to regulate outsiders without hurting feelings.

Given the way things were, it wasn't hard to blame the local folks for expecting us to solve all their problems; or the kids for wanting a place to come to where, no matter what they did, they wouldn't get whipped. Besides, Skeeter, Beanie, Peanut, Meatball, Sammy, Sweet Thing, and the rest may have stolen our time, but they stole our hearts as well, and as fond as we were of them, they reciprocated tenfold. It was hard to say no to their hungry-eyed devotion. It wasn't hard either to blame the racist system, which was designed to crush people, for the pandemic apathy and rampant alcoholism that plagued Burgland.

Once I had sized up the staff, I broke us down into four categories: the WiFos, the LoFos, the MoFos, and the Mau Maus. The white folks were the four volunteers, although we certainly had our differences; the local folks—Gayl, Lance, Leetonia, and Mary Allen—were the ones who believed in free-spirited participatory democracy and the inherent wisdom of the black community; the motherfuckers, which included Marcus, Jason, and Wachula, were the increasing number of drunks, goof-offs, and don't-give-a-damns; and the Mau Maus were Feelgood and Poe, who wanted to impose revolutionary discipline on our helter-skelter cadre. We WiFos generally sided with the LoFos, while Feelgood liked to stack meetings with MoFos who weren't even on the staff and then use them to get his way. Esther was caught in the middle as she did her best to hold the various groups together. More often than not, her efforts boomeranged.

One day Bob Moses, returning with Gayl from the Freedom School convention in Meridian, made a surprise visit to the house. He sat, with characteristic self-effacement, in an unconspicuous corner of the room during our staff meeting and rarely spoke. Nevertheless, it was hard not to keep glancing over to see how he was taking things. He looked far more weighed-down and worn-out than when I last saw him and his thick black eyebrows lowered like an impending storm.

Gayl opened the meeting by pointing out that we had paperwork piling up in the back room that had to be dealt with.

"I'll take care of it," Esther said.

"Why you?"

Gayl glowered at Esther with obvious hostility.

"It's easy for me. I'm a fast typer."

"Are you saying we're slow?"

"I didn't mean to imply that. You can do it if you want."

"Thank you very much, but I can't type."

"Well, what do you want to do then?"

"It's not what I want to do. It's what you want to do. You want to control the information. You want to be spokesman for the group. You want to take over."

"I just want to answer some letters and write some reports," Esther said with exasperation. "It's two weeks since the bombing and we still haven't sent out a decent press release. We've got to have some efficiency around here."

"And you're going to provide it?"

It was painful for me to listen. Esther and Gayl were the two most solid and competent people on the project, but they were always at cross-purposes. I wanted to say something, but I was afraid that if I came to the support of Esther, I would offend Gayl.

"Why not let some of the local people do it?" Lance suggested.

"They're not on the staff," Lenny pointed out, "and besides, they haven't the skills."

"Well, show them."

"It's not that easy," Esther responded. "We're short of time. If I have to rewrite everything, I might as well do it in the first place. But if you don't want me to, I won't."

"Leave it to me," Feelgood announced, ending that discussion—but we all knew that probably nothing would be done.

"I hate to bring this up, but have any of you noticed personal possessions missing?" Esther asked. "I'm afraid some of my jewelry has been stolen."

"Who are you to talk about stealing?" Gayl demanded.

She was still steaming over that trip Esther and Feelgood had taken to New Orleans.

"It's true," I said. "Stuff has been stolen from the Freedom House."

"I thought everybody was told not to bring jewelry," Feelgood said.

"I didn't bring much," Esther explained, "just my favorite necklace and a few rings."

"Feelgood will buy you another necklace," Poe said, his gold tooth flashing beneath dark glasses.

"It was from my grandmother."

"What do we do about a person who steals?" Lance asked. "Last time I was in jail I came back and all my clothes were gone."

"You sayin' one of us did it?" Jason asked.

"Nobody's accusing anybody," I said.

"That's right," Lance added. "If we can't trust each other, who *can* we trust?"

"What bothers me," Bob Moses broke in, irritated by all our bickering, "is that people steal my time. They don't really talk of themselves, from the center, they talk from the periphery. They steal because there isn't enough time to go around, and the needs of people that don't get answered cause them to steal. People steal because they have already lost themselves. In our society we steal whole people's lives away. I don't know if we have the right to own anything."

Moses's open-ended philosophizing left us hanging in air. No one knew what to say in response. Finally, I spoke: "Canvassing is a daily drudgery. But I think we're getting somewhere. Before long black folks around here are going to have the vote, but once they've got the vote, then what? Are we doing enough to prepare them for integration?"

"Next summer will be better," Misty stated. "The project will really draw the Greeks."

"The what?" I did a double take.

"You know, the fraternity guys."

"What good are a bunch of frat rats from 'I Felta Thigh' and 'I Tappa Keg' gonna do?" Lenny demanded.

"Even if they persuade just one person to register, that's something," Misty said.

"Bullshit," Poe shouted. "We've got enough honkies down here as it is."

"I disagree," Esther said. "I think we can use all the help we can get."

"Who's 'we'?" Gayl asked.

"Us," Esther said with emphasis. "The project."

"All this country gets off on is images of blue-eyed blondes ministerin' to the poor oppressed black folks," Poe asserted

"My eyes are at least as dark as yours," Esther replied.

"Don't fool with me," Poe warned. "You white gals are just down here for some black cock."

"Don't you wish."

Poe gave Esther a this-chick-can't-be-for-real head shake.

"You think what you're doin' is romantic," he said with cutting sarcasm. "Black is what's happenin'. The Negro is in vogue this summer. Mississippi is the 'in' place to be. You get to write yo letters home postmarked from some 'Black Belt' hot spot and back on campus you can brag about how you made that civil rights scene. But when something else becomes hip, you'll split. I'm on to you honkies. Look at you in yo bare feet, workshirts, and blue jeans. You think it's beautiful to be poor? Well let me tell you, there's no glory in bein' poor. It's a grind, man. And I didn't learn that in no sociology course; I lived it. Poor people don't need no bleedin'-heart liberals comin' down to 'identify' with their plight."

"What *do* they need?" I asked.

"Money."

"What do you suggest?"

"You really want to know?"

Poe looked at me intensely.

"Yes."

"Rob a bank."

"We only came to help," Misty said.

"Lawdy! Lawdy! Our troubles are over!"

"I think that when the local people see whites working beside them and sharing their problems, they feel better," I explained.

"So you feel better too?"

"It works both ways."

"Person-to-person contact is important," Esther added. "When people get to know each other, prejudice is broken down."

"Only it ain't person to person, it's master to slave."

"I believe that whites and blacks can learn to live together," Leetonia affirmed.

"That's because you're half-white yourself," Poe shot back, indifferent to whether he was hurting Leetonia's feelings, but she held her ground.

"I think we have more in common than people realize. I'm tryin' to show that."

"Don't try too hard."

"These kids comin' down here is a fine Christian thing," Mary Allen said in her jovial grits-and-gravy voice. "They listens to us and they always asks what we wants. Folks here is real grateful they come. I pity Mississippi when these kids leave. I don't know what gonna happen then."

Poe, his face filled with foxy cunning, seemed to derive perverse pleasure from responding to all our arguments. Feelgood, by his side, smiled grimly as Poe pressed the attack. Moses radiated gloom as he sat silently in his corner.

"I don't dig havin' black folks playin 'all the supportin' roles so y'all can star in yo own successful experiment in interracial living," Poe said. "We ain't runnin' no summer camp for do-gooders and social workers; we're committed to workin' for social change."

"I'm committed to that too," I said.

"For two months."

"I might stay longer."

"Don't do us no favors."

"If I stayed, it would be for me too."

"Naturally."

"I don't see why you have to be so hostile," Misty said. "You should see the way the faces of my girls light up when I come in the room."

"I have. That's what bothers me. I've also seen the way they stroke yo hair and touch yo skin."

"What's wrong with that?"

"You're white."

"We just want to be accepted at face value," I said.

"That's exactly what I'm doin'," Poe asserted. "I see all yo white faces and I accept the fact that you don't belong here."

"Why can't you accept us?" Misty pleaded. "The community has been wonderful to us. They're so terrific! So spiritual! They've welcomed us with open arms."

"Don't kid yourself," Poe replied. "They ain't makin' a big fuss because they like you personally."

"I don't believe that," Misty pouted.

"Suit yourself, but don't say you wasn't told."

Feelgood chose this moment to speak with measured deliberation.

"Integration is not a revolutionary objective," he announced while Poe nodded in approval. "It assumes that stuffs gotta be done for black folks because they got no identity or culture of their own."

"That's right," Poe said. "They gotta be indoctrinated and shipped out to the suburbs so they can wear Bermuda shorts and learn to play croquet. Forget it, Jack. I ain't buyin'. Do you think a dude in a brick house is gonna give a shit about the brother pickin' cotton?"

"Who are we to say black people shouldn't have those middle-class material things we take for granted?" Esther asked. I secretly rejoiced to see her, for once, publicly questioning Feelgood.

"We don't want to be like you," Poe said with icy intensity. "We ain't adjustin' to no white world. Yo life is a lie and we ain't livin' no lie. We played the slave for you too long already. Now it's time for you to adjust to us. This ain't no time for mouth-to-mouth resuscitation; I'm talkin' toe-to-toe confrontation. It's time to tell you honkies to move over or we gonna move on over you."

"The best way to show that white superiority isn't so is by working side by side," Esther pleaded. "All we have is each other. We must learn to live together. We can't let this turn into black against white. We have a job to do."

Esther looked imploringly over at Bob Moses. He was obviously uncomfortable in the face of all our personality conflicts, but it was Gayl who came to her defense.

"It is not enough to be physically integrated," she said. "We need to be morally and philosophically integrated too. We need to keep focused on the same prize."

After a long moment of meditative silence, Moses said a few words about the convention challenge, and then he addressed himself to the long-range issue of whether SNCC should stay in small towns or start working in the cities.

"Our strength is in the rural areas because there people's lives have more integrity and wholeness. Families stay together and black farmers own land. How do you develop a community focus in cities where technology flattens everything and people have no sense of participation? We have legitimately earned our rep in the Black Belt, and so that is a good reason to continue working the rural areas, but don't we also have a commitment to try to work in the cities? The problem is we know Albany and Selma and McComb, but what do we know about Atlanta, Birmingham, Detroit, and Chicago?"

Once again, Moses had gone abstract and philosophical on us and thrown our staff meeting into a different dimension. Still, I had to admit that he was raising important questions. Everybody had jumped on Feelgood when he said his job was to think, but in truth that was what Moses did best, that was how he led. He should have been left alone to do our deep thinking, leaving someone else to deal with the petty personal problems and daily administrative crises of the Summer Project. After the meeting I had hoped to get a chance to relax and talk to Moses at length. I had a fantasy that maybe he would pull me aside and say, "Hey, Tom, I've got a raft on the Mississippi; let's you and me drift on down the Father of Waters and meditate on the meaning of things," but instead all there was time for was a "How's it going, Tom?" "Okay,

Bob" before he closeted himself with Feelgood for an hour and then a car came by to whisk him back to Jackson.

Gayl came up to me with her usual look of sorrowful solemnity. "I have something for you."

She handed me a letter simply addressed to "Tom."

"Where did you get this?"

"A girl from Tallahatchie asked me to give it to you."

"Jasmine? Where did you see her?"

"She was at the Freedom School convention. She was one of the stars. She gave a speech about the importance of Africa. It was very good, very polished. But I think she had some coaching. Every time I saw her, Ledell Simmons was by her side. I warned him about jailbait, but, my she is pretty! How do you know her?"

"She was one of my students," I mumbled faintly.

"Lucky you."

I thanked Gayl and then found a quiet place where I could read Jasmine's letter:

Dear Tom,

I'm sorry we didn't get time to talk more before you left because I feel like there was a lot more we had to say, but since then seem like things been happening so fast in my life I don't really know where to start. After you go I was sad for days and then Ledell ask if I wants to go to the Freedom School convention in Meridian and I say yes, so we be spending a lot of time on that and I see how much it is we have in common and how we agree on most everything and see the world in the same way. Then when he say I love you I was so shook I don't know what but this warm feeling come over me and I know I have found what I been searching for all my life. I love him, Tom, and he love me back. He is a good God-fearing man who has stood up for our people and a very nice person who treats me with respect. He has taught me how to be serious about our freedom and also he is fun to be with and he wants to take care of me. I ain't tole him nothing about us but I think he knows cause of how sad I was. You is a sweet boy, Tom, the nicest white boy I ever met, and I will always remember you. Before you came Grandma say be nice to you for you may not be long for this earth, but what I feels for you is much stronger than that and I will always treasure you in my heart. I know there ain't no point in thinking about some other life I might of had, I only got this one and I want to make the best of it. I am very happy now and I hope you are not hurt by this letter. When I think about what might of been, I can't help but cry. I do wonder how all this is gonna turn out, but this ain't no time to talk about regret. I done made my choice. There is so much more I want to say but I can't tell you all I feel on this paper.

Best wishes to you and may God bless you and take care of you.

Jasmine

I suppose that deep down I had known that this would happen, but I kept it from myself, pretending that our relationship had a future. I felt empty, as if holding on to love were like trying to carry water in your hands. The whole project didn't mean anything to me; I wanted to pack my bags and hop the next bus and forget that I'd ever been in Mississippi. Instead, I walked over to the train tracks and stared a long time at the rails glinting in the sunlight. At dusk I returned to the Freedom House and sat in on a jam session without saying a word. That night I dreamt of Jasmine rising naked from the baptismal river and walking slowly toward me while her white robe drifted downstream.

5

"McComb is about played out," Feelgood announced. "I want y'all to start workin' the rural."

"The rural" was anywhere outside the relative safety of the larger towns. In the Delta it was the plantations, where the SNCC guys would first have to case the place, making a map of all the entrances and exits, planning step-by-step exactly where they would go. At night, they drove a fast car with no lights and kept the motor running as they whispered to people in darkened rooms about freedom.

The rural areas of Pike County probably wouldn't be as dangerous as those plantations, because some blacks owned small farms and had guns and many more were poor and unemployed and lived hidden on little side roads where few whites ever went. But Feelgood wasn't a man to play it safe.

"We gonna work Pike County, and we also gonna work Amite County. Those crackers over there have had things their own way for too long."

Feelgood's strategy was risky, but in my present devil-may-care mood I was ready for danger and the thought of going where Bob Moses had gone was a challenge I couldn't resist.

Our first assignment, Craw Dad Bottom, a row of shacks in a swamp, was a study in misery. I had seen poverty in McComb, but these people were destitute. Their tin-roofed, tar-papered shacks with broken stoops or sagging porches were so weathered and worn they looked like they would collapse at the next strong wind and rot into the ground.

Inside, it was worse. Sometimes the floor was merely packed dirt; more often it was ill-fitting, splintery planks, so fragile the house shook at every step, and with cracks wide enough to turn an ankle in. The slat walls were insulated with cardboard and papered with sheets torn from old magazines and catalogues. Often there was no ceiling; shafts of sunlight sliced through gaps in the rusty roof, and wasp nests were visible in the rafters. The front room would have a battered couch, a table made out of orange crates, and a blaring television—even Craw Dad Bottom had electricity. Burlap sacks served as curtains for the windows, which had neither screens nor glass, and tow and feed sacks were piled in the corner to make a pallet for the children. There was normally a cot in the tiny kitchen, too, and it wasn't rare for several bodies, often half-dressed and completely drunk, to be sprawled on a bare mattress on the one bed in the one bedroom. Clothes hung on nails and the only pictures, usually of Jesus or JFK, were cut out of newspapers and scotch-taped on the walls.

The smell was unforgettable: a combination of wood smoke, moonshine, old sweat, stale urine, soiled diapers, rotting newspapers, flour paste, bacon grease, and cooking beans (with some dog and chicken odors thrown in for good measure). This was either intolerable or strangely appealing, depending on the blend.

At the first shack, a young boy whose face was disfigured with scars and running sores saw us and crouched down in the yard in fright. A woman wearing a head rag and a tattered slip came to the doorway; peering out behind her were three naked children. Like most of the kids we saw, they looked sick and malnourished: bloated bellies, skinny limbs, big joints, visible ribs. One boy had a distended navel and a puffy eye almost closed with pus. Teeth, an unmitigated disaster; eyes, dull and lackluster; skin with an eerie sheen. A sparsely feathered hen, clucking like she owned the place, was the only one who wasn't afraid. When we tried to talk about voter registration, the boy in the yard stared at us and began laughing wildly.

It was hard to believe that life had done *that* to a group of human beings.

"I doesn't vote," was all that the woman would say, and her eyes said, "Go away."

The mother at the next place unselfconsciously nursed a two-year-old boy while she told of her troubles.

"My baby be down today," she said. "He feel hot."

"Does he have a fever?"

"I believe he do. He cry all the time."

"Do you know what's wrong?"

"The nurse lady say he got intentional worms."

"Does he have much appetite?"

"No, he don't. I give him my milk, but he don't take it."

"What about the other children?"

"They eats fine. The problem is what to feed 'em."

"What did they have today?"

"I gives 'em a candy bar for energy in the mornin'. An' some pop. They loves that Nehi grape. We gots some grits an' gravy for dinner. Y'all want some Kool-Aid? I just made some."

"Thanks, that would be nice."

She handed us scratched plastic glasses. Her children looked at us with thirsty eyes. We took a sip, then gave the Kool-Aid, which was also grape-flavored, to them.

"Now y'all share that," the woman said, and they did: five children, from three to eight, with two glasses.

"Melvin, don't you take too much," she said to her oldest boy. "He got sweet blood."

"Sweet blood?" Esther asked.

"Thas right. Only we can't afford no sugar shots."

"You mean diabetes?"

"Thas right. They's lots with sweet blood 'round here."

"Melvin, seem like he always got somethin'. He got bit the other day an' his leg was all swole up. It be better now."

Melvin turned his leg to display an ugly wound.

"Has he had a rabies shot?"

"No, Mam. It weren't no rabbit. He was dogbit."

"Are you on welfare?"

"Oh, no, Mam. I works for what we got."

"Where?"

"Blue Moon Saloon. Twelve hour every day, fifteen dollar a week."

"So you live on sixty dollars a month?"

"Thas right. I pays for food, clothes, an' rent outa that."

"You pay rent for this place?"

"Fifteen dollar a month. An' you see how it is, this dump ain't fit for a dog."

"Do you ever run out of money?"

"Oh, Lord, all the time, Mam. We don't never not run out. It just goes an' then it's hard. We like to froze las' winter. Didn't have no wood."

"Have you ever tried to vote?"

"Oh, no, Mam. I don't want to get in trouble."

"May I ask how old you are?"

She looked to be about forty.

"Twenty-two, Mam."

Esther couldn't conceal her shock.

"You don't have to call me 'Mam.' We're the same age."

"Yes'm."

"You know if everybody could vote," I said, "something could be done about your problems."

"Yassuh. You sho is right. Don't give up on what you doin'."

We tried to explain to her about the convention challenge and the freedom registration forms, but she began to stare off to the side and stopped listening.

"I can't get my mind around all that," she said dejectedly. "I got these chillrun to think of."

"Is there anything we could do to help?" I asked.

"I'd sho like to have some wood for the winter."

I promised to see what I could do.

Lenny, who had gone to the next shack, joined us in the street.

"It's the Night of the Living Dead over there," he said. "I mean I knocked and somebody opened the door, but like nobody's home!"

"So what did you do?"

"I kept talking and they kept looking at their shoes and saying they didn't want anything to do with 'that mess.' They weren't signing up for freedom ever. Finally I said, 'Oh, I understand, you're not signing up for freedom ever and under no circumstances, right? What you need is the form for folks who don't want nothin' to do with that mess, right?' So I pulled another Freedom Form out from the bottom of the stack, and they signed it."

"I don't know about that, man," I said.

"That was a shitty thing to do," Esther added.

"You're right," Lenny admitted, "but it seemed like a good idea at the time. I mean, if anything makes me give up on Mississippi, it's not going to be the harassment of white racists, but the apathy of people like that."

"There's a reason for how they are," I argued. "Three hundred years of oppression. These people are paralyzed with fear. Apathy isn't indifference or laziness, it's ambivalence. You want to do something, but you're deathly afraid to do it. As a result, you expend all your energy fighting yourself, your psyche shuts down, and you can't move."

"I took the psych course too," Lenny said. "But still it's damn hard to deal with sometimes. This is one of those days. The whole fucking system stinks."

"Where's that famous Lenny Swift sense of humor?" I asked. "You didn't used to be this bitter."

"Mississippi will do that to you. Let's finish this street and get the hell out of here."

Most of the shacks were so appalling we stopped being shocked. You had to be hard, abrupt, almost jaded, to see what we witnessed. At one place I knocked and the door opened but I didn't see anyone. Then I looked down and saw a legless woman at my feet! She had had a double amputation because of advanced diabetes. On the bed behind her was an old man who had had a stroke and was paralyzed on his left side. Somehow they managed to take care of each other. They both signed Freedom Forms.

Another woman with ten children told Esther she had had eight miscarriages as well. Chickens grubbed in the yard and cockroaches, large as my thumb, walked the walls. We watched the children, seated on the floor, eating rice and beans with a spoon, using hubcaps as plates. A line of ants had gone to work on what they dropped. She had just begun to tell us about her "sis-sy-a-shun" when the man of the house arrived.

"Why should we vote?" he demanded. "The whites always keep us down. I hate them greedy suckers, hoggin' all the good things an' makin' us work for chump change."

"But that's why the vote is so important."

"I don't want none of yo white man's freedom. None of this booze-wah, this middle class. Thas a lotta crap."

"What's your answer?"

"They ain't none. The way things is, thas how they gonna be. In this country the colored people catch hell, an' thas it."

And so it went. Only one family in Craw Dad Bottom was willing both to sign the Freedom Form and to register at the courthouse. They were down but not out. You could see it from the outside. Their shack was the same size and shoddy materials as the others, but it was surrounded by a fence decorated with milk of magnesia bottles, and the packed dirt of the yard had been swept with a dogwood broom. Spare truck tires and a discarded bathtub served as flower holders. There was a big zinc wash pot in the backyard and fresh clothes on the line. The front room had a full complement of handmade furniture and an old rug covered the floor. The father had even built a little loft over the living room, log-cabin style, where the children could sleep, and the bed in the bedroom and the cot in the kitchen were covered with clean sheets.

"We may be poor," the woman said, "but we ain't cheap and we ain't beat. If y'all can take the trouble to come all this way to see us, the least we can do is do something to help ourselves."

We found that same spirit among the black farmers of Amite County. One old man, when he saw us walking down the dusty road, left his mule in the field and came over to ask if he could sign up. In three days we had even gathered enough voter registration commitments to plan a Freedom Day for Amite County on August 15 at the Liberty Courthouse. One small black man, who lived up on a slight hill off a side road, couldn't stop smiling from ear to ear as we talked about the importance of voting. We asked if he wanted to sign.

"Well, I reckon so," he said, still smiling.

We handed him the form and he wrote his name: E. W. Steptoe.

"Aren't you afraid out here?" I couldn't resist asking.

He showed us his arsenal—at least one gun in every room—and then remarked, "A man who ain't willin' to die for what he believe in ain't fittin' to live."

I knew enough about what had happened when Bob Moses came to Liberty in 1961 to look at him with unfeigned awe. It was hard enough just to survive in Mississippi, but Steptoe had always had the courage to be a leader.

"I really admire the stand you've taken," I told him.

"Somebody gotta eat the poison off the pie," he replied.

We lived in the present tense, the tense here and now. We lived in fear, not just of the bullet that had our name on it, but of all those addressed "To Whom It May Concern" as well. Under the circumstances you'd think we would have been as cautious as possible, never taking any unnecessary chances. Instead, after a week or so of playing it safe and expecting the worst, a kind of giddiness set in—a perverse desire to court danger. To Feelgood, for example, a car wasn't a means of transportation, rather he saw it as a way to push life to the edge and run risks with death. All the SNCC guys drove like that.

Our impulse was to break the rules, to do all the don'ts—especially when it came to sex. The assumption was that if everybody got laid, nobody would get screwed. The black guys looked for white gals ready to go all the way for integration, and the white guys were all too willing to take advantage of the instant crushes the teenage black girls had on them. If you believed in equality, why not? The place to make the beloved community was right there on that mattress on the floor.

I was reluctant to see my relationship with Jasmine as a part of that pattern. Were we attracted to each other merely out of some illicit urge to defy a taboo? I didn't think so. At the same time I felt betrayed that she could find someone else to fall for so quickly. After what had happened with Michelle, I was doubly vulnerable to rejection, and I vowed to be more cautious with my heart in the future. That went especially for Esther. As much as I was afraid of being shot in Mississippi, at the moment I was even more concerned about being shot down! But why couldn't Jasmine have given us a chance? If affections were so fickle, what hope was there for building a better world based on love? Lenny advised me to take a cynical stance; he believed that after sex a woman should change into three men and a deck of cards.

Lenny and I slept in a converted toolshed that shared a flimsy wall with Feelgood's bedroom, so I soon came to know more than I needed to about Esther's relationship with him. Except when they whispered—and Feelgood rarely whispered—I could hear every word they said. They made love, fought, apologized, made love again, and fought some more. I lay awake as they argued, wondering what I would do if Feelgood actually hit Esther. Their voices rose and fell, punctuated by long pauses and soft cries, and their quarrels only sharpened my own agony, but I couldn't stop listening:

"I'm sorry, baby,"

"You don't look sorry."

"I'll make it up to you."

"How?"

"Like this."

"No, I don't want that."

"I've had a rough day, baby."

"Give me time."

"I ain't got that kinda time."

"What do you want from me?"

"More. I want it all."

"All you want to do is screw."

"You the one beggin' last night."

"You think I love the rough stuff best. If you loved me, you wouldn't treat me this way."

"What way? Like this?"

"Stop it now. I mean it."

"I want you now, bitch."

"Maybe I am a bitch for sleeping with you."

"Don't make me hurt you, girl."

"You already have, remember?"

"I was drunk, baby."

"You don't care how I feel."

"I'm crazy about you."

"You're just on edge, that's all."

"That bugs you, don't it?"

"No."

"Seem to."

They were both addicted to the high drama of it, and in truth, so was I. Sharing vicariously in their emotions was better than missing Jasmine and feeling sorry for myself. Suddenly Feelgood started to shout, "Get out! Get out!" and Esther ran sobbing to the porch. I went to comfort her.

"I don't know what to do," she sobbed. "He's got me so wound up I can't think straight. I never know what he's going to do next. He's angry all the time. Nothing I do seems to please him. I'm afraid he's going to hit me. When he's angry, he's scary."

"Why do you put up with it?"

"Because I love him."

"But he treats you rotten."

"He can be sweet too."

Esther spoke imploringly, in low, intimate tones, as if she expected me to verify her statements, but I crossed my arms and looked doubtful.

"I've seen him bawl his eyes out like a baby and dance for joy," she insisted. "He can be so frank, so tender, so uninhibited. He really wants me. I know that. He wants me so much it's frightening, and very exciting!"

Esther's face glowed in the moonlight. She looked radiant; tears only added to her beauty. I wasn't sure how to respond. Although she was praising Feelgood, the man who abused her, I wished she were talking about me.

"He hasn't been himself lately," Esther offered in explanation.

"I wouldn't be too sure," I said. "I think he's more himself than ever."

"What do *you* know? . . . I can be such a bitch."

"Do you believe that?"

"He's always getting mad at me. I can't do anything right."

"That's hard to believe."

"It's true. You should hear him."

"I have," I said, looking away into the night.

"God, are the walls that thin?"

"I'm afraid so. I can't help but hear. Why do you stay?"

"Part of me wants to go, but another part wants to be with him. He's not like that all the time. He can be very loving. Other times I feel like I could be anybody."

"Who's white."

I hadn't meant to be so blunt. Esther looked down, hurt.

"I suppose. But I don't think of it that way. I don't say, 'Hey, I'm sleeping with a Negro.' I say, 'I'm sleeping with Feelgood.' He's got me so confused I don't know if I'm coming or going. I find myself crying for no reason. Yesterday I slept away the whole afternoon."

"You can't go on like this," I argued. "Feelgood is a time bomb; he can really hurt you. . . . There must be something you can do to avoid it."

"I deserve it."

"You don't really believe that!" I cried, my voice rising.

"Today I do."

My heart went out to her, but I also felt a kind of envy for the way Feelgood could keep a woman as strong as Esther under his thumb.

7

The next time we headed for Amite County, Feelgood was at the wheel. He had taken the Edsel to Willie Dillon to see if that mechanical wizard could restore its youth. His "garage" consisted of a block and tackle rigged from a sturdy branch of a large oak in his front yard. He worked at night under a lightbulb that tapped directly into a convenient power line. How he could accomplish so much with so few tools was a mystery to me. When he was finished, that old Edsel ("Hear that freedom car a-rattlin'") had a lowered cylinder head, a dual carburetor, new valves, points, plugs, tires, and a tightened suspension that jarred hell out of passengers but kept the car from knocking off its muffler and oil pan on those rutted backcountry roads.

"If you gonna work the rural," Feelgood said, revving the engine with satisfaction, "you gotta have a fast car."

Esther, Lenny, and I were in the back, Leetonia was in the front with Feelgood. She had relatives in Amite County and said she could direct us to a Baptist church that was having a revival as well as two other churches that had recently been burned.

The Zion Hill Free Baptist Church had been torched the night before. Only the brick walls remained to pen in a pile of ashes and cinders. One of the deacons had rescued the cornerstone and was cleaning it off on a rough-hewn picnic bench.

"Better watch your step," the deacon said in a troubled voice. "They tryin' to get somethin' on y'all."

"Who?" Feelgood asked.

"The sheriff. He was pressin' us with all kinds a questions about the COFOs. He wanted to know if we was havin' any civil rights meetin's. We told him, 'No, we ain't.' He was tryin' real hard to get to us to say that when we turned y'all down, y'all threatened to burn us down. I told him I couldn't testify to what wasn't the truth."

"What'd he say?"

"He say, 'If this nigger won't testify, we gonna get one who will.' They sure do want to get you folks out of town."

Our next stop was the Rose Bower Missionary Baptist on the edge of Amite County, a church that had barely escaped the same fate as Zion Hill. I could still see traces of the evidence: a fuse that ran along the rubberized carpet runner to a large pile of powder near the pulpit. Fortunately, the fuse had fizzled out before it reached its destination, but the resultant flash fire had scorched the floor, charred the pews, and caused enough heat and smoke to kill all the wasps nesting in the ceiling. They lay in heaps as a grim suggestion of what might have happened had the church been fire-bombed during a service.

A shroud of doom hung over us as we left the church and headed deeper into the lonely roads of Amite County; soon we were lost and we stayed lost for a long time.

The problem was we were traveling blind. There were no street signs and no names on the mailboxes. It was hard to tell from the outside which unpainted shacks belonged to blacks and which to whites. Almost all were in a similar state of disrepair and decay. The same was true of country stores and cafes. Finally we saw a black woman out back of a small cafe called Slim's Grill. I volunteered to ask directions.

The second I was inside the screen door I realized my mistake.

"What chew want?" a woman behind a small counter asked in a scratchy voice.

Three men in CAT-visored caps and farm overalls turned to stare.

"I was looking for a church."

"Which one?"

"A Baptist church. They're having a revival."

"Well, *we* ain't havin' a revival."

"Say, what kinda church you lookin' for, boy?" one of the farmers asked. "Where you from?"

"Ohio," I said, instantly regretting my answer.

"You ain't one of them civil rights, is you?"

"No sir, I'm just passing through. I guess I'm in the wrong place."

"I reckon you is."

I stepped back into the sunlight and jumped in the car. One man watched us speed away. About a half-mile down the road we saw two black women sitting on a porch; we pulled in the dirt driveway. Feelgood, Leetonia, and I went up to talk to them.

"These white folks around here so mean," one woman confided, eyeing us with alarm. "They'll run us off this place if they see us talkin'. You just don't know."

They hadn't heard about the revival and refused to have anything to do with voter registration. We asked where the nearest black farmers lived. They pointed in the direction from which we had come. Just then a green pickup truck with a tall, two-way radio aerial screeched to a halt, blocking us in the drive.

A couple of bare-chested young guys with sandy crew cuts stood up in the back of the truck, grinning like crazy. One of the farmers I saw at Slim's Grill sat glumly in the front. A heavyset man in a Stetson hat got out of the driver's seat and walked toward us.

"What seems to be the trouble here?"

"No trouble," Feelgood said. "We was just talkin'."

"Nigger, don't you know enough not to speak unless you're spoken to? I was speakin' to my people here."

The two black women tried to smile, but they looked terror-stricken.

"Alma, have you let them talk you into that mess?"

"Nawsuh."

"You didn't invite these niggers and this white trash here?"

"Nawsuh. We don't want 'em."

"Don't we treat you real good? Aren't y'all happy?"

The two women said that they were happy.

"What do you have there?"

He took the clipboard out of my hand and scowled at the freedom registration forms. His face became flushed and his hands started to shake.

"Alma, did you sign one of these?"

"Nawsuh, we ain't sign nuthin'."

"See, they don't want what you're sellin'."

"It doesn't cost anything to sign," I said. "It's free."

"Cost some their lives. I ought to cram this filth down your throat till you choke. You are the lowest slime that breathes, do you know that?"

"That's news to me," Lenny said from the car window.

The man whirled around and shouted at Lenny, "Get out of there so I can smear your ass in the dirt."

"Maybe some other time," Lenny said, rolling up his window.

"If you knew who I was, you wouldn't think this was so funny."

Feelgood and Leetonia took advantage of the man's divided attention to get in the car. When he saw that I was still standing by the door, he ran around to the passenger's side.

"I ought to slap your brains out."

"Wait a minute," I protested, "can't we talk this over?"

He grabbed for my shirt, but I shoved him away and ducked into the front seat.

"Get out of that car you son of a bitch."

Suddenly he pulled back his fist and punched it into the window. The glass gave an inch and fractured into a spider web of a thousand slivers, but didn't shatter.

"Johnny, bring me my goddamn gun," he shouted.

"Holy shit!" I cried. "Here come the others."

"Stay cool," Feelgood commanded, "that's what I was waitin' for."

He slammed the car into reverse, stepped on the gas, and went barreling backward down the drive, veering off at the last second to miss the pickup and jump the ditch. He skidded to a stop, put it in gear, and we went fishtailing down the road, peeling rubber. I turned around and saw the man in the Stetson pushing cartridges into the side of his rifle.

"They're gonna kill us all!" Leetonia sobbed.

"They have to catch us first," Feelgood said.

The Edsel was doing nearly ninety on the paved road, which was straight, but hilly. As we cleared the next rise, we could see them coming, two hills back.

"We're shooting sparks out the back," Esther cried.

"The exhaust pipe hit the ditch," Feelgood explained as calmly as if he were giving a lecture on auto mechanics. Despite myself, I had to admire his cool.

"But it might fall off."

"It's *gonna* fall off."

"Then what?"

"We'll go faster."

Sure enough, the exhaust pipe did snap off and went scraping down the road behind us. The Edsel's motor roared and blew black smoke out the back, but we were indeed going faster. Feelgood pushed that old buggy to the limit. Trees and fields and shacks flashed past while my heart pounded at a wild rate.

"Damn, it's heatin' up. Don't lock up on me, baby! Keep pumpin'."

We could all feel the car begin to lurch and lose speed.

Leetonia started to moan.

The pickup truck was only one hill back and coming on strong. The young toughs hung over the sides and waved their shirts in the air. I kept my eyes glued on the farmer in the front seat, dreading to see that rifle poke out his window. The Edsel waned on the inclines now; they had no trouble catching up, ramming us once from behind, then swooping past and slowing down, daring us to try to get by. Our fair-haired friends shook fists and shouted obscenities, then they got a bright idea: they hefted a rotten watermelon, probably on hand for a spree of nigger-knocking, and lofted it in our direction. It split on the windshield, splattering pink flesh and blood down the hood.

"Fuck this," Feelgood said, swerving sharply down a side road. The pickup made a U-turn and followed in hot pursuit. We were kicking up such a cloud of dust, and the road was so rocky and bumpy, that they couldn't quite catch us. The Edsel was still missing a cylinder, but it had enough get-up-and-go for that dirt run.

"If we can make it to a main road," Feelgood said, "we just might be all right."

I looked ahead hopefully.

The road dead-ended in a field.

Feelgood jammed on the brakes, spun the car in a hairpin turn, and opted for a hard-charging route across the open field, aiming for the road we came in on. The pickup did the same, only at a tighter angle to cut us off. They were gaining and would have caught us if they hadn't hit an extra-deep furrow. Dust exploded in all directions and the pickup bounced into the air, slammed back to earth, and flipped over on its side, sending the two punks sailing headfirst into the mud.

By the time we reached the paved road, we still couldn't see them coming.

"What a relief!" I sighed.

"Someone's following us."

"This is no time to joke, Lenny."

"I'm serious."

We heard the shrill siren and saw the highway patrolman waving us over.

"Stay in the car," Feelgood warned.

As we waited for the officer, the pickup truck came slowly out of the dirt road, stopped to look our way, then headed in the other direction.

The cop ambled toward us like a lion on the scent of zebra. He was wearing mirror sunglasses. All I saw was my own face, shrunken and doubled, reflected back. I focused instead on the thin, hard line of his mouth.

"Whooah, what have we here! Girl, what are you doin' with your dress up?"

Leetonia's skirt was slightly above her knees. She tugged it down and put her face in her hands.

"Y'all been over in those woods? I bet you mixers know how to mix it up all kinds a ways."

"All we're doing," I said, "is helping people to vote."

"You're just askin' for trouble comin' in here."

"Did you see that pickup truck chasing us?"

"Nope—but if you want me to issue you a speeding ticket, tell me all about it."

"It's against federal law to harass voter registration workers."

"Boy, if you think J. Edgar Hoover gives a shit what happens to you, you got another think comin'. I'm the law here. Consider yourselves under arrest."

"What for?"

"We'll let the judge decide that."

We followed him to a little crossroads town: a few scattered houses and a mom-and-pop general store with metal cola signs for siding and a single gas pump out front. Pop, it seemed, was also the justice of the peace.

"Who you boys work for?" he asked.

"COFO."

"They work for CORE," he told Mom, who served as court stenographer.

"What you doin' out here?"

"Voter registration."

"You got that?" he asked Mom. "Voter restoration."

"If we are under arrest," Esther said, "we have a right to know what the charge is."

"What do you want to book them for?" Pop asked the patrolman.

"Willful trespass," he said. "A couple of nigger ladies down the road phoned in a complaint."

"How do you plead?"

"We were discussing voter registration with two women when a man in a Stetson hat came up and threatened us," I explained. "We were chased down the road by armed men in a pickup."

"Did you see any of that?" Pop asked the officer.

"Nope."

"Charge them with willful trespass," Pop told Mom, who filled out the form. "Bond is fifty dollars."

"Apiece? We don't have that much money."

"Well, how much do you have?"

We counted and came up with seventy-eight dollars.

"Bond is seventy-eight dollars."

"We're gonna need some gas to get home," Feelgood said, breaking the stony silence he had maintained since our arrest. I thought they would jump all over him for not saying, "Sir," but Pop and the patrolmen didn't seem to notice.

"Bond is seventy-three dollars. I'll fill you up at the pump out front."

8

After escaping from Amite County with our skins intact, we held a party. The exhilaration of the car chase had us all hopped up. To come down off that adrenaline high, we decided to get gloriously smashed and dance the night away. We had jars of homebrew locally known as "busthead," beer in quart bottles, and Marcus brought a small plastic bag of marijuana and proceeded to roll and pass around some fat joints. It was my first taste of the evil weed.

"Smoking reefer is basic," Lance said, passing his to me. "You can't groove to the music without it."

The smoke grated in my throat, but a pleasant, prickling sensation simmered across my scalp and sent warmth all the way down to my groin. I was in the mood to sink into the couch, beer in hand, as the waves of sound from the stereo washed over me. Maybe if I got sufficiently stoned I would forget about how lonely I was and how much I missed Jasmine.

Leetonia began dancing with abandon to the music. Her short skirt whipped around her butterscotch brown thighs and her light blouse clung to her breasts. All eyes focused on her, but it was understood that she was Lance's girl. They had been carrying on a courtship that consisted, as far as I could tell, of casual hand-holding and animated conversations.

"I'm watchin' you, girl," Lance said.

"I know you are." She flashed him a wide, inviting smile.

"I love the way you move, baby. Let's boogie."

Misty came in with Jason's arm wrapped possessively around her neck. Her face was flushed, yet every blonde curl was in place. She reminded me of one of those inflamable ice goddesses Hitchcock was so fond of: pure and cool on the outside, but a hint in the eyes and lips that someone had been whispering dirty secrets in her ear.

She watched Lance and Leetonia shake and shimmy with admiration.

"You've got to show me how to do that!" she said.

Misty was a snappy dancer who caught on quickly, but she was only a weak imitation of Leetonia. There was a lot of laughter and friendly banter about how if it wasn't for Chubby Checker, white girls never would have learned how to "shake that thing." Several of the local teenagers kept cutting in on each other to dance with Misty, while Jason stood aside and moped. During the slow numbers, they hung on to her so tight you couldn't see daylight from neck to knee. Marcus, Poe, and a McComb guy named Terry Reese, sitting beside me on the couch, couldn't resist making comments.

"That bitch is beggin' for a righteous poppin'," Poe said with a merciless leer.

"I'd sure like to make her moan and groan," Marcus said.

"I don't go for those pasty-faced broads," Terry said.

"Not me," Poe said. "That broad's ripe to give it up."

"That's Jason's chick, man," Terry drawled.

"Hey, Misty, c'mere," Poe called.

Misty walked over. She was wearing skintight cutoff blue jeans and a V-necked T-shirt. She blanched when she saw the way Poe was eyeing her and took a hesitant step backward.

"What is it?"

"Dance with me."

Misty glanced expectantly over at Jason.

"It's cool wit' you, ain't it, man?"

"I don't mind," Jason said, looking like he minded a great deal.

Poe pulled Misty to him and, pressing his thigh between hers, began dry-humping to the slow tune. I could see what was coming, but I knew that I'd probably only make the situation worse if I intervened.

"Stop it," Misty cried, pushing him away.

"Leave go mah girl!" Jason commanded.

Poe spun on him, glassy-eyed and grinning madly. "You play pussy with me, nigger, you're gonna get fucked."

"I'ma show you who you be messin' with," Jason warned.

"Let's get it on," Poe said in a raw strident voice. "Go for what you know."

"You go ahead," Jason challenged. "Hit me. See what happen."

"Y'all quit that now," Gayl said in a measured, deliberate voice. "I'm sick of all this fussing. Y'all are doing the same thing we're struggling against. This is a time of uniting, not fighting among ourselves."

"Keep yo fat butt outa this," Poe said.

"Don't you trifle with me," Gayl snapped, fuming with anger. "I'm tired of all you men talking black and sleeping white."

"What'sa matter," Poe muttered, "don't you want it all?"

"I think I know a nigger from Gimmie, Mississippi, when I see one."

"I wasn't born in this nasty-assed state," Poe said. "I'm from Baltimore."

"That's just one more thing wrong with you then," Gayl said. "Your mama should have taught you by peach switch not to be so greedy."

"Not me."

"Well I do believe you've got a few licks still coming to you," Gayl said with a sad shake of her head. "Now get on outa here and leave this white girl be."

Jason left with Misty, Esther and Feelgood were off somewhere by themselves, Lenny was passed out in the back room, and Gayl sat in a corner and scowled. I felt like I was in a land of strangers, a million miles from home.

9

"It is a privilege to be in a place so filled with the power of the Lord," I said, feeling instantly inspired by the congregation's responsiveness. It was the Monday evening before Freedom Day and everyone could feel the spirit moving in the hall. "Tomorrow you have an opportunity to do something for the books. You have a chance to leave a legacy of freedom for your children and their children's children. The Lord said that faith can move mountains, and we know that's true. But He also said that faith without works is dead. The way we show our faith is by putting it to the test. Tomorrow that test is down at the courthouse, inside the registrar's office, and it has twenty-one questions. Now I know a lot of you are afraid, and we're afraid, too, but that's where faith comes in. Do you really believe that the God who saved Daniel from the lion's den and Shadrach, Meshach, and Abednego from the fiery furnace isn't going to look out for you? The Bible says 'knock and it shall be opened.' Well, tomorrow we're going to go down to that courthouse and knock on that door and keep on knocking, and if we have faith and if we do our work, it *shall* be opened. Amen."

"The Lord moves in mysterious ways," Lenny whispered when I sat down.

"You gotta go with what you've got," I replied. I had to admit that there was something miraculous about the way the faith and love of these people could lift me out of the doldrums and give my life direction.

Esther came to the podium and with cool efficiency explained the logistics of getting people to and from the courthouses in Magnolia and Liberty, making it very clear that being on time was important: if everyone showed up together while the reporters and television cameras were watching, we would be much safer and we might make the national news. Then it was Feelgood's turn to speak.

"They's a lotta people in this town rockin' on porches sayin' 'Yassuh, Yassuh,' who if they went down tomorrow and told the man, 'Nawsuh, I ain't satisfied,' they would rock that old courthouse til its walls came a-tumblin' down. The potential power of our people is tremendous, and power is what this thing is all about. I hates to say it, but they be some in this room who won't be goin' down with us tomorrow. We need everybody, but we ain't gonna get everybody. Why's that? Because we not only got a problem with the man, we got a problem with the Toms. Thas right. We know damn well we got some Toms among us. There is the black Tom: now I ain't talkin' 'bout the color of his skin but of his evil heart. There is the gray Tom, you know the kind, they as gray and shifty as smoke and they drift away when you need them most. There is the yellow Tom. Now I ain't sayin' that they is chicken, but they sure do have some henhouse ways. There is the green Tom, green with envy. If you got anything he don't got, he want it, and if you take one step to get ahead, he'll stab you in the back. Last but far from least in they own eyes is the purple Tom. They think they royalty, that perfume's they natural aroma. I'm talkin' 'bout that better class of 'Knee-Grow' who think they's too good for that mess. All these Toms is Satan in his coat of many colors, and we must put them behind us."

Even though there were a few Uncle Toms of various shades in the audience—folks who said they were with us "one hundred percent" and then did nothing but undermine our efforts—I was afraid Feelgood might destroy the enthusiasm we were generating by dwelling on the subject and threatening to name names. I shouldn't have worried. Feelgood knew how to make an audience squirm and then how to make them sit up straight.

"The time has come to start makin' yo own decisions. Stop listenin' to the bosses and start payin' heed to yo own heart. But you say, 'The man's got me down! He's on my back! What can I do?' Well, I think you already know what to do. Stand up! Stand up and start walkin' toward dignity. You know if you turned back now, you couldn't sleep with yourself. And if you can't sleep with yourself, ain't nobody else gonna sleep with you neither. You have to keep on keepin' on. So we shall leave this house of worship and tomorrow we shall walk down the mean streets of Magnolia and Liberty until we reach the courthouse of injustice and there we shall *demand* the right to vote!"

We all began to sing "Everybody Wants Freedom," and Feelgood called on the area captains to have their people stand— "Beat one wants freedom!" "Beat two wants freedom!"—until we were all standing, clapping, shouting, and dancing in the aisles.

An old man asked to speak.

"I've lived in Amite County all my ninety-two years, and I never voted. You say I should. I say I'm ready."

"Are you ready to spend a night in jail?" Feelgood shouted.

The Freedom School students shouted "Yes!" and waved their toothbrushes in the air.

Then we sang "My Country 'Tis of Thee," a song I've never taken very seriously, but in that packed hall, soaked with sweat but soaring with spirit, it was strangely stirring and meaningful. We singers—black and white, rich and poor, male and female—were from different parts of the country and different backgrounds, but it was *our* country, and if our grief was collective, so was our joy. A few days before I had felt like an outcast of the universe, now I was sure I was at the heart of the beloved community.

10

"All these handkerchief heads, clappin' hands, an' singin' spirituals, what kinda scene is that?" Poe asked Feelgood as we gathered after the rally. "Why you doin' this shit, man?"

Feelgood looked uncomfortable. He was as brave as any SNCC guy in the state and had a knack for speaking to the people, but Poe knew that his heart really wasn't in the kind of civil rights work we were doing.

"I promised Bob I'd stick it out this summer," he said.

"Moses is a purist," Poe said. "An innocent. He thinks the 7th Cavalry is gonna come ridin' to the rescue. Hell, man, this ain't no 'Freedom House,' this is a foxhole; we in a war here, and the enemy is white."

"I don't want to go back on my word." I'd never seen Feelgood so defensive. "Moses made a deal with Kennedy that we'd work within the system."

"Kennedy's dead, and Moses is next. They set him up, man. They sent him down here to die."

"What do you mean by 'they'?" I asked, knowing full well what he meant.

"You, and all the rest of these honkies down here pretendin' to help us poor black folk," Poe said scornfully. "You're all part of the same scam."

"What're you talking about?" I was determined not to let Poe destroy our renewed sense of unity.

"All you honkies got that master's mentality. You think these black cats need watchin'. You think you know what's best for us—that's paternalism, Jack, plain and simple."

"We're down here putting our lives on the line," I said, "because that's the only way to show that integration can work."

"That's right," Esther concurred. "And there have been important changes. The civil rights bill . . ."

"Integration may be the *law* of the land," Feelgood said, "but it sure ain't the *reality* of the land."

"You said it, man." Poe smiled with approval. "Exactly so. The black masses can't relate to SNCC because it's actin' out a fantasy—this is a racist society and this black and white together boogie-joogie don't fool nobody. The time has come to unmask the cast of lyin' characters and tell the honkies to get out of the picture. This scene is ours, dig? From now on we will determine our own destiny."

"Who died and left you king?" I demanded. "What gives you the right to say what's best for black people? I know many who are happy we're here."

"Yeah, I know them too. They're all named 'Uncle Tom.'"

"So everybody who doesn't agree with you is an Uncle Tom?"

"Were you born here? Are you black?"

"Of course not."

"Then shut the fuck up."

"Wait a minute, I'm not finished."

"Yeah, you are."

"I haven't finished my argument." I was surprised by the threat in my voice.

"I don't give a shit for your argument. I know all about what you doin'. You got a guilty conscience, and you're down here tryin' to absolve the crimes of yo kind. You're the gentle face of genocide." Poe looked proud of himself for serving up that last phrase.

"I think I have the right to say something about mass murder," Esther cut in. "If you want to make comparisons, the Jewish people have suffered a great deal."

"You Jew?" Poe stared at Esther with his red underwater eyes. "You don't look Jew. Don't give me no jive about some old-timey holocaust. I'm talkin' about here. I don't see no Jews sufferin' in the U. S. of A."

"How can you talk like that?" Esther cried. "We are all human;

we all suffer. To say that one group has a monopoly on suffering is offensive."

"The more white folks I offend, the better," Poe said. "Ain't that right, Feelgood?"

"Right," Feelgood said. "Babies, it's not my ambition to be a credit to my race."

"You're history," Poe said. "The time has come to pick up the gun and begin the armed struggle. No more sit-ins. I'm ready for a shoot-out. We got to get us some crazy killin' spooks who'll set the 'Man' to shakin' in his shoes all night long. Free the black colony! No mercy for the class enemy! Bring this evil system to its knees! Tear the motherfucker down brick by brick and build it back from the bottom up. And we gonna treat the honky white man like the war criminal he is. He is a rabid racist dog and a blood-suckin' beast who deserves to have a stake in his heart and his head chopped off and sent back to England!"

"Do you want to lose?" I asked. "I'm just a foot soldier here, but I don't think the best strategy is to deliberately shoot off your toes. A race war would be a disaster."

"What about the convention challenge?" Esther asked. "Moses said he thought we had a chance to be seated."

"If you think I'm goin' to Atlantic City and beg, you're crazy. I'm goin' up to Newark where I know some hope-to-die brothers who is ready to be washed in the blood of the 'Man' or go down side by side tryin'."

"I'm tired of Yankees telling us what to do," a voice behind me asserted with such force it put a stop to our argument.

I turned around to face Gayl, with her usual expression of painful perplexity.

"You mean us whites?" I said.

"No. I mean northerners, period. Black *or* white. You, too, Monty. I'm sick of listening to you. We always think the Yankees got some fancy new idea that will save us, and so we start doing what they say and forget who we are. It's not just y'all. It predates the project. It goes way back and it gets very confusing. Take Bob

Moses, for instance. He isn't from the South but he acts like he was and we love him like one of our own. When he married that girl from Chicago, that hurt. We thought he was ours. We've got to learn to stick by our own and be strong, like we've always done, and not ask for outside help. I think you folks have probably done more good than harm down here, but the time has come for y'all to go home."

Maybe Gayl was right. Maybe sticking it out and fighting on would be stupidity rather than courage, stubbornness rather than loyalty to my principles. I was more than willing to let the local people take it from here if I thought that would be best for them. And if that was what they really wanted, then I could leave Mississippi without feeling guilty for abandoning the cause. If I could just get through Freedom Day alive, I would have done my bit for civil rights, and I could retire from the field with honor.

11

I had just fallen asleep when I was awakened by a BOOM! BOOM! BOOM! that could mean only one thing. Who? Where? Was anybody killed? The explosions came from three different directions: the first was close enough to rattle the windows, the second sounded like it was on the other side of Burgland, and the third was far away to the south, possibly in Baertown. We dressed in a rush and went running up Denwiddie Avenue toward where we thought the nearest bomb went off.

The target was a cement-block building in the heart of Burgland that housed a grocery store and, on the second floor, the Eureka Masonic Lodge, where Bob Moses started his voter registration work in 1961. Right across the street was the church where we held Freedom School classes. The blast had broken every window in the building and blown the double door in front off its hinges and into the store, smashing a produce counter. Wide cracks laced the interior walls. Fruits and vegetables were scattered all over the floor and flying debris had shredded a row of breads and cakes.

An angry crowd of about a hundred people began shouting at

the police, who seemed more interested in investigating the usually off-limits Masonic Lodge than in looking for genuine clues. But before a serious confrontation could develop, even worse news arrived: "They've bombed Mama Quin's house," someone shouted, "and killed her children."

Mama Quin was the Movement's pillar of strength in McComb. She fed us in the cafe she ran—South of the Border—just as she had looked after Bob Moses three years earlier, and she organized the black community in our support. Her daughter had participated in the McComb student walkout in 1961 and was a teacher in our Freedom School. The police had tried to shut her down by pressuring her white landlord and planting liquor on her premises. Mama Quin had stood up to their threats, but last week she had told her landlord she was ready to close. "Good," he replied, "now I can tell the chief of police and the sheriff and your place won't be bombed." What she hadn't told him was that as soon as she left South of the Border, she planned on opening her own cafe.

We all charged up the hill toward her house, straining to outrace the sirens headed in the same direction. From a block away you could see that something was terribly wrong. The roof had collapsed in front like a clam shell, crushing one half of the house.

"That's the kids' room," a woman screamed, pointing at the worst part of the wreck.

"They're okay," a man assured her. "I don't know how, but they got out."

Mrs. Quin's two youngest children and their baby-sitter had been asleep in the front bedroom when the bomb ripped through the house, bringing the ceiling down on top of them. Four-year-old Anthony had been pinned to his bed by fallen plaster until he was rescued by neighbors, and Jackie, aged nine, complained that her ears hurt, but they had survived the blast without serious injury. I thought back to the bombing of the Freedom House as I gazed at the wreckage, feeling a growing anger. When would this madness stop? The fury of the crowd was contagious: this bombing was not intended to frighten, but to kill.

When the police arrived, already wearing riot helmets and pointing their shotguns at the sky, the crowd was reluctant to let them through. Weren't they in cahoots with the Klan? Maybe one of them was the bomber! Wouldn't they intimidate the victims instead of investigate the crime? That certainly had been the pattern in the past. With a lot of shouting and shoving and an occasional shot fired in the air, the cops finally cleared the area around the house, leaving the crowd in an ugly mood. An FBI agent, stooping to inspect fragments of the bomb, had his flashlight knocked from his hand by a thrown brick. A few stones, aimed at the police, smacked against the side of the house, but mostly the people fumed in frustration and shouted out their rage. When the state highway patrol arrived on the scene, they immediately set up roadblocks and checkpoints to contain and harass the crowd.

The police made it obvious that they could not care less who threw the bombs; it was us they were after. The crowd was an inch away from going on a rampage.

The chief of police singled out Mama Quin, who had rushed home when she heard the explosion, for intense questioning.

"Tell these people to clear on out and go home," he ordered. "We don't want them here."

"Well I do," she replied. "They are my friends and I want them to stay. The ones who should go are all these police. Why aren't they lookin' for who did this?"

"If you tell your people to leave," he said, "I'll see what I can do."

"My friends are at home right where they are. They will stay here."

"You know we wouldn't be havin' all this trouble if there wasn't that mixin' goin' on over on Wall Street."

"I'm not concerned right now about the Freedom House. I'm concerned about my house and my children, who were almost killed tonight. If you would forget about 702 Wall Street and start thinking about 304 Summit Street, we'd all be better off."

"I'm not so sure those kids were in that house."

Mama Quin did her best to ignore his provocation.

"All I can say is that I ask God every night to protect them and He did."

If anything was obvious about the bombings and beatings, the cross and church burnings that had plagued McComb, it was that the Klan was behind it. Who else could synchronize three bombings in three parts of town? The only question was which Klan, or which klavern of which Klan, was behind it. Who picked the victims and gave the orders? The refusal of the police to confront the Klan indicated either total incompetence, blind racism, deliberate evasion, or direct implication. True to form, they capped their investigation by taking two of Mama Quin's children down to the station for interrogation.

Meanwhile, Esther, Lenny, and I hopped in a car heading to Baertown to check out the third bombing. We found what we most feared: Society Hill Baptist Church had been demolished by a powerful bomb that had brought the roof crashing in on the cellar. Only the rear wall and the steeple were left standing above the rubble. We gazed down into the pit of twisted wreckage, spying here a part of a pew, there a page from a hymnal or a shred of altar cloth. Piano wire spiraled up from the debris like exposed nerves.

Once again a large crowd was gathered and the police were pushing them back and cussing them as if they had no right to be angry. The sheriff stood off to the side grilling C. C. Bryant and the pastor, Reverend Taylor, as if they were to blame.

Even though the church had closed its doors to us and C. C. Bryant, and the NAACP had kept a disapproving distance from the Summer Project, they had hosted our rally earlier in the evening and many of their kids attended Freedom School, which meant that Society Hill was still the center of the Movement in Baertown. I only hoped that all the bombings wouldn't leave everyone too terrified to participate in Freedom Day.

"If you damn niggers would call my office instead of the FBI, Aaron Henry, or Washington, we would catch these bombers," the sheriff told Bryant.

"If we weren't insulted and suspected, maybe we would be more willing to cooperate with you," Bryant said.

"You damn well better cooperate with me," the sheriff snarled. "If you don't start cooperatin' with us, more than this is gonna happen to you."

"Sheriff, are you threatening us?"

"I'm just givin' you some advice. Looks like you niggers is bombin' each other to get the government to declare martial law here. You probably planted that bomb yourself."

"That's crazy talk," Bryant argued. "No Negro in Pike County can buy dynamite."

"Can't you see that only the Klan could be doing these things?" I shouted.

"I wouldn't know about that," the sheriff said, giving me a slow appraisal, "but if I was as trashy-lookin' as you are, I'd keep my mouth shut."

"Sheriff, it's been a long night. I haven't had much sleep."

"Looks to me like you're a little short of soap too."

"What does that have to do with anything?"

"Don't you see the connection? Your presence here is offensive to the civilized white community."

"Are you saying that these bombings happened because I don't use enough soap?"

"I'm sayin' I've had my eye on you for some time. You know we've got a new 'key' club here in Pike County, it's called the county farm. You don't need a key to get in, but you sure as hell are gonna need one to get out."

I left the sheriff and his cronies chuckling over his witticism. Because we usually saw only their ugly side, it took a conscientious effort to remember that except for the race issue, Mississippians were friendly people who went to church, loved their children, and worked at regular jobs. They drank beer, watched TV, and rooted for the home team; they worried about sore throats and runny noses and scratched where it itched; they loved to hunt and fish and swap stories. Had I come to Mississippi under different circumstances, they would have welcomed me warmly as one of their own. Had I stuck out my hand, they would have shaken it.

12

It was noon when our small caravan of cars pulled up in front of the Liberty Courthouse where the Amite County sheriff was waiting. He was so agitated his hands trembled.

"Now, we gonna do this my way or we ain't gonna do it at all," he said. "If you try to cross me, I promise you there's gonna be some slow walkin' and sad singin' tomorrow."

Apparently he had deputized every white man in town. They stood posted all around the lawn, baby-blue riot helmets gleaming in the sun, guns and blackjacks hanging from their wide leather belts, billy clubs at the ready. A gang of young toughs itching for a fight—T-shirts rolled up to bare their biceps, hair slicked back in Elvis pompadours—stood on the corner, waving a Confederate flag. One caught my eye, gave me an evil grin, and drew his finger across his throat. An NBC camera crew and several of the veteran civil rights reporters, smelling blood, had arrived early too. A gray-haired man who had done a story about the Freedom House told me that if anything photogenic (i.e., our heads versus their clubs) was going to take place, it had to happen before midafternoon to make the six o'clock news. That was an honor that I dreamed not of; all I wanted was to get out of Liberty alive.

The sheriff and his deputies were obviously under orders to be on their best behavior. When the toughs began slinging racial epithets at us, they were herded away. A car with shotguns poking out the windows, which came charging down main street in our direction, was diverted down a side street before the TV people even got their cameras turned around. That was the key—as long as the media stayed, we were safe. By means of several walkie-talkies, we could contact them as well as the people in line. Lenny kept up a running commentary on his, trying to make what was shaping up like a tedious day sound like the World Series: "Ladies and gentlemen, the line is moving! Mr. Knox is at the door. Yes, fans, he's going, going, gone—that's one more citizen inside the courthouse!"

Our chief antagonist that day was the fierce heat. While the cops enjoyed the shade of the trees on the courthouse lawn, we simmered and sweated on the baking sidewalk in front of the hardware store across the street. It was even rougher on the people waiting in line to register. I was in awe of their patience, dignity, and determination. They were admitted one at a time; it took some an hour to fill out the form; and if they left their place for any reason, they knew that the sheriff might not let them return. When Esther tried to bring them ham sandwiches and lemonade, she was stopped and turned back.

"Why don't you photograph that," I asked one of the cameramen, who had spent the day smoking cigarettes and drinking Cokes. "You see the petty cruelty?"

"Big deal," he said, looking bored. "You think 'Cop Denies Negroes Lemonade' is gonna get air time on Huntley-Brinkley?"

A middle-aged woman who saw what happened reprimanded the sheriff until he finally let Esther bring refreshments.

A man in a crumpled white suit with a perpetual smile on his face scrutinized us from a safe distance, first with binoculars then with the telescopic lens of his camera. I began to mimic everything he did. If he lifted the binoculars to his eyes, I made an imaginary junior-birdman pair with my hands and did the same. If he prepared to take a picture, I picked up my camera, jumped in front of whomever the man was focusing on, and took his picture back. Finally the man stashed his equipment in the trunk of his white Oldsmobile Supreme, parked in a no-parking zone near the courthouse, and walked over.

"I hate to inconvenience you," Lenny told him with mock seriousness, "but all photo opportunities must be arranged through our agent."

"Lemma ask you boys somethin'," he said, his wide smile still in place. "Did you ever know a white man who would keep a nigger from votin'?"

"Not personally," I said.

"Well, then why are you boys down here? Are you Americans?"

"Yes, sir."

"Man, I find that hard to believe."

"What do you think we are?"

"Traitors. You know it hurts when one of your own race betrays his country."

"What's so un-American about helping people vote?"

"Look at that old burr-head standin' out there, too dumb to come out of the sun. What business does he have votin'?"

"He has every right that you do."

"You think a damn no-account nigger is as good a man as me? They're different from us. Did you ever see a blue bird livin' with a red bird?"

"No," I said, "but I've seen a parrot repeat every stupid thing he ever heard."

"Do you boys know who I am? My name is Jackson Finch. Does that ring a bell? They say I'm the big nigger-hater 'round here, is that right?"

"We wouldn't know."

"These hot young bucks is the ones. They want to climb on our women. We taken the biblical position on that—God never intended it. You know that church that got burned down near here?"

"We sure do."

"Well, I give that preacher some money to build him another one. Say, what do you boys think of Mississippi hospitality? Y'all been treated good?"

"Some are treated better than others."

"Man, I wouldn't know about that. Could be they asked for it. We got a great country here and we don't want to lose it. We don't ever want to see the day when hook-nosed kikes and bonedumb niggers try to tell us what to do."

"What do the Jews have to do with it?" Esther asked.

"Why, they're behind the whole thing," he said expansively, welcoming the chance to enlighten us. "Roosevelt was a Jew; his real name was Rosenfelt. It all started with him. I thank God that I was born a white, Anglo-Saxon, Protestant man. Are you boys communists?"

"Are you in the Klan?"

"That's a secret."

"What's your office?" Lenny asked. "Inferior Lizard or Grand Klutz?"

The man kept smiling all the while he was talking, as if we were discussing the beauty of the flowers. Nothing we said in reply seemed to register.

"Hot as a bitch, ain't it?" he said, wiping his brow with a pink handkerchief and squinting at the sky. "But I do believe its gonna cloud up and crap pickaninnies any time now. If I was you, I'd leave on out of here before that happens."

He returned to his car, started the engine, but didn't go anywhere. He just sat inside, enjoying the air conditioner, still smiling.

A dark armada of thunderheads came sailing in shortly afterward. The sudden downpour sent everyone sprinting for the courthouse porch. The sheriff threw up his hands at the futility of trying to keep the packed crowd segregated. He finally ordered the auxiliary cops to line the halls and kept us outside on the steps, where we got soaked by gusts of windblown rain, which felt refreshing. Once the sun reappeared I would dry off in no time.

The courthouse wits overflowed with jokes about how we were overdue for a shower. One man was inspired to bring a box of soap from the cleaning closet and toss the bars at us from an open window. Lenny picked one up, took off his shirt, stepped out in the rain, and went right ahead and scrubbed off. This was considered hilarious. He even asked for shampoo, but when they produced ammonia instead, he graciously declined.

As soon as the storm hit, the media people left, but I still thought we were safe because of the restraint shown so far and the presence of several FBI agents. Conspicuous in their look-alike shirts, ties, and haircuts, they did nothing but observe and take notes. One agent came into the courthouse and asked the sheriff about the men in the hall. The sheriff said they were all level-headed family men helping out with crowd control. That seemed to satisfy the agents, who drove away shortly thereafter.

We were waiting for the last of our people to finish registering so we could leave too. Finally, the ninety-two-year-old man walked out, tickled to death that he had completed the form. He clasped his hands and bent his knees as if he wanted to jump up and down, but his feet never left the ground.

"How did it go?" I asked.

"I voted and voted and voted," he said. "I voted all I could."

At that moment several things happened simultaneously: a cream-colored ambulance pulled up beside the courthouse; the sheriff shouted into a megaphone, "This is an unlawful assembly"; and I heard the first "thonk" of wood against skull. The auxiliary cops poured out the front door, swinging their billy clubs at anyone they could reach. Screaming people clutched their heads and scattered in all directions. I spun on my heel and ran for my life.

I was almost across the lawn when one of the Elvis clones who had been heckling us earlier stepped from behind a tree and hit me in the face with a Coke bottle. My left eye blinded with blood. I reeled into the arms of his buddies, who manhandled me across the street and smashed me backward through the large display window of the hardware store.

I curled up in anticipation of further blows.

"Are you hurt?" a woman asked out of nowhere.

"Yes."

"Good!" she hissed. "You deserved it!"

I was sitting on the floor, attending, with Lenny's assistance, to lacerations on my arms, a blood clot on my eye, and a gash on my forehead, when a deputy came up and told me I was under arrest for breaking and entering.

"That's a crock and you know it," Lenny said.

"You keep your cocksuckin' mouth out of this, motherfucker."

Lenny picked up his walkie-talkie and reported my arrest and what the deputy just said.

"You're under arrest too."

"What for?"

"Cussin'."

Outside, Elvis and his buddies had vanished. Apparently throwing me through a plateglass window had satisfied their spirit of derring-do. A nurse with a concerned face bandaged my forehead, put a patch over my eye, and cleaned the cuts on my arms.

"Don't touch him," I heard a woman's voice screach. "Let him bleed."

"You ought to be ashamed of yourself," the nurse cried. "He's a human being!"

The deputies decided that nothing less than a hammerlock and a choke hold would suffice to escort Lenny and me back to the jail, which was adjacent to the courthouse. Two grinning men were dragging Feelgood feetfirst in the same direction. Esther was pleading with them to let him walk. The beatings had stopped. Cops milled around, smacking their billy clubs in their palms and looking smug. A few were herding all the Amite County people into a blue bus with bars on the windows. As far as I could tell, most of them were not injured. Leetonia was leading them in singing "We Shall Not Be Moved" while they waited their turn to get on board. When the bus pulled out, destination unknown, we heard them singing, *"We shall go to jail some day ay-ay-ay-ay."*

"Is this your camera?" one of the men not in uniform asked me.

"Yes, I dropped it. Thanks."

"Don't thank me."

The man put the camera on the courthouse steps and pulverized it with a nightstick.

"He doesn't like photography," I explained to no one in particular.

At the booking table, a cop with a broad, painful, keyboard smile ripped our SNCC "One Man—One Vote" pins off our T-shirts.

We were booked: breaking and entering and obscenity over the air waves, respectively. They confiscated all our clothes and issued us a pair of shorts, a roll of toilet paper, and the last threadbare strands of what had once been a towel.

Feelgood, still in his street clothes, was being interrogated in the next room.

"Watch out when they put you in the cell," Feelgood warned. "They'll bang the door open with your head and slam it on your fingers."

"You with the fuzzy lip, what's your name?"

"Raymond Fleetwood. What's yours?"

"Don't talk back to me. Half of the last nigger that did that was found in the Homochitto Swamp."

"What was his name?"

"God damn it, if I wanted you to know his name I would have told you. Do you want to die young?"

"No, sir."

"Don't you sir me, you sonofabitch. I've got a good notion to make you a pet of mine."

The man pushed Feelgood against the wall and frisked him. Then he pressed his nightstick against his throat and took him upstairs. Another guard directed Lenny and me down a hall and through an iron door. True to form, he tried to hit our heads on it, but we were too quick for him. What we couldn't avoid was a last swift kick in the ass as we were shoved into the same cell.

No one who has been in jail can ever forget that heart-stopping clang of metal on metal that lets you know you have just been swallowed alive.

"Welcome to the Bum Rap Hotel," I said.

Our cell was a dismal affair: a cold slimy concrete floor; four perforated metal bunks, one covered by an old urine-stained mattress leaking dark cruddy cotton from a rip in its side; a dripping sink that could not be turned on or off; a filthy seatless toilet that, with infinite patience, could be induced to flush; a blanket crumpled in the corner that smelled so foul we were afraid to touch it for fear we'd find something dead in it; and a rusty bucket with a tin dipper—our water supply for the indefinite future. Light came from a naked bulb in the hall and a small barred window up by the ceiling. Three of the walls were painted a bilious green, which mercifully was peeling back to the original cement block. Muralists had scratched to their heart's content sundry private parts and perverse boasts ("I fucked and sucked my thirteen-year-old niece. That was sure some fucking and sucking for a fifty-five-year-old man"). One had the touch of a poet:

> *By all forgot*
> *We rot and rot.*

Lenny and I stewed in our own sweat for several hours. The three other cells on our floor were empty. All I could hear was a shuffling of feet upstairs, where I dreaded to imagine what was happening to Feelgood, and the occasional barking of the police dogs in a kennel near our window. We didn't even know if they had arrested Esther or not. The Amite County people, I was told while being booked, had been taken to the penal farm in Pike County. That made me especially anxious to contact our lawyer, but the sheriff said he didn't want us using his phone. I figured that the others would tell where we were anyway, but when nobody came and nobody called, I started to get very tense and jumpy. Why were we being held incommunicado? Wasn't that what happened to Mickey, Andy, and Jim?

"What do we do now, Lenny?"

"Part of the time I'll sleep out," he said, testing my memory of Dr. Shaw's Shakespeare class, "the rest I'll whistle."

What he did instead was crouch in a corner and look very distressed. "I wish they'd just kill us and get it over with," he muttered.

"Hey, maybe we should sing something so that Feelgood and Esther, if she's here, will know where we are."

We had belted out a few stanzas of "We Shall Overcome" before a guard appeared at the end of the hallway.

"Sing all you want now, tonight it's gonna be our turn."

Lenny acted as if he were unfazed.

"What's for dinner?" he asked.

"Grits and chicken gravy."

"One of my all-time favorites."

After a while, the guard returned with two tin pans filled with a god-awful glob of congealed crud. Lenny extracted a morsel with his wooden spoon and took a tentative taste.

"Excellent! Just the way I like it: strained so that only the slightest hint of chicken remains and the grits chilled to obtain a lumpy texture. My compliments to the chef. Bon appétite!"

"As far as I'm concerned," the guard said, "you're not a white man, you're just a nigger and you're gonna stay a nigger."

"Damn! And here I thought you were my Fairy Godmother!"

The guard glowered at Lenny, then turned without speaking and walked out.

"Lenny, for Christ's sake, do you *want* to get us killed? You can't talk to these people that way."

"I know. I know! But when I see those bastards I get so wound up I can't help myself. If I didn't mouth off, I'd freak out."

Ten minutes later the guard returned with the cop who had harassed us earlier. He was carrying a thick leather strap that he slapped against his thigh for emphasis.

"What did you do to Feelgood?"

"I'll tell you this, he ain't feelin' so good right now."

"Where's Esther?"

"That was a shame, what happened to her. Nigger we put her with hadn't had a woman for a long time, but we didn't think he'd do *that* to her."

Neither of us believed him.

"We have a right to see a lawyer," I said.

"Boy, I ought to gouge your eyes out," he said as soon as he saw that I didn't evade his gaze. "You know what time it is?"

"Story time?" Lenny volunteered brightly.

"You like to play, don't you, smart boy? You think all this is a joke. Well, we got a little game which I believe will hold your attention."

"You've already got it." Lenny looked glum now.

"What's your favorite TV show? You like the *Beverly Hillbillies?* They're funny. We're gonna plug in a set in that room down there and turn up the volume real loud so you don't miss none of the punch lines."

"Don't do me any favors."

"Don't go, Lenny."

"Shut up, or you'll be next. He don't got no choice. He's goin' down that hall on his feet or his face one. What'll it be?"

They shoved Lenny down the hall. When the door opened, I saw our smiling friend, Jackson Finch, waiting for him. The door slammed, and through the crack at the bottom, I could see the shadows of moving feet. I heard the murmur of interrogation, the WHAM and WHACK of flesh on flesh, then they turned the TV up and the sounds of the beating were drowned out by hillbilly jokes and canned laughter:

"Cousin Ezra, you're right on time."

"Is Elly May ready?"

"Sho is! Been ready since she was twelve!"

(*Snicker, snicker*)

"Say, where's the john?"

"Down the hall, to the right."

"In the house!"

(*General hilarity*)

The door opened again to let in another cop, and I saw Lenny slumped in a chair with blood on his head. When they dragged him back ten minutes later, he was still bleeding and barely conscious.

"God damn you fuckers to hell," I shouted. "You had no right to do that."

"Shut your mouth or we'll do you the same way," the short cop said.

"Let him go," the other guard said. "He already got himself beat up once today."

I put Lenny on the mattress and used the towel and the bucket of water to wipe the blood from his face. He had a golf-ball-sized bruise popping out of his scalp, a cut and swollen upper lip, and both his front teeth were chipped. I asked him where else he hurt, but he could only groan. He took one of my hands in his and held on tightly.

An hour later our lawyer arrived. He was an elderly man with world-weary pouches under his eyes, but he was obviously shocked by our condition.

"What happened here?" he demanded of the guard.

"They was roughhousin' around in there. I think that red-headed boy slipped on the floor and hit his head on the bunk."

"What's your name?"

The guard didn't answer.

"You don't have a name?"

"I can be just as polite with you as you are with me."

"Don't talk to me about civility. Those boys were beaten without provocation. I have a court order for the immediate removal of my clients."

I could hardly believe the sense of release I felt as I helped Lenny down the hall to the sheriff's office. When they brought Feelgood in, he walked very slowly, bending to one side. The sheriff blandly told our lawyer he had cracked a rib while resisting arrest. Feelgood and Lenny were taken to the hospital in McComb. I was sent to the county farm.

13

In former days the Pike County Penal Farm had been in the hands of Jehu "First Bale" Brabham, who was notorious for the way he drove his mules and inmates to harvest the finest cotton in the fastest time. Shut down for fifteen years, the place had been renovated in the wake of Bob Moses's incursion into McComb in 1961. The rats, mice, flies, mosquitoes, and other assorted bugs who had claimed squatters's rights in the interim proved reluctant to vacate—to say nothing of the six-foot-long snakeskin I found in my cell.

Esther was there, safe and sound, along with the Amite County people and about thirty others arrested at the Magnolia Courthouse. They housed all of us, segregated by race and sex, in the large central building. Everyone had been prepared to go to jail for a night and be bailed out the next morning, but the variety of charges—from parading without a permit to conspiracy to overthrow the government—and the higher bail—averaging $500 per person—made that impossible. As a result, morale was low and some of the young men were in an ugly mood. I was depressed because I would probably miss the Democratic National Convention in Atlantic City. Mary Allen and E. W. Steptoe were especially anxious, because they had been chosen as MFDP delegates.

To lift everybody's spirit, we sang for hours that evening, making that old jailhouse rock, but in the morning, after a night of sleeping on cold concrete, our voices were shot and people spent the next two days speaking in a hoarse whisper. The nurse from Amite County came out to take off my bandages and inspect my eye. The blood clot had dissolved, but there was still some blurring on my left side, which she said would go away in time.

"I want you to know," she said, "that even though I don't agree with everything you believe in, what happened to you in Liberty was unforgiveable. I know those people; they are good people, but when it comes to this issue they can't be reasonable."

"I've noticed, but thanks."

Lenny arrived after a long morning at the dentist with temporary caps on his teeth. The first time I asked, he refused to speak about his beating. That was strange; Lenny was always articulate. *What could they have done to him that he didn't want to discuss?* Feelgood was brought in the next afternoon with a bandaged nose and a military posture necessitated by the wrap on his cracked ribs.

"I've had it worse," he remarked offhandedly, but his nonchalance was belied by the murderous look in his eye.

"What about you?" he asked Lenny.

"I made that mother catch his breath."

That was the Lenny I had been waiting to hear from.

"Too much, man," Feelgood chuckled, then grimaced from the pain in his side.

Later I asked Lenny how he had felt.

"Only my laundress and I will ever know how frightened I was," he said.

It was a good line, but I didn't laugh. I don't think he ever wanted to talk about it again. He was deep in a funk he couldn't shake off, and I felt myself slipping into the same despair.

The county farm was a drag. The sun beat down and the humidity didn't let up even at night. The flies swarmed around my head and the mosquitoes sucked my blood. There was no escape from the stench of stopped-up toilets and sweaty bodies.

The women made the best of things. Some of the girls spent hours playing improvised clapping and card games through the bars. Esther woke up one morning being serenaded with "Happy Birthday" and pelted with paper flowers made out of toilet paper. They organized chores and kept their cells clean, although one day a woman had hysterics over all the roaches and refused to touch a broom.

The men didn't know what to do with themselves; they stood around in glum clumps, usually not even talking, waiting for the next lousy meal. The day they varied the routine and brought in hamburgers and hot dogs from a restaurant in Magnolia I thought I was in heaven. One afternoon they loaded about ten of us in a truck and set us to digging a drainage ditch. In the early evening I sometimes played volleyball with a rope and a rolled sock, but mostly I just sat, doing my own time.

Lenny and I talked a lot about the situation in McComb and whether we wanted to stay with the project or quit at the end of the summer. On the one hand, the black community welcomed what we were doing and didn't want us to leave; on the other hand, the tensions with the SNCC veterans were getting worse. They were tired and we were tired and the stress of living in constant fear and not seeing enough progress had stretched everyone to the breaking point. Basically, my feeling was, *I've had it, let the local people carry on, because I don't think I can take it any more. If I stay, I'll either go crazy or burn out.* Besides, some of Poe's arguments made sense: as long as white people were around, SNCC wouldn't get full credit for what it was doing and the black community wouldn't learn to rely on its own leadership.

When our lawyer finally arrived, the decision to go or stay was taken out of our hands: he said that Liberty intended to press charges against us. They had FCC regulations to throw at Lenny, and the owner of the hardware store was willing to testify that I maliciously lured some innocent bystanders with wavy hair to toss me backward through his display window for the nefarious purpose of shattering glass and stealing tools.

"If we can get the case removed to federal court," the lawyer explained, "none of this will stand up. But in the meantime, they can make things pretty rough on you. Now I'm working on a plea bargain that will get everybody out at once. Will you go along with that?"

The worried look in his eye told me there was a catch.

"What do we have to do?" I asked.

"You have to leave the state. They agree to let you go, but if you come back, they will press charges."

"What if we don't agree?"

"They'll not only keep you here as long as they can, but the rest of the people too."

That left us no choice. The brave black people of Pike and Amite County, who just wanted to be first-class citizens, did not deserve to spend another minute in jail.

"Has Esther agreed?" I asked.

"She's not involved."

"What about Feelgood?"

"Same thing. The resisting arrest bit won't wash, but they think they have you two in a corner."

"Why go to all that trouble?" I questioned. "We're not crucial to the Movement."

"As far as they're concerned, the more COFOs they can get rid of the better."

"Do we have to sign something?" I asked.

"This deal won't be on paper."

An hour later, when Feelgood announced that everybody was getting out, a great shout went up and hoarse voices rose once more in song: "Woke Up This Morning with My Mind Stayed on Freedom."

A police cruiser drove Lenny and me to the Freedom House to pick up our things. The Edsel was still parked out front. In my absence, someone had torched it and slashed the tires. I inspected the charred chassis, trying to decide if the ovoid grill looked more like a horse collar or a toilet seat. One of the lasting effects of Freedom Summer for me was going to be higher car insurance premiums. After we packed our bags, we were promptly escorted to the bus station.

"Can we get to Atlantic City from here?" I asked.

"If I had my way, I'd send you both to Siberia, Alaska," the man at the ticket window snarled, serving up our last taste of southern hospitality.

"When is the next bus?"

He knew exactly when the next bus was leaving town.

Bob Moses

Greenwood and Liberty, Mississippi

July 1963–May 1964

1

For the past two years I had been seeking a tactic that would force the government's hand. If we kept demonstrating, everybody would be arrested, and the local people weren't willing to spend months in a cell. If the SNCC staff by itself continued to take risks, some of us would surely be killed; that was too high a price to pay, especially if our deaths didn't change anything. We needed to cultivate local leadership, that was clear, but some new factor in the equation was needed. We couldn't survive the stress and strain of the struggle for much longer if all we had to show for it was our own personal growth.

One sweltering day in July a group of us were sitting around in Greenwood discussing strategy when a preoccupied-looking guy came in, carrying a battered briefcase with papers jutting out the seams. His suit looked slept in; he wore white sweat socks and saddle oxfords. He pulled up a chair, poked up his thick glasses, passed a hand through his thinning, rust-colored hair, and said, "Go on with what you were saying."

We shrugged at each other and kept talking. *New York Jew,* I thought. *He won't keep quiet long.* I had the feeling I had seen him before.

"My name is Allard Lowenstein," he said after a few minutes. "Ed King sent me."

Ed King, the chaplain at Tougaloo, was one of the few white men in Mississippi we trusted. A couple of months before a car chase in Jackson had forced him into a collision; he survived, but one side of his face was left permanently disfigured. We looked at this stranger with new interest. He proceeded immodestly to make it known that Frank Graham, Norman Thomas, and Eleanor Roosevelt were friends of his; that he had organized sit-ins in North Carolina and worked against Franco in Spain and apartheid in South Africa.

"Have you read my book, *Brutal Mandate?*" he asked. "Marlon Brando's going to star in the movie version." He retrieved a copy from his briefcase as proof and told us how he had smuggled a "Cape colored freedom-fighter" out of Johannesburg to testify at the United Nations. While he spoke, I had the eerie feeling that there was a ticker tape in his head converting it all into headlines:

LOWENSTEIN ARRIVES IN NICK OF TIME
MISSISSIPPI: NO GAINS WITHOUT PAINS

Allard was pushy, but he wasn't all bluff; he really did have political contacts in important places. He was also a shrewd observer who quickly sized up the situation: SNCC was physically exhausted, spiritually flat, and literally bankrupt. Nothing we tried—picketing, marching, protesting—was working.

"This is intolerable," Al said, echoing my sentiments. "Something must be done."

I told him that a SNCC law student had discovered an obscure Mississippi statute dating from Reconstruction that permitted anyone unfairly denied the vote to cast a ballot "under protest" and that we wanted to test its validity in the upcoming gubernatorial election by running our own slate of candidates and by holding a "Freedom Vote," parallel to the official one, for all the disenfranchised blacks of Mississippi.

"That's good," Al said, vigorously nodding his approval. "In

South Africa, blacks held a 'Day of Mourning' to protest their exclusion from politics; a 'Day of Voting' is better."

"The problem is we need a big turnout," I said. "Otherwise the point that black people would vote if they had a chance will be lost. But how are thirty-five SNCC field-workers going to canvass the entire state?"

"I can get you as much help as you want." Al spoke with supreme confidence, his arms folded like a smug Buddha. He had a way of flexing his biceps and blinking his weak eyes that simultaneously called attention to his wrestler's body and his bookworm's face.

"Whites?" I wondered how large a following such a man could command.

"Of course. Look, I've been a dean at Stanford and I've taught at Yale; I'm a former president of the National Student Association. If you give me the go-ahead, I can deliver some exceptional young men, future leaders."

Al's eyes glowed with the prospect of America's best and brightest coming to the rescue of SNCC's beleaguered garrison.

"We've had a policy that Mississippi is too dangerous for whites," I said. "If you'd seen how Bob Zellner got beaten to a pulp in McComb, you'd know why."

"These will be the sons of America's elite," Al replied. "If anything should happen to one of them, the *New York Times* will cover it."

He seemed to assume that once a problem was reported in the *Times* a satisfactory democratic solution was at hand.

"Actually, we already have a few whites working in our Jackson office," I admitted. "Maybe the time has come to test them in the field."

Al was a take-charge kind of person who believed in executive orders and flowcharts; he became increasingly frustrated while SNCC devoted lengthy sessions to discussing the issue of whites in the Movement until we arrived at a consensus. He could hardly believe it when the day finally came that I pulled out a cheap tablet of multicolored paper and jotted a letter authorizing him to begin recruiting.

The Freedom Vote was launched with Aaron Henry—the outspoken NAACP leader from Clarksdale whose home and pharmacy had been frequently attacked—running for governor and Ed King for lieutenant governor. The campaign provided us with a program we could grow with and organize around. Even though it was only a mock election, it gave people an opportunity to vote for the things they believed in. The "official" Mississippi election was filled with mudslinging. The Democrat and Republican candidates called each other the lowest and most loathsome names they could think of: Rubel Phillips denounced Paul Johnson as an "integrationist" only to be accused, in turn, of being a "moderate"!

Our polling places were in the black community where people felt secure. We set up ballot boxes in churches, general stores, barber shops, pool halls, and funeral homes; we even had a "Votemobile" that traveled to remote rural areas. No matter how few votes they gathered, the SNCC workers went around telling the people a whisper of freedom was in the air and that we would never let another election pass without being heard.

In late October, about two weeks before the election, preppy types from both coasts, looking a little lost without their surfboards and sports cars, began to show up in Jackson. I briefed them on what was ahead and sent them out to various towns to help bring in the vote. Apparently some of them were under the impression that the Freedom Vote was an Allard Lowenstein production, with SNCC supplying the supporting cast. One volunteer said as much to Jim Forman.

"If Lowenstein tells you to go to heaven and Moses tells you to go to hell," Forman growled, "you'd better start packing your summer clothes."

"There's something fishy about Lowenstein," Forman told me. "I don't trust him."

"He's got connections," I said. "We need the support of people who know people."

"He's got too many, if you ask me," Forman replied. "I think his powerful friends sent him down here to check up on us, maybe even subvert us."

"We'll see," I said. "At least he's brought in the students."

There was no mistaking the upper-crust collegians as they walked the dusty roads passing out flyers and urging people to cast their ballot. Mississippi whites were upset by the "outside agitators," and the police cracked down. Six Yalies were arrested the second day they were in the state. Most received blunt lessons on the Southern Way of Life.

"It's okay to buy a Coke in a nigger cafe but not to sit in one," a Jackson cop told a Stanford student. "If you want to live with niggers, do it outside Mississippi."

"Either you stay in the white section or get out," the Clarksdale police chief told another volunteer. "If you live with the niggers, you're gonna get stabbed in the back."

The most serious incident involved George Greene, a SNCC worker in Natchez, and Bruce Payne, a student from Yale. They were in a harrowing ninety-mile-an-hour chase between Port Gibson and Fayette that included gunfire; shots were fired at others as well; a few were beaten; many blacks were threatened with reprisals if they voted; yet all in all the degree of intimidation during the Freedom Vote was less than I anticipated.

"This is worse than South Africa," Al said to me at the height of the trouble. "There the aroused conscience of the world spoke out, but here, nobody cares."

The first time Al saw pickup trucks with shotgun racks circling the SNCC office in Jackson, he dropped to the floor and announced we were in a state of siege. It *was* a tense night; we'd held a big rally in the black community and the Klan was on the prowl.

Al got on the WATS line and called the attorney general.

"Bobby, this is Al, down here in the SNCC office in Jackson. We're barricaded behind some overturned desks and chairs. The Klan has the place surrounded. You've got to do something. This is an absolute nightmare! A reign of terror! Unless you take immediate action, our chances of surviving the night are less than fifty-fifty."

Then he phoned Yale and ordered in reinforcements!

As it turned out, Lowenstein's "Last Stand" that night was a nonevent; the Klan eventually drove off and we went back to work.

It wasn't that Al lacked courage—I had seen him confront the police with cool diffidence on several occasions; he simply liked to see himself as a protagonist at the epicenter of the action. The students he brought in certainly did add drama and draw national attention—the press trailed after them like caddies on a golf course. The problem was, the media thought **WHITE STUDENTS IN MISSISSIPPI** was the whole story. In Jackson, when Aaron Henry spoke, the TV cameras zoomed in on the students in the audience and ignored the speech. In Yazoo City, the NBC crew stayed with the white students canvassing, even though blacks were being beaten a few blocks away. It seemed that violence in the South wasn't newsworthy unless the blood being shed was blue.

More than eighty thousand voters cast ballots in the Freedom Vote; with a larger staff, that figure might have been doubled. For the first time since Reconstruction, Mississippi Negroes were participating in politics in significant numbers. And SNCC was moving beyond isolated black communities, working in all five congressional districts and using the vote to organize on a statewide basis.

Al was elated by the success of the campaign.

"Stanford and Yale saved the day," he told me.

"Eighty thousand black people had something to do with it."

"Sure, I know," he replied, "but it's the force of idealists from outside that can change things and end the intimidation."

"So what do we do now? We've lost our voter registration funding because of our direct involvement in the Henry campaign. Without money, we can't operate."

"Start planning for next summer," Al insisted. "I can bring in thousands of students if you give me the go-ahead. We can force a showdown with the Dixiecrats at the Democratic convention in Atlantic City next August."

"That's a big change," I said. "I don't know if SNCC will go for it."

"They will if you make them," Al said.

"Nobody in SNCC makes anybody do anything," I replied, repressing my irritation. "We'll talk it over."

2

Every positive advance in 1963 had triggered a violent response. Kennedy's civil rights speech brought the murder of Medgar Evers; the March on Washington was followed by the four girls killed in the Birmingham church bombing; a few weeks after the Freedom Vote came the assassination of Kennedy himself. It was a grim SNCC staff that assembled in Greenville to discuss our next step. The situation in Mississippi was desperate; if we didn't come up with a new strategy, we faced the bitter prospect of defeat.

A heated debate broke out over whether or not we should bring large numbers of white volunteers to Mississippi the next summer to precipitate a major confrontation.

"If they wants to come, I say let 'em come," Fannie Lou Hamer said. "We needs all the help we can get."

"I don't want their help," Hollis Watkins protested. "Y'all saw what happened when Al and his 'all-American boys' dropped in for a few days, grabbed the headlines, and left, taking credit for a victory we won with our own sweat and blood."

"That's right," Willie Peacock added. "These hotshot Ivy League dudes simply *assume* they're in charge. They'll undermine the local leaders we've worked so hard to establish and try to steal SNCC away from us."

"No pampered, know-it-all kid is gonna tell *me* what to do," Fannie Lou replied. "I say the time has come to try something new."

"White students are more trouble than they're worth," Hollis argued. "If they move into the community, the police are gonna come down extra hard on anyone who helps them. That'll just scare people off."

"It didn't always work that way during the Freedom Vote," Larry Guyot pointed out. "A lot of people responded positively to the students."

"Yeah, I know," Hollis admitted, "but that was sick. People smiled and filled out ballots because the person telling them to was *white*, not because it was the right thing to do."

"You saw the way reporters followed the white students during the Freedom Vote," Jim Forman said. "Imagine the coverage we'd get when those students get beaten up."

"That's a sorry state of affairs," Charles Cobb replied with disgust, "if that's what it takes before anybody pays any attention."

"This is a racist society," Jim Forman responded. "That's the way it operates. We have to use the oppressor's weapons. The problem, as I see it, is one of discipline. Will all these students follow orders? Who will give those orders? If we are going ahead with this, we'll need to select and train about twenty subsection leaders first, and then conduct an orientation for everybody else. Otherwise there will be no unity."

"It's too big an undertaking on too short notice," Bob Zellner stated. "What we'll have is undisciplined and untrained students wandering around the state creating chaos and confusion. We can't organize or administer that many volunteers. What will they do? Who pays their bail? Who notifies their parents if they get killed?"

"We would have to be up-front with them about that," I said, breaking the long silence that had followed Zellner's last remark. "Anybody who comes to Mississippi would have to face the fact that they might get killed."

"There's no 'might' about it," Guyot asserted. "If we bring all those students in here, hell, we *know* somebody is going to die."

"We also know that *now* is the time," Marion Barry added. "Next year LBJ is up for election; we have to put him to the test."

"I don't like it," Willie warned. "SNCC is a *black* organization fighting for the rights of *black* people. To destroy the myth of white supremacy, we have to keep it that way."

"If we're trying to break down this barrier of segregation," Fannie Lou replied in an anguished voice, "we can't segregate ourselves."

"SNCC is ours," Hollis said. "It's the only thing in this damn country that *is* ours. Let them work with their own people."

"I'm for that," Ivanhoe Donaldson agreed. "How come whites can work in the black community, but blacks can't work in the white community? It's a one-way street. What I dig about SNCC is blacks doing their own thing."

The debate surged back and forth over a series of meetings. To concede that we needed whites was humiliating; it was like admitting that all our sacrifices had been in vain. I withheld my own opinion, feeling that those staff people who carried the burden on their shoulders of implementing the project should make the decision. But finally I was called upon to summarize the discussion and state my position.

"We need a breakthrough," I said. "We can't keep beating our heads against a stone wall. Bringing in the students could focus all the emotions that have been building here in Mississippi. The students will be a spotlight: they carry the rest of the country with them; they have important connections; what happens to them will be seen all across the nation; and the more America sees of Mississippi, the less they will like. The students have the means and desire to come; their presence will inevitably bring about a confrontation. That might force federal intervention or at least allow us some room to negotiate. On the other hand, the federal government appears to be either unwilling or unprepared to act. This may not be the time or place for a showdown. SNCC could lose its identity and autonomy; we could have a bloodbath on our hands with consequences out of our control.

"I have considered these pros and cons, and I support the Summer Project for the following reasons: I cannot be a part of a racist organization. To reject whites and select people solely on the basis of color, rather than their personal qualities, is exactly what we are fighting against. If you want to run that kind of organization, then count me out. Mississippi is *America's* problem. We need to show by our example that black and white can work together, so that the nation will see that this is not a case of black against white, but of rational people against irrational people. Only in that way can we rise above race, catch the conscience of the country and draw the full power and authority of the federal government unequivocally to our side."

"Bob is right," Julian Bond added. "I think the presence in Mississippi of one thousand whites will cause a lot of *good* trouble. We need to teach this fat, rich, powerful country what it's like to be poor, powerless, and hungry. The best way to do that is to bring their kids down here and rub their noses in the nitty-gritty."

Although major misgivings remained, SNCC agreed to proceed with the Summer Project. We were going to give integration one more chance. After we had finally reached consensus, all the staff joined hands to sing "We Shall Overcome," raising our voices sharply at the verse *"black and white together."*

Even after the project was approved, debate continued on how to implement it. Al was very involved at this stage, urging the National Council of Churches to fund us and insisting that the Democratic convention in Atlantic City should be our ultimate target. Our plan was to try to participate in the precinct meetings and the state convention of the regular Democratic Party. If permitted to attend, we would introduce a resolution pledging loyalty to the national party; if turned away, we would document our rejection. Anticipating our exclusion, we would simultaneously form a parallel political organization, the Mississippi Freedom Democratic Party, which would present itself in Atlantic City as loyal to the national party, representative of a substantial black electorate, and morally more deserving than the Mississippi regulars of being seated at the convention. An executive committee, headed by Ella Baker, was chosen to coordinate the challenge. The white volunteers would spend their summer both registering blacks at the courthouse and recruiting them for the MFDP. They would also teach Freedom Schools, establish community centers, and generally act out the proposition that the condition of Mississippi's blacks ought to be everybody's concern.

When it came down to specifics, Al got cold feet. He thought that once black people were allowed to vote, Mississippi's problems would be solved. But Al feared that we were moving in dangerously radical directions, and he wanted to sound an alarm. I tried to convince him to stay with us; I valued his talents as a recruiter of students, a bridge to the liberals, and a savvy political strategist.

"I know that you and Jim don't get along," I told him, "but you know it takes public tensions to bring about political change—it only stands to reason that there will be private tensions as well. Don't drop out; we need your voice in the dialogue."

"Letting the Lawyer's Guild represent you is unacceptable," Al asserted, jabbing anxiously at his glasses. "They have notorious fellow-traveling ties."

"You know our position," I replied. "Whoever wants to help is welcome."

"In that case, why did you drag your feet about bringing in the students?"

"SNCC believes in decentralized decision making," I said. "It took us a long time to thrash out our differences."

"The staff shouldn't make those decisions," Al grumbled. "That's your job."

"I'm just a field secretary like everybody else. You've got to understand that my leadership in SNCC must be low-key or this project will never come off."

Al still wasn't satisfied.

"I also have a problem, Bob, with what materials will be taught in the Freedom Schools. It makes a big difference whether they read Karl Marx or Thomas Jefferson."

"You're in no position, Al, to tell us what Mississippi Negroes need to know," I said without even trying to hide my anger.

"Maybe not, but I do know something about political organization.

SNCC needs structure. You can't ad-lib an operation this big. You should have an advisory board made up of the best people in the country. . . . If only Eleanor Roosevelt were still alive!"

Al's eyes always lit up when he mentioned her name.

"That is not what SNCC is all about," I explained again, feeling increasingly frustrated. "We believe in participatory democracy, in letting the people decide."

"You listen to the people only when they agree with you," Al retorted. "That's dictatorship in disguise. A leader should frankly admit that he's a leader—and lead."

"It's not my leadership that's at stake. The point is you don't trust us; you think we have a hidden agenda to radicalize blacks and overthrow the country. To prevent that, you're trying to find a devious way to take control of SNCC away from us. We won't permit that. Nor will we let you use SNCC and the MFDP to 'deliver' support to Hubert Humphrey and your liberal friends. Either you work *with* us or you leave."

Al left.

In truth, we did see ourselves as revolutionaries. There was nothing moderate about Mississippi; only a radical solution made sense. But revolution means different things to different people, and I, for one, knew that eventually we would have to work out some kind of understanding with the type of liberals Al represented. Although some of the staff may have fantasized about Mau Mau bands in combat camouflage establishing guerrilla bases in the Mississippi swamps, the rest of us were more pragmatic, believing that the power of the vote and community organization would improve things over time.

Clearly, the political system in Mississippi had to go, but what should replace it?

There was a simple truth in what Mississippi Negroes said about their own lives that no existing system of government was prepared to listen to. Those people didn't need anyone from the top telling them what to do; they just needed the confidence to stand up for what was pure and poetic in themselves. None of us could comprehend the meaning of the revolution we were making. None of us had the answers to the technological changes sweeping over our lives and restructuring society. The key was to move beyond outdated alternatives. It wasn't enough to put our bodies on the line; we needed to use our minds and imaginations. Our job was to confront present evils and initiate the annealing process.

"Only when metal has been brought to white heat," I told the SNCC staff in December, "can it be shaped and molded. This is what we intend to do in the South and the country—bring them to white heat and then remold them."

3

In the spring, SNCC proceeded to recruit northern students. We planned to build on the idealism demonstrated by the March on Washington to show that northern whites and southern blacks could work together to ensure that all Americans, in the presidential election year of 1964, were entitled to vote.

We consciously faced the grim reality that someone might be killed. At orientation we would tell the volunteers that their lives were in jeopardy and teach them how to protect themselves. We realized that we were in a war, and we wanted to be sure that everyone was prepared for whatever dangers lurked ahead.

The cold-blooded killing of Louis Allen on January 31 made it clear that blacks in Mississippi could still be murdered with impunity because they lacked connection to the larger society and protection from local racists. After he witnessed the murder of Herbert Lee in Liberty, Allen felt guilty about lying to support Hurst's claim of self-defense.

"I don't want to tell no story about the dead," he told his wife, "'cause I can't ask them for forgiveness."

Allen grew up in Amite County. He was a logger and a responsible family man. He bought a small home and some land. When that was paid off, he borrowed money to purchase a chain saw and a pickup truck and logged for himself. He was never in trouble with the law, but when word leaked out that he was having second thoughts about his testimony before the grand jury, he found his life in danger. One of Allen's uncles drove out the Gloster road to his home, a weather-board and tar-papered cabin, and told Allen's daughter that a friend of his heard that some men, including the sheriff, were out to get him. The girl ran into the woods to where Louis was logging and warned him. After that, Allen stayed back in the forest as much as he could and rarely went to town.

Allen had always sold his logs to the Sam Mabry Lumber Company. One day they told him that they could take only two of his truckloads a week; then it was one a week; then they wouldn't finance him to buy a strip of timber to work. The two gas stations in town cut off his credit. The squeeze was on.

One day Allen stopped in Liberty for supplies. As he was passing the jail, someone called out to him from a cell window. He went over and a woman who had been caught shoplifting gave him a piece of paper with a phone number on it and asked him to call a friend of hers in Jackson to tell him where she was. He took the card and made the call.

That night, as Allen and his wife were watching *The Untouchables*, they heard a car honking in the driveway.

"Don't go, Louis," his wife said.

"I better see to it."

Deputy Sheriff Daniel Jones and Layten Bates were standing in the yard.

"What do you want?" Louis asked.

"You're under arrest."

"What for?"

"Interfering with the law."

"For *what?*"

"You heard me."

"You takin' me to jail?"

"That's right."

"Can I get my hat?"

"No."

Allen turned to his son.

"Go fetch my hat, Henry."

At that moment Jones struck Allen across the side of his jaw with a five-battery flashlight the length of a nightstick. Allen staggered around to confront his attacker.

"Don't you touch that white man, nigger," Bates warned, drawing his gun and pointing it at Allen's chest, "or I'll drop you right here in this yard."

"I think you busted somethin'," Allen moaned. His lip was bleeding and his jaw had already begun to swell.

They took him to the Liberty Jail and wouldn't call a doctor. The next day his wife and son went into town to see how he was.

"Is Louis in jail?" she asked Jones.

"You're damn right he is! And that's where he's gonna stay."

"But he ain't done nothin'."

"Y'all better get the hell back across the river, or y'all be in jail or dead one."

Two days later, Allen's lawyer arranged to have Louis released after paying a fine. His face was badly bruised and he was in pain. They took Allen to Jennie Field, a woman doctor in Meadville who treated blacks fairly. His jaw was cracked and had to be wired in place. When he got out of the hospital, he went into hiding, logging as far back in the pine forest as he could. He kept to himself and hoped in time things would blow over.

That November, Daniel Jones cornered him again. Allen had stopped for gas at Hawkins's service station. He didn't see Jones in the repair shop until it was too late.

"Louis, you're under arrest."

"What for?"

"I'll show you."

Jones opened the passenger door to Allen's bobtailed Ford logging truck, reached in the glove compartment, and pulled out the pistol Louis kept there for protection.

"Concealed weapon!" Jones announced in mock surprise. "That's serious."

At the jail they told him his license plate had expired. When

Allen wrote a check to pay for a new one, they said his check was bad and charged him with that too.

"What's my sentence?"

"Eight hundred dollars or ninety days in jail."

"I don't have that kind of money."

"You've got a truck; you've got a shack; you've got a bit of land. Sell them and get out of Liberty."

Allen told his son to ask men he had worked for to lend him the money.

"I'm not fooling with it," said one. "Louis is a good worker, but he should have kept his mouth shut."

"I could, but I'd rather not," another said. "I don't want to do something I might regret later."

"Your father is worth more dead than alive," the last man stated. "You better leave him sit where he's at."

When his son told him what the men had said, Allen scowled and looked at his hands.

"Don't ask any more white men, Henry," he said bitterly.

Rumors circulated that a mob was planning to storm the jail; the black community made a concerted effort to obtain his release. It took three weeks to gather enough donations, but finally Allen was freed. Immediately, he loaded his family in his truck and headed for Baton Rouge. Meanwhile, Jones had been elected sheriff. Allen certainly didn't want to be in Liberty when he took office. In fact, he was so frightened for his life that he hid under a blanket until he had crossed the state line. Then he sat up and said, "Thank you, Jesus."

Work was hard to find in Baton Rouge and word came that his mother, back in Liberty, was dying of cancer.

That night Louis and his family returned to Liberty. He thought no one had seen them, but the next morning Donis Hawkins drove up to the house and honked.

He stuck his head out the window and pointed at Louis's three-year-old daughter.

"You see that little baby standing out by that woodpile?"

"Yassuh, I sees her," Allen said.

"It would be mighty bad if she got herself burned up, now wouldn't it?"

"It surely would."

"'Cause she's an innocent baby, but she could get burnt up just like that." Hawkins squinted up at Allen to see how his words were registering. "I could tell you more, but I'm not going to. If I was you, I'd get my rags in a bundle and clear out."

Allen knew that Hawkins wasn't making idle threats. Not long after Leo McKnight tried to register in Liberty, he and his family had all died when their home mysteriously caught fire in the middle of the night. Allen was tempted to leave right away, but his mother was so close to death, he decided to stay by her to the end.

After his mother's funeral, Allen planned to move to Minneapolis where his brother lived. He went around to his former employers to ask for recommendations. All the men he'd worked for treated him like an outcast in his own town.

"How do I know I ain't helpin' a communist or something like that?" one of them said, refusing to look Louis in the eye.

When Allen came home he put his head in his hands and wept.

"Louis," his wife said, "I've never seen you cry before."

"I don't want to die," he said. "When you're dead, you're dead a long time."

Later, Allen heard his dogs barking and the mules snorting in their stalls.

"Turn the porch light off," Louis said. "I feel like I'm bein' watched."

He slipped out a side door, but in the dark, he couldn't see anyone. He sat alone for a long time in the backyard, brooding.

"I'm gonna try one more white man," he told his wife. "Mr. King knows how good I can drive a dozer. If he'll recommend me, I think I can get a job doin' construction."

As he walked to his logging truck, Henry called out, "Take a pistol, Daddy."

"What good is a gun gonna do me?" he said. "I put my trust in God."

"You be careful, you hear?"

"Don't you worry; I'll be back soon."

About eight-thirty that evening Allen returned. He drove partway up his long drive, pulled the emergency brake, leaving the lights on and the engine running, and stepped out of the truck to lift the loops of his barbwire gate. Somehow he must have sensed that he wasn't alone. Maybe he heard them; maybe he saw them; maybe they said something before they opened fire.

The first shot missed. Allen dove under the front of his truck. The next two loads of buckshot slammed at short range into his face and head. They must have taken their time about it, coming in at close range and squatting down to shoot. Maybe they made him beg.

From the house back in the trees, a hundred yards from the road, Mrs. Allen heard the shots. She went to the window and saw headlights down by the gate. She probably had a hunch what had happened, but she was too terrified to walk down the drive and make sure. Instead she paced from room to room, trying to deny her forebodings. She returned to the window again and again, watching those two beams by the road grow dimmer and dimmer.

Around midnight Henry and his cousin, John Wesley Horton, returned from a dance and found the truck in the drive. They tried to start it; the battery was dead. To clear the drive, Henry released the brake and John pushed. The truck rolled back toward the road, exposing the body in a pool of blood.

"They killed him, Mama!" Henry cried when he reached the house.

Mrs. Allen screamed and ran for the door. Henry caught her.

"You can't go down there, Mama. You don't want to see him like that."

"What are we gonna do?"

"We've got to tell the sheriff," Henry said.

"Jones?" his mother cried. "Not that man!"

"He's the sheriff," Henry said. "We got to."

Henry drove to the home of Sheriff Jones, who lived two miles closer to Liberty on the same road, to report the murder. John stayed with Mrs. Allen in the house.

Jones and eight other men he had impanelled as an inquest jury inspected the scene of the crime. Allen, they ruled, had died at the hands of an unknown assailant.

The morning after the murder, Sheriff Jones came to see Mrs. Allen.

"Elizabeth," he said, "the FBI is gonna come snoopin' around here, and you better be careful what you say. If I was you, I wouldn't mention that business about Herbert Lee and Louis's testimony. And don't you go doin' what Louis did, tellin' the jury one thing and the FBI another. Anything you give them, they're gonna turn over to me, because I'm the one investigatin' the case. No use bringin' that old account up now."

Two days after the murder, three FBI agents arrived. I urged them to make a thorough investigation, but instead, they only talked to the people Sheriff Jones told them to, and they didn't even bother to look at the body or study the crime scene.

I went to the funeral at the Star Hill Methodist Church. The casket was closed.

I began investigating on my own. Mrs. Allen told me how Sheriff Jones and his friends had been hassling her husband for two years because they believed he was a tip-off man for the FBI. Henry told me that a cream tan '61 Ford with two men in it and a black '60 Ford with one had stopped in front of the Allen driveway a day before the murder. Another neighbor had seen the same two cars following Louis's truck returning from Lloyd King's place. Informants told me that an hour after the shooting, the two cars came down a road behind the Allen home, drove into Liberty, and parked at the courthouse.

"It's a puzzling case," Jones told the press the day after the funeral.

"What about the rumor that Allen wanted to change his testimony in the Herbert Lee case?" one reporter asked.

"That's news to me," Jones stated. "To the best of my knowledge, Louis never messed with that civil rights stuff."

"Has he had trouble with the law?"

"Quite a bit," Jones said. "Quite a bit, yes sir—bad checks, stolen goods, concealed weapons. We had to keep an eye on him. He and his wife didn't get along, you know. She come in here last month with cuts and bruises on her head, said Louis had gotten after her and called her names in the streets of Liberty."

The reporters wrote it all down. When I urged them to investigate the case more closely, they ignored me.

"I'll be workin' full-time on this," Sheriff Jones assured them, "but it's gonna be a tough one to crack. You see, I don't have a single clue."

4

The slaying of Louis Allen touched me deeply, because it was another repercussion of my decision to bring the Civil Rights Movement to Liberty. His death was not an isolated incident. Five nights before his murder, fiery crosses burned in thirty-five locations in Pike and Amite counties to show everyone that the invisible empire was ready to assert itself again. We found leaflets that stated, "The Klan is now awake after a thirty-five year sleep. It is reorganized, revitalized, and among you. By sinister means we shall heal the sore of the communist-led nigger conspiracy that poisons our way of life."

Others had already died by "sinister means" in the Liberty area: Eli Jackson, Denis Jones, Lula Mae Anderson, Clifford Walker. I will always be haunted by the poor victims whose names no one bothers to remember.

Beyond doubt the terrorists in southwestern Mississippi were operating with pattern and direction. Any Negro associated with the Movement or with enough economic security to have some breathing space could be their next victim. Those they hadn't killed had been beaten. Archie Curtis, Willie Jackson, Alfred Whitley, James Winston, Roland Sleeper, Wilber Lewis—they were all dragged out into the swamps and whipped.

Since the killing of Louis Allen, Sheriff Jones had been stopping by the homes of those local people who had shown the most gumption, giving them deadlines to leave Amite County. He drove out to Parish Hill Baptist Church and told them they better not hold any more evening services there unless they wanted to die. Negroes were afraid to be seen on the streets of Liberty after six for fear of being beaten. They were even afraid to *leave* town for an afternoon, because anyone who had been away was looked on with suspicion. Everyone was living in a state of sheer terror; everyone, that is, except Steptoe.

The previous week Sheriff Jones had driven out to Steptoe's farm.

"I want to talk to you, Steptoe," he said.

"Okay. Have a seat and go ahead."

"This is a private conversation."

"My home is a private home; you can talk to me here."

"You're not gonna lie to me."

"No."

"You know I'm the sheriff and I can arrest you and carry you to jail."

"Yes, I know you're the sheriff."

"Steptoe, I understand that some of these students coming in are gonna stay here."

"Yes, that's right."

"Who are you gonna keep?"

"Well, who come in, that's who I'm gonna keep."

"Are you gonna house white students?"

"Yes, it don't make no difference to me what color they are; I'm gonna house whatever students come in."

"How many are you gonna house?"

"I don't know, as many as my house can hold."

"Both boys and girls?"

"Yes, whatsoever they are."

"What about white girls? You gonna keep them?"

"Yes. Look, Sheriff, my wife raised four, and she raised them as respectable and decent as any other girls in this county, or in this country, and these folks that's comin' here, my wife is capable of seein' to them just like she done her own girls."

"Steptoe, don't you know you're gonna get killed?"

"Oh, yes, I know my life is overdue."

"What would it profit you to get killed?"

"I'm an old man, Sheriff, my life is too far spent anyway. But the young peoples will live to enjoy what I'm doin'."

"Look, Steptoe, I'm gonna have to come down here with a truck and haul all these dead people off."

"Well, you may have to do that. I won't say you won't, but I'm gonna house these students. Let me say this, Sheriff. If your kids was down here, and didn't have no place to stay, I would be less than a man not to take them in."

"Steptoe, that's a different situation. I live here; this is my home."

"Yes, I know that. I live here just like you, and I'm not plannin' to move. These people comin' in here are doin' the very things you people in this state and in this country should have done years ago. If you had done *what* you should have, *when* you should have, there wouldn't be no students comin' here to help us through this struggle."

When Steptoe told me what he had said to Sheriff Jones, I was deeply troubled.

"Steptoe," I said, "three years ago I made a vow to you that I would return to Liberty. But I don't want to see you dead. It may be too dangerous for you to house the volunteers for the Summer Project."

"If I was afraid, Bob, I wouldn't live here. I'd live someplace else."

"I know you're not afraid, but the lives of all those students are in my hands. I'll have to think about it and make a final decision at orientation."

"Whatever you say, Bob, I'll do."

Nothing convinced me more of the need to bring in the students than the death of Louis Allen and the courage of Steptoe. With Allen's murder, it seemed like we had come full circle and were back to where we were when they killed Herbert Lee. I felt like Sisyphus, shoving the stone uphill only to watch it roll back down again. In order to break Mississippi, we had to find a new way to apply pressure. The students were our best hope and our last chance to shatter the closed society. Yet I knew that no privileged group in history had ever given up anything without exacting some kind of blood sacrifice.

Tom Morton
The Convention

Atlantic City

August 22–27, 1964

1

Atlantic City squats on sand at the end of an excursion line from Philadelphia and New York. Once the top resort on the eastern coast, since the Great Depression the city had suffered a steady downhill slide: it was now a tawdry tourist trap of faded splendor and huckster chicanery. Back in the twenties, however, when most of the big hotels were built, it might have been the ideal spot for a Jay Gatsby to rendezvous with his long-lost love, Daisy Fay, taking a plush suite at one of the ersatz Taj Mahals facing the Boardwalk.

The Democrats had chosen this town of the slow burn and the fast buck for two simple reasons: the city made the highest bid and boasted the largest indoor auditorium in the world (or at least in New Jersey). Convention Hall, a thirteen-story, city-block pile of brick and cement, could seat 20,000 on its football-field-sized floor and house an army of behind-the-scenes operatives in its maze of adjoining rooms. To ensure no hitches to his glorious coronation, LBJ and the media had wired the place with 100,000 circuit miles of cable and installed 3,000 telephones that enabled the president's men to keep constant tabs on their big roundup of delegates, gathered to nominate LBJ by joyful acclamation.

The fly in this ointment (anointment?) was the Freedom Democratic Party. We had come to challenge not only the lily-white Democratic Party of Mississippi, but also the whole segregated system of the Solid South that made the power of the Dixiecrats in Congress possible. We planned to put our case before the credentials committee, lobby the state delegations, and stage demonstrations to win sympathy for our cause. We were determined to accept nothing less than the ouster of the regulars and the seating of the MFDP in their place. If that put LBJ's predicted November landslide victory in jeopardy, that was his problem; all we wanted was justice.

Bob Moses and our attorney, Joe Rauh, had worked out the details in the spring. At that time Moses saw the challenge as a means of dramatizing the situation of black people in Mississippi before a national audience, but Rauh was more optimistic; he thought that if we could get our case to the floor of the convention, we might actually win. When the Summer Project brought so much attention to Mississippi, the odds in our favor began to improve. Twenty-five congressmen representing nine different states signed a statement urging that the MFDP be seated and several state delegations, including all-important California, took straw polls that showed we had strong backing. So it was with considerable hope—a rare commodity among the battle-hardened SNCC veterans and COFO volunteers—that we came to Atlantic City and set up operations in the dingy Gem Hotel on the black side of town.

Lenny's father, who was working behind the scenes to secure the vice presidential nomination for his longtime friend Hubert Humphrey, drove Lenny and me up to Atlantic City on Friday evening. Since there was no vacancy at the Gem Hotel and the only alternative was sleeping on a pew in the nearby Union Temple Baptist Church, we agreed to share his room at the Pageant Motor Inn. After a week in jail and two months of Mississippi insomnia, I couldn't resist the temptation of clean sheets and a fresh mattress. As it turned out, the motel, a four-story affair with a swimming pool on the roof, was located right behind Convention Hall and smack-dab in the middle of the action.

Everyone agreed that LBJ had this convention locked up, and Atlantic City, I soon found, was not a spot conducive to agonized reappraisals. As I strolled around on Friday evening, the first thing I noticed was that the street names had been the inspiration for Monopoly, that developer's dream of a game the whole family could play, swapping phony money for real estate in prime locations. Here was Park Place circling the classy Claridge Hotel where Martin Luther King was staying, while Baltic Avenue's ramshackle low-rent district bordered the railroad track. And, of course, the big money was on the five-mile-long boardwalk lining the golden beach. After Mississippi, this neon-drenched gantlet of crass commercialism was profoundly unreal. All those ghostly white faces! If people noticed me at all, it was with mild curiosity or indifference rather than hate. Amid this nonstop three-ring circus, civil rights workers were just one more sideshow.

Everything was for sale. The spiel of the carny barkers drowned out the surge and crash of the surf; the odors of snowcone syrup and cooking oil submerged the smell of the sea. On garish display beneath flashing lights and pounding music were all manner of gewgaw, gimcrack, froufrou, and folderol to gull the gullible, bamboozle the rubes, and con tourists into believing they were having a good time. For the pensioners on package plans and small-town folks who'd never seen a floor show, the Steel Pier offered Glenn Miller's big band sound and Milton Berle cracking jokes, while the 500 Club countered with the crooning of Eddie Fisher. The more sporting might play Bango ("the most fascinating game on the Boardwalk"), take a turn at the pokerino tables, test their hunches at the racetrack, or catch Sally Rand doing her fan dance at the Globe Burlesque.

For the kiddies, there were funlands and Ferris wheels, pinball machines, shooting galleries, and penny arcades. At the Steel Pier, they could gulp pop and popcorn through sixteen hours worth of movies; gape at Dixie Blandy, the world champion flagpole sitter;

or witness with their own eyes a white horse, ridden bareback by a little lady in a skimpy bathing suit, plunge off a fifty-foot tower into a tank of water. And if that didn't hold them, they could play skee ball on the beach while their parents went shopping. You could pay an arm and a leg for the pelts of endangered species and the latest Dior fashions from Paris or try your hand at hard bargaining for teak figurines, Ming vases, and Persian rugs in the numerous open-front auction houses.

But the big selling items on the Boardwalk that year seemed to be JFK memorabilia and "LBJ for USA" logos. The latter adorned buttons of all sizes, cowboy hats, straw boaters, pennants, glass-ware, ashtrays, cuff links, candy bars, and "El Bubble" (a bubble-gum cigar). LBJ's mug shot was everywhere: on hats, lampposts, store windows, the two-seat wicker chairs the weary could be pushed along the boardwalk in, and the ten-passenger jitney buses on Pacific Avenue. Two humongous twenty-eight by forty-foot most-wanted posters hung modestly inside Convention Hall. True believers could even purchase an oil portrait of LBJ's beagles—"Him" and "Her"—with ears at rest and the White House north portico in the background.

The really kitschy stuff was devoted to JFK. For those who didn't want the presidential face engraved on silver goblets, etched on Wedgwood plates and plastic plaques, or sketched in pastels, there were embossed Kennedy half-dollars for the grown-ups to cherish, chocolate Kennedy coins for children to chew, bulbous Kennedy busts with a future as paperweights, and framed "Special Delivery from Heaven" doggerel to be enshrined over the davenport:

> *Sorry I had to leave right away.*
> *I look down and smile at you every day.*
> *Little Patrick also asks to say "Hi."*
> *I love you. I'm happy, so please don't cry.*

Then there was the question of food and lodging. Atlantic City meant time-nibbled, stale gingerbread hotels and saltwater taffy "cut to fit the mouth" or sold in "mail-it-home" two-pound kegs. You could eat chickenfurters at the snack-a-teria or breakfast on barbecued ribs at the Bamboo. Some waited hours to be served by black waiters in pith helmets at the Gunga Inn while others munched a knish at Saul's Delicatessen. Most settled for fudge, frozen custard, cotton candy, candied apples, and butter crunch, but for the gourmand the pièces de résistance were chocolate-covered frozen bananas and foot-long hot dogs boiled in champagne. At Captain Jack's bar I overheard a disgruntled journalist, back from covering Barry Goldwater's nomination at the Cow Palace, mutter into his scotch on the rocks: "The hotels charge tomorrow's prices for yesterday's rooms and the food is thirty-five hundred miles from San Francisco."

Three beers later, I sat on the boardwalk and watched the promenade. Although I saw lots of camera-clad vacationers in flowery aloha shirts or polyester stretch pants, old-timers predominated: geezers in shabby straw hats with baggy pants held up by one suspender, affable grandfatherly lions whose white spats matched their last wispy thatch of hair, ample-bosomed matrons straight from a Victorian novel, prune-faced spinsters, frumpy puddings, wilting lilacs, shy women in sunbonnets, and blue-haired biddies in tennis shoes. In this motley throng, the men wearing makeup were either congressmen or queens. The delegates, even if they weren't sporting badges, were fairly obvious: the women ranged from pale, powdered dowagers in faded sequined gowns, who had probably voted for Woodrow Wilson and taken tea with Eleanor Roosevelt, to dreamy virgins in cashmere sweaters and matching skirts still waiting for the right unicorn to come along. One fine-boned peacock, mink stole tossed athwart her regal neck, sharp eyes flashing and chin held high, went click-clicking her high-heeled way down the boardwalk without stepping in a single crack. Two floozies in pink and gold-lamé Capri pants, eyebrows plucked and repenciled higher, eyes cosmeticized into Eyes, blonded beauty-parlor beehives holding their improbable shapes against the wind, were followed by a lovely bevy of "Jersey Johnson Girls," as shapely as starlets, in white cowboy hats and boots, blue silk blouses and short red skirts, prancing their peppy way along as they sang, *"Hello, Lyndon. Well hello, Lyndon. It's so nice to have you back where you belong."*

The male delegates were proud to show they'd given the motel shower a workout. Groomed and shampooed, well-scrubbed faces aglow with good living, even if LBJ had them in his pocket, they swaggered as if they were power brokers: trim well-tanned middle-aged men, muscle tone intact, who looked like they'd just stepped off the tennis court; elegant execs straight from the boardroom in cool white suits with an argent streak in their coiffured hair; beefy guys in golf shirts and Bermuda shorts who knew their way around the union hall, parading their beer guts and granite calves as if they were the insignia of success; young lawyers on the make, or take, still in the Kennedy mode: shirtsleeves rolled up for action, a shock of boyish hair tossing on their brow for sex appeal, ready at the first sign of a photographer to wade along the shoreline to demonstrate their spiritual depth; and glad-handing, backslapping gregarious booster types wearing shiny seersucker or madras jackets with skinny ties. One pink-faced citizen, in particular, caught my attention. He was wearing an "All the Way with LBJ" button as big as a dinner plate over his belly, a "Wallace and Powell: A Balanced Ticket" button on his hat, and another on his chest picturing a bucktoothed, guffawing donkey saying, "Hi, I'm a delegate! Where's the party?"

2

Saturday morning the excitement in the air at the Gem Hotel was palpable. The MFDP delegates, who had exchanged their cotton dresses and coveralls for their Sunday best, knew that today was the day they would finally present their case. SNCC veterans and Freedom Summer volunteers were bear-hugging and embracing each other like long-lost relatives. I wrapped my arms around Feelgood, dapper in a tan three-piece suit, but quickly eased up when I remembered his bruised ribs. Esther, looking radiant, kissed me so warmly on the lips I felt my heart flutter. Mary Allen, in a pleated, peach-colored dress and flowered hat, beamed with delight to be a delegate. I ran my eyes anxiously over the crowd searching in vain for Jasmine. Just to think of her pierced me like a spear and made me ache with longing. I wondered if Mrs. Mays or Midnight Grimes might have been selected as delegates, but I didn't see anyone from Tallahatchie. Few people spoke of Mickey, Andy, and Jim, but beneath our apparent happiness we were all tasting the same bittersweet twist of fate: our three friends were dead but we had survived to tell the Mississippi story.

After lunch we walked a block to the beach and then, with Martin Luther King, Aaron Henry, and Joe Rauh in the lead and Bob Moses inconspicuously bringing up the rear, we marched down the crowded boardwalk a long mile to the convention hall, singing freedom songs all the way.

The packed ballroom was tense with anticipation—Judgment Day was at hand. The press was already playing up the hearings as the only sour note in LBJ's symphony. The contesting delegations sat facing each other and the credentials committee occupied the middle, surrounded by reporters and TV crews, who pushed their cameras into any open spaces and brandished their microphones like war clubs. I was pressed against a side wall, with only a partial view. I kept glancing over at Bob Moses, to see how he felt about his brainchild coming to fruition, but his placid face gave no sign.

LBJ had entrusted the job of finessing the situation to an old pro and crony, seventy-five-year-old David Lawrence, a former mayor of Pittsburg, governor of Pennsylvania, and delegate to every national Democratic convention since 1924. A broad-faced, bigheaded man with thinning white hair and wearing rimless spectacles, Lawrence knew how to pour oil on troubled waters. "Everyone wants a harmonious convention," he announced, "and we'll have that. We will accept the nomination of Lyndon Johnson by acclamation. We will approve the man he selects for vice president by acclamation. We will adopt the platform by acclamation. There will be no contests."

Joe Rauh, looking like a Saint Bernard who had chugged his brandy keg and replaced it with a floppy bow tie, was tall, barrel-chested, coarse-featured, and direct, as befitted the man who also served as a lawyer for the United Auto Workers. He introduced Rita Schwerner. "I would like you to know," she told the hushed audience, "that to this day the state of Mississippi and the county of Neshoba have not even sent me a copy of the death certificate of my husband." The members of the credentials committee, who had listened with rapt attention, were obviously moved. Somehow that small, deliberate oversight was more revolting than a full recital of the gruesome details of the murders themselves.

I was disappointed when Rauh introduced several national civil rights leaders to provide moral support. With the exception of Martin Luther King, their remarks were uninspired. I would have much rather heard from Bob Moses, who had brought all these things to pass, or from local leaders like E. W. Steptoe and Hartman Turnbow. Why weren't they asked to speak? Wasn't the whole point of participatory democracy that sharecroppers could speak for themselves?

Then came Fannie Lou Hamer.

Short and heavyset, with a pronounced limp and large, sunken eyes that had a hauntingly trancelike quality as though she were an oracle from Delphi, she spoke with a husky, pain-laden voice that could sound all the modulations of the blues. Perspiring under the intense lights of the television cameras until it seemed as if her whole body wept, she told how, when coming back from a voter registration school the year before, she had been arrested in Winona, Mississippi.

I felt suddenly woozy as images of the Liberty Jail and the sounds of Lenny being beaten down the hall came back to me. I focused my eyes on Mrs. Hamer's glistening face so intensely the rest of the room turned dark and all I was aware of was her voice.

"And it wasn't too long before three white mens led me down a hall and it was two Negro prisoners in this cell, in their twenties. The patrolman said 'Take this,' and he give one a long, flat, leather blackjack, wide and heavy like lead at one end. And the Negro said, 'You want me to beat her with this?' And he said, 'You damn right, and if you don't, I'll use it on you.' He had no choice, you see. So he said, 'Get over there on that cot.' And I said, 'You mean you would do this to your own race?' and the white man said, 'Do it! You heard what I told you.' So I stretched out on that bunk flat on my stomach and that man begun to beat me. I tried to put my hands to my side where I had polio when I was six years old, but he beat on my hands till they turned blue-black, he beat my arms till they had no feelin'. That man beat me till he give out. Then the second Negro was made to beat me. I took the first part of it, but I couldn't stand the second. I buried my head in the mattress and hugged it to kill out the sound of my screams, I couldn't stop screamin' it was so bad, and after the second Negro give out, they taken me back to my cell 'cause I couldn't but barely walk and I couldn't sleep it hurted so. My hands was navy blue and so swole I couldn't bend the fingers, and my body where I was beat was just as hard as bone.

"And after I got out of jail, half-dead, I found out they'd shot Medgar Evers down in his own front yard. Now we tired of all this killin'. If the Freedom Democratic Party is not seated now, I question America."

The credentials committee sat in stunned silence, turned to stone. The Mississippi regulars, when their time came to testify, made no effort to refute Mrs. Hamer. Rather, State Senator E. K. Collins categorically denied that Negroes were discriminated against, asserting that the MFDP was "a group of dissatisfied, power-hungry soreheads," while the white people of Mississippi were "by far and large the biggest-hearted people in the world."

"Are you telling us, then, Mr. Collins," a delegate from Indiana asked, "that every Negro of voting age has free access to the Democratic Party organization in Mississippi?"

"Absolutely," he replied, "just as free as you would have if you moved there."

At that remark I laughed out loud.

"Then your state convention was open to Negroes?"

"Yes, absolutely."

"Were any Negro delegates there?"

"No delegates, but they were there as spectators."

That pretty much summed up E. K. Collins's case: Negroes in Mississippi were free to participate in politics provided they didn't participate.

3

Lenny and I slept in late on Sunday. We had been up half the night at the Club Harlem on Kentucky Avenue celebrating the profound impression the MFDP had made before the credentials committee. Feeling upstaged, LBJ had called an impromptu press conference right in the middle of Fannie Lou Hamer's presentation to divert the TV cameras from Atlantic City, but the networks reran her entire testimony on the prime-time news anyway, triggering an avalanche of telegrams from across the nation that demanded the seating of the Freedom delegation.

In the early afternoon, we sat with Mr. Swift in our hotel room, watching Hubert Humphrey on "Meet the Press" tell three NBC reporters why he wanted the vice presidency and how he defined his role:

"Above all, a vice president should be loyal," Humphrey gushed. "He must have a quality of fidelity, a willingness to literally give himself to his president to be what the president wants him to be—a loyal, faithful friend and servant."

"Rosencrantz and Guildenstern couldn't have said it any better," I remarked.

"Fido the Friendly Lap Dog," Lenny sneered. "How can you support him, Dad?"

"Hubert really wants the job," Mr. Swift said sadly as he packed his pipe and lit it. "He's saying what he knows Lyndon wants to hear. I wish him luck."

"I don't see why he has to grovel," I said.

"It's more complex than it seems," Mr. Swift explained. "Being second-in-command has never been easy."

"Brace yourself," Lenny warned. "Dad always wanted to be a professor."

"Not really." Mr. Swift smiled in my direction. "I like being close to the action and knowing the actors firsthand. In the final analysis, politics does indeed come down to personalities. Hubert and Lyndon go way back. They're both poor boys who grew up in small towns during the depression. They know what hard times are like and how it feels to kick around the country on an empty gut and what it takes to work your way up and make good. When they entered the Senate, Lyndon took Hubert under his wing and taught him the ropes. Lyndon taught Hubert how to be an insider."

"Humphrey strikes me as a cheerleader," I said, "always looking to the bright side."

"You're right, Tom," Mr. Swift granted. "Hubert would probably call jumping off a cliff a progressive step. He's got the gift of gab, and he actually enjoys the rubber-chicken circuit, hitting the hustings and pressing the flesh. But he knows his man. Rumor has it that when Lyndon was born, the obstetrician thought he had two umbilical cords, but on closer inspection, one proved to be a telephone line. He's an authentic political animal."

"I think he's a bully," I said. "Like that business of pulling his beagles' ears."

"He's one personality inside another," Mr. Swift said. "Scratch the bullyboy and you get a crybaby, and so forth. He's a thin-skinned man with an overbearing ego. He likes to stretch people on the rack and watch them sweat. Have you noticed? The names of his wife and daughters all have the same initials—Lady Bird, Lynda Bird, and Luci Baines. Think of Lyndon as an ambitious Texas rancher: he wants his brand on everything."

"He sounds like Attila the Hun," I said. "Why is that cause for celebration?"

"Because Lyndon is the first president since Madison who actually understands how the government operates. I don't mean in general but in specific. He knows what it takes to get his way. If he has to twist your arm or scratch your back or squeeze your nuts, he'll do it—and you damn well better like it. Lyndon is an FDR man: He believes that the national government can accomplish things that enhance a community—things individuals can't do for themselves. He believes that government can be a positive force for good—that's to his credit."

"He still doesn't sound like the kind of man who ought to be president."

"*Ought* has nothing to do with it," Mr. Swift told me. "We're talking about *is*. It is my considered opinion that worlds that exist have more reality than worlds that don't. In a world where many are not good, doing good is a tricky business; you have to differentiate degrees of evil and distinguish bad from worse. Incidentally, it's envy and spite that drive Lyndon to some of his best actions. He's insanely jealous of the Kennedys, for example, and so he tries to outdo them—hence the civil rights bill and the Great Society legislation. Remember, Johnson is not running against Jesus, but Goldwater. Barry's not a bad man, but like a lot of Americans, he's missing a few floors; all he sees are white hats and black hats; he doesn't understand human nature or how the world goes."

"He's guilty of innocence," I said, feeling savvy after my summer in Mississippi.

"Yes, you could say that." Mr. Swift welcomed my phrase. "No one would ever accuse LBJ of innocence. Lyndon loves to swap stories about what makes people tick. He knows that telling a person to go to hell and making him do it are separate propositions. 'Come, let us reason together,' he likes to say. But the corollary is, 'until you do what I want.'"

"If LBJ is so powerful and so concerned with the common good," Lenny objected, "why doesn't he seat the MFDP and tell the regulars to go to hell?"

"That's the tricky part." Mr. Swift grimaced at the intricacy of it all. "Lyndon doesn't just want to win, he wants to win big. He wants to be president of *all* the people. He wants to carry every state. Everyone knows he's president because Lee Harvey Oswald cast an unscheduled ballot. Lyndon has the usurper's craving for legitimacy; he wants a huge mandate to prove his right to wear the Kennedy mantle."

"Which is why Bobby Kennedy won't be on the ticket," I added.

"Exactly," Mr. Swift affirmed, "that and the fact that the two men despise each other. Lyndon was so afraid Bobby would give an emotional speech and stampede the delegates that he put off the tributes to Jack until the last day—after the nomination. Even so, watch the JFK film closely Thursday evening; Bobby won't be in it—that, too, is Lyndon's doing."

"I still don't see why it's so important to the country for Johnson to win in a landslide," I said. "None of the polls I've seen give Goldwater much of a chance."

"The problem is not so much Goldwater as the people who are behind him. Did you see them in San Francisco?"

"We didn't have time to watch television in Mississippi, Dad," Lenny commented.

"Well, the people behind Barry are dangerous, fanatical. They know exactly where the grapes of wrath are stored."

"So Johnson's strategy," Lenny surmised, "will be to present himself as the wise old skipper whose steady hand will keep the ship of state on an even keel, while Barry's crew will be pictured as a bunch of loose cannons crashing around on the poop deck."

"It looks to me like Goldwater's painted himself into a corner," I said. "How can he possibly win?"

"Ah." Mr. Swift smiled. "That's where you fellows come in."

"Us?" I asked in surprise. "What do we have to do with it?"

"The hidden ingredient in this election is what I call the 'Woodwork Factor,'" Mr. Swift explained. "It is an article of faith among the Goldwater people that there is a host of true believers out in the heartland, who have been waiting all these years for Goldwater. He provides them, the theory goes, with a choice, not an echo. And so on election day they are going to come crawling out of the woodwork, sweep Barry to a stunning upset victory, and redeem the land from its sinful ways."

"But the polls don't support that," I protested. "They show three times more Republicans planning to vote for Johnson than Democrats switching to Goldwater."

"You're right," Mr. Swift admitted, "but some of the most subtle and in-depth pollsters have found one issue that could swing it the other way."

"What's that?" I asked.

"Race," Mr. Swift said. "The only way LBJ can lose this election is if race becomes the central issue."

"How do you know?" I asked.

"Ironically, the March on Washington has some unforseen consequences: it established an expectation of good behavior for Negro protest and now anything that exceeds that norm offends white people. The riots this summer have caused a tremendous reaction."

"White backlash," I said.

"Well, it's real," Mr. Swift said. "Some white Democrats have already switched to Goldwater, and a lot more are tempted. Another major riot this year and they'll jump."

"Which is why he's not going to back the MFDP," I said.

"Exactly," Mr. Swift replied. "Some southern governors told LBJ that if he seated the MFDP, the South would walk."

"But you don't know what Mississippi is like," Lenny protested. "Those people deserve to be seated."

"Believe me," Mr. Swift insisted, "a strong moral case was made on Saturday. Lyndon had been planning to give the MFDP kind words and free passes to the gallery, but because of Fannie Lou Hamer, I don't think that will wash in the credentials committee. You need only eleven votes to force a floor fight. If that happens, and things turn nasty, all bets are off."

"Look, all MFDP delegates want is a chance to represent their state," Lenny said. "Don't blame us if this racist country is about to self-destruct."

"I don't blame you," Mr. Swift said. "I simply want you to realize that actions have consequences. LBJ has more on his mind than the justice of your cause. There are more Negroes in New York City than in all of Mississippi. If their situation is not dealt with soon, this country could come apart at the seams. So you see, a lot is riding on this convention being harmonious. That's why Lyndon has ordered Hubert to settle the seating issue."

"Humphrey!" Lenny and I cried out.

"Lyndon's last pound of flesh," Mr. Swift said dryly.

"I still don't see why seating the MFDP should offend the rest of the South," I said. "Everybody knows Mississippi will vote for Goldwater in November."

"A peasants' revolt alarms all landlords," Mr. Swift remarked. "Seating the MFDP would establish a precedent."

"Great!" Lenny cried. "The more challenges the better. I think you're more concerned about due process than real progress. The time for fence-sitting is over. Which side are you on?"

"The Democratic Party does have a heart," Mr. Swift replied with regret in his voice, "but this is an inopportune time to test it. When a democracy is confronted with a complex problem that requires that the majority of the people surrender certain long-held privileges and prejudices, the chances are you're not going to have a happy ending."

"What you call politics sounds like apologetics for the status quo to me," I argued.

"Not really," Mr. Swift insisted. "I'm rooting for the MFDP more than you realize. This old party needs some shaking up."

"Maybe the best way to give hope to the black people of the North is to seat the MFDP and show that the Democratic Party really does care," I suggested.

"You're both young men," Mr. Swift said, waxing sentimental. "You're both filled with promise; you think all things are possible on demand. Well, I was young once too; I understand how you feel."

"No you don't!" Lenny shouted. "Not anymore. Your Hubert Humphrey may have been a good man once, but I think he's sold out."

"I don't agree," Mr. Swift said, "but sometimes I do think that youth should be held liable for breach of promise."

"It's America that's broken its promises," I said. "We're trying to fix that."

"Come on, Tom," Lenny said as he stood up and headed for the door. "There's no point arguing. I'm tired of listening to this crap."

We stalked out, leaving Mr. Swift alone with his pipe to brood upon the grand scheme of things.

4

"I'm sad to report," Aaron Henry announced loudly to the MFDP delegates gathered Sunday evening in the basement of the Union Temple Baptist Church, "that we have been rejected by both the Democratic Party of Mississippi and the national Democratic Party."

A murmur of foreboding and dismay ran through the room.

"The credentials committee has proposed that the regular" *(a roar of "no" and "boo")* ". . . that the regular Mississippi delegates be seated, provided they take a loyalty oath; that we be seated as 'honored guests'. . ." *(hoots and catcalls);* " . . . and that discriminatory state delegations be banned from future conventions."

People all around me shouted out their disapproval and their determination to protest.

"The country is watching what we do here," Doc Henry continued. "And I want to say that we have not come to Atlantic City to accept the same back-of-the-bus treatment we get in Mississippi. They want to give us free passes to the gallery, so we can sit and watch others vote, but we've been watching from the balcony all our lives."

At least a dozen members of the credentials committee had privately pledged to vote for the proposal to seat the MFDP, but Doc Henry warned that if their names became known they would be subjected to tremendous pressure from LBJ to back down.

I watched Bob Moses slowly walk to the front of the room and wait until we were ready to listen. It irritated me that people kept talking and only relucantly gave him the respect and attention he deserved.

"We have come here to bring certain realities to the attention of America," Bob Moses commented softly, his large brooding eyes absorbing everyone. "We must not permit ourselves to be pushed aside or swept under the rug. To apply pressure of our own, we must be seen. Until the MFDP is seated as a legitimate Mississippi delegation, I suggest that we stage a constant vigil in front of Convention Hall."

And so, around midnight, about a hundred of us marched from the church, carrying placards and singing freedom songs, to Kennedy Plaza, a semicircular colonnade across the Boardwalk from the entrance to the hall. We placed pictures of Mickey, Andy, and Jim beside a bronze bust of JFK, already turning green from the salty sea air, and then stood silently side by side. Thousands of strollers stopped, to stare or offer encouragement, but for the first few hours, none of us said a word, letting our signs do the talking:

VOTE MISSISSIPPI FREEDOM—UNSEAT RACISM IN AMERICA
STOP HYPOCRISY—SUPPORT DEMOCRACY
FREEDOM'S NAME IS MIGHTY SWEET—SING IT FOR MISSISSIPPI
ONE MILLION MISSISSIPPI NEGROES DESERVE REPRESENTATION
HOW MANY MORE MUST DIE?

As late night dragged on to early morning, and the spectators and reporters drifted away, I wedged my placard in a crack in the boardwalk and sat down in a circle with other volunteers huddled against a cool breeze blowing in from the ocean. We spent the early hours swapping stories about Mississippi and speculating about what we thought the credentials committee would do. Someone supplied me with an army blanket, a can of V-8 juice, and a ham sandwich. At dawn, coffee and doughnuts miraculously appeared, lifting our spirits enough to sing in the sunrise.

It got so hot so fast I envied the bathers on the beach. The girls were wearing two-piece suits that year and sporting late summer tans. Their squeals of delight as they splashed about and jumped waves carried all the way up to where I sat sweating. I tilted my sign to block the sun. *What business did I have telling self-satisfied delegates in suits and ties that they ought to care about poor people from towns so small they weren't even on the map?* It seemed futile, a hopeless cause. *What chance was there that the drab, humdrum world of politics would respond to the magnitude of their plight?* All morning I had watched biplanes skim the breakers, pulling rippling streamers that advocated "Decency" in the platform, the Holy Bible in the public schools, Bobby Baker in the "vice" presidency, and Olivo in your hair. That was American politics, a series of glib slogans for mass consumption, not a compassionate response to serious problems. *Perhaps democracy was nothing more than a method of implicating the American people in the incompetence of their leaders.*

At noon, Feelgood and Esther walked over arm in arm with big smiles on their faces.

"Come on," Feelgood said. "We've got something to show you."

He was trying to be upbeat, but his voice sounded tired and defeated.

We walked across the boardwalk to a parking lot where lo and behold the charred chassis of my burned-out Edsel was sitting on a flatbed truck, beneath a "Mississippi Horror Museum" banner. Grim reminders of terrorism were on display: two wooden crosses wrapped in singed burlap sacking and the scorched brass bell from the firebombed church in Neshoba County that Mickey, Andy, and Jim had gone to investigate that fateful day in June. Summer volunteers stood by the exhibit, passing out flyers to the curious about voter intimidation and the convention challenge.

"How did you get it here?" I asked, feeling a tightening in my throat.

"Lance and Leetonia arrived this morning." Esther looked at me intently. "They had to sneak it out of Mississippi in a closed van."

"I didn't remember that it was burned so badly."

"We added a few touches," Feelgood admitted with an uneasy laugh.

The Edsel looked so woebegone my eyes welled up. My battered buggy was a rattletrap that stalled more than it started, but at least it was still doing its bit for civil rights. Somehow I felt strangely heartened.

A blue-suited delegate inspected the wreckage and stated authoritatively to his wife, "That's the car they were driving."

"Who?" she asked.

"You know—them—the three boys."

"Oh!" She looked at the Edsel with open-mouthed awe. "How horrible!"

"They didn't have a chance," he said with finality.

I kept quiet. What did it matter what the truth was? They wouldn't have understood anyway.

"Do you think the MFDP will be seated?" I asked Feelgood.

"Of course not," he replied with a conspiratorial grin. "The Democratic Party doesn't give a shit about niggers."

"Why isn't Poe here?" I asked.

"He's up in Newark with some of the bros. They'll show if they're needed."

"Moses still thinks we have a chance," I said.

"Bob is kidding himself," Feelgood replied in a mordant voice.

Later, Lenny and I bought souvenir T-shirts; Lenny's had a bug-eyed picture of Barry on the front and said, "In Your Gut You Know He's Nuts"; mine showed Goldwater's face in the shape of a mushroom cloud with the words "In Your Fright You Know He Might." We figured we'd get some laughs; instead, we arrived just as a scuffle broke out between some Young Democrats and a half-dozen neo-Nazis. A freaked-out guy wearing combat boots, an army fatigue hat, and a brown shirt with a swastika armband broke free of the crowd and charged at me swinging a sign as if it were a battle axe. Fortunately, the police were already on the scene; they grabbed him before he could strike and hustled him off with his buddies, leaving their "Down with Traitor Johnson" and "Wallace Über Alles" signs on the ground. The papers had warned that extremist groups and agent provocateurs from both the left and the right were plotting a race riot, but this fight was stopped so quickly that many bystanders probably never realized anything had happened at all. I saw one teenager with a torn shirt and a cut on his hand, but other than that, no one was hurt and our vigil continued without interruption. In fact, as the day wore on, bus loads of SNCC and CORE people from Boston and New York joined us, until we were several hundred strong. I must admit that I resented their presence. Just as the SNCC veterans hadn't wanted us volunteers butting into their business, now that I was a two-month veteran myself, I was uncomfortable with these outsiders. Mississippi was ours.

In midafternoon, Fannie Lou Hamer, Aaron Henry, Joe Rauh, and Bob Moses came out to tell us about a meeting they had had at the Pageant with Humphrey. It was maddening to be always out on the boardwalk when I knew that the important things were happening behind closed doors inside, so I listened with great interest.

"I'd heard so much about Humphrey and what he'd done for civil rights," Mrs. Hamer explained. "But here sat this little man with his round eyes full of tears and he told me if we didn't stop pushin' he wouldn't get to be vice president and do good things for the world. I said, 'Senator Humphrey, I lost my job in Sunflower County, but I think I did what was right, and God's takin' care of me. Do you mean to tell me that yo job is more important to you than the lives of all the black people in Mississippi?' Well that knocked him back. He said, 'What will you settle for?' I said, 'Seats.' He said, 'Two.' I said, 'Seat sixty-eight in two seats? We need sixty-three thousand seats, that's how many signatures we got!' He said, 'I can't do it.' I said, 'Senator Humphrey, if you don't seat us you may become vice president, but you will never be free to do the things you want to do.' He didn't like to hear that, but I was talkin' the truth. I said, 'Senator Humphrey, I'm gonna pray to Jesus for you.'"

Mrs. Hamer shook her head sadly, then she led us in singing "This Little Light of Mine, I'm Gonna Let It Shine"—*"This little vote of mine, I'm gonna let it shine,"* and *"We are first-class citizens, we're gonna let it shine,"* and on and on until we were hoarse.

"Did you hear that, Lyndon B. Johnson?" Feelgood shouted toward the huge Convention Hall. "Do you hear the voice of the people?"

5

By Tuesday, paranoia ruled. Our vigil continued, people slept in shifts at the church and took turns on the boardwalk, but after two days of sweating in the same clothes, everyone was tired, irritable, and hopelessly grungy. The well-dressed delegates looked askance at our straggly hair, stained T-shirts, and grimy blue jeans. I was in a surly mood. If one of them had asked me, "What are you protesting against?" I would have snarled like Marlon Brando in *The Wild One*, "Whadda ya got?" The seating question should have been settled days before. Instead, Humphrey had swept the issue off center stage by establishing a five-man subcommittee, headed by one of his top aides—Walter Mondale. Their report had been postponed. Why the delay? Rumors were flying and suspicions were high that some kind of dirty deal was in the works. The fear spread that we had a traitor in our midst.

Rumors flashed along the boardwalk that a new compromise, one that took seats away from the regulars, was imminent. At ten we met with Rauh to discuss options. Bob Moses asked the MFDP delegates what they were prepared to accept: would they accept two seats, he asked, and they all said no. Rauh promised to heed their advice at the credentials committee meeting. We were told that Humphrey wanted to meet with Aaron Henry and Ed King in his suite that afternoon. Moses looked alarmed; he said someone from SNCC should be present; everyone agreed that it ought to be him.

By this point I was dead on my feet from lack of sleep, so I returned to the Pageant to take a nap. When I arrived, Mr. Swift was leaving for the President's Club Clambake on the beach; he was in a cheerful mood.

"Three thousand lobsters fresh from Casco Bay in Maine," he said heartily. "I can't wait. And a Perle Mesta party after that. By the way, here are two floor passes for tonight. If your idea of a good time is listening to party underlings recite the platform's deathless prose, be my guest."

I woke up in midafternoon, showered, shaved, and spiffed up in suit and tie for a last-ditch lobbying effort. I turned on the television to see if I had missed anything.

Walter Mondale, outside the credentials committee room with a very perturbed Joe Rauh in the background, was making a statement to the press: "It may not satisfy everyone," he said. "It will not satisfy the extremes on the right and the left. But it is a sound compromise, an honorable solution that recognizes the legal status of the Mississippi regulars and the strong and compelling moral case of the Freedom Party."

The compromise called for the seating of two members of the MFDP, Aaron Henry and Ed King, as delegates "at large," the seating of those members of the regular party who would sign the loyalty oath, and an antidiscrimination rule for future conventions. The committee had accepted the compromise unanimously.

"Oh, Jesus, Rauh broke his promise," I said out loud. "What's going on?"

I was on my way down the corridor when I heard a sharp cry: "You cheated! You cheated! You double-crossed us!" Suddenly Bob Moses burst out of Hubert Humphrey's room. "You lied to us! You set us up!" he shouted and slammed the door with resounding force. The mouths of the Secret Service men standing guard outside dropped; they didn't know how to react. Then Moses staggered down the hall in my direction like a wounded man.

"Bob, what happened?" I said, reaching out to him.

"Get out of my way," he warned with a stricken look in his eye as he brushed past. "Don't touch me."

The shock of seeing Bob Moses furious left me unstrung. My heart was thudding and my knees were weak. My impulse was to slip to the floor and sink into the carpet, but I stood rooted to the spot as in one of those nightmares when the more you struggle, the less you can move. I watched Moses's back recede down the hallway. For an indefinite period of time, I was oblivious, unaware of my surroundings; all I saw was a figure growing smaller and smaller as it left me behind. I felt rejected by the person who ultimately was responsible for my being there at that very moment. I thought how absurd the world was: I had just been shoved aside by the man I most admired in the world, and he had been betrayed by people he thought were his friends, and so on—hitting and missing, we ricocheted at random through life like so many billiard balls. *What was the point?* I thought. *Whom could you trust?*

Still in a daze, I hiked down several flights of stairs, pushed open an unmarked door, and found myself on the mezzanine in the midst of a reception for Bobby Kennedy. I leaned over the balcony rail just in time to see him, dressed in an elegant black pinstriped suit and standing on the ornate, curved stairway that led to the lobby, tell the packed crowd, "I'm delighted to see so many bosses here to welcome me." He flashed a shy, charming smile, which exposed two big gleamingly white front teeth, and passed his fingers through the brown cowlick flopping on his forehead.

I followed my nose to the open bar and hors d'oeuvres in the ballroom and then stood in a receiving line that started out in the hall. The only person I recognized was John Kenneth Galbraith, a remarkably tall man whose long, thin face floated above the throng. When my turn came, Bobby Kennedy stuck out his hand and fixed me with keen light-blue eyes as large as prize agates. "I appreciate your support," he said, in a voice that was at once high-pitched and frog-croaky, and smoothly passed me on with practiced ease to his frankly pregnant wife, Ethel.

That evening Lenny and I arrived at the convention on time to hear the temporary chairman, John Pastore of Rhode Island, call for a voice vote on the credentials challenge. Everybody in the hall, from the spectators in the galleries to the alternates in the back, shouted their "aye" and "no" along with the official delegates. It sounded close to me, but Pastore didn't hesitate: "I believe the ayes have it," he cried, banging his gavel. "Yes, the ayes have it." Looking up at the huge twin photos of Big Bubba Johnson that loomed behind the rostrum—which reduced Pastore, already a small man, to insignificance—I could have sworn that one of those shrewd gambler's eyes, inherited from forefathers who had spent their lives squinting at the big Texas sky, winked.

The main item of business was the reading of the platform—a process tedious enough to drive us outside. On the Boardwalk I heard the sounds of "We Shall Overcome" rising loud and clear, appropiately enough, from the Mississippi Avenue side of Convention Hall. At least fifty people had joined hands around Aaron Henry, Fannie Lou Hamer, and Ed King as they tried to push their way up the delegates' ramp into the building, but they were being blocked by a line of police who stood shoulder-to-shoulder behind a wooden barricade.

"We have tickets and are entitled to admission," Doc Henry shouted, but the officer in charge replied that he had orders to admit no one because the hall was filled to capacity.

"What's going on?" I asked Esther, who looked flushed with excitement.

"We're taking the seats," she cried. "We've got floor passes, and when we get in we're heading for the Mississippi section."

Feeling as exhilarated as a Bolshevik storming the Winter Palace, I raced to the next entrance and was admitted without incident. As soon as I stepped on the floor, I saw Feelgood and five of the MFDP delegates working their way down an aisle toward the Mississippi standard, followed by Lenny. We sat down in an empty row of seats behind the three members of the regular party who had signed the loyalty oath. For a few minutes no one noticed that anything had happened. Then a television crew spotted us and the rush was on. Cameramen, looking like invading Martians with their protuberant lenses, bristling antennae, and bulging backpacks, fought each other to monopolize the best angles. Delegates from nearby states stood on chairs to see what was happening; many applauded their approval; others were knocked to their knees in the confusion and almost trampled. Well-wishers came over to shake our hands. The sergeant at arms—a tall, balding man with horn-rimmed glasses who looked like a college professor— was in a quandry; he knew we shouldn't be there, but anything he did would be seen in living rooms across the nation. One of LBJ's floor managers, a brash man with a walkie-talkie, thrust himself forward and ordered a check of everyone's credentials.

No one moved.

"We have a right to sit in this section," Mary Allen, the delegate from McComb, said. "If you want me to leave, you'll have to drag me out."

She lowered her head, as if in prayer, and began to softly sing "We Shall Overcome."

"Remove these people," he commanded.

Several men grabbed Feelgood and tried to wrestle him out of his seat. Realizing that his ribs couldn't take any rough stuff, he let them escort him away, but the MFDP delegates linked arms and refused to budge.

"Under the circumstances, any precipitate action would be unwise," the sergeant at arms said, sounding like a college professor too.

At that, the LBJ man rushed away, barking all the while into his walkie-talkie. He was shortly replaced by a cooler head who decided to handle the matter with kid gloves, at least until the television cameras went away.

Meanwhile, more MFDP delegates had infiltrated the floor and squeezed into the remaining Mississippi seats, the three regulars having slipped off into the crowd when the fun began. Finally, Aaron Henry arrived, sending the media into another frenzy.

"They wanted to seat us at large," Doc Henry told the newsmen, "but we want our seats in Mississippi. The seats are here and so are we; I don't see why that's so exciting."

Actually, he looked more excited than the reporters. He was

dressed in a light-blue suit and wearing an "All the Way with LBJ" button on one lapel and a March on Washington white-hand-clasping-black-hand button on the other, with a silken pennant in place of a tie that read "Free Mississippi."

In the background, rising above the pandemonium on the floor and drowning out the reading of the platform, I could hear our sympathizers in the galleries chanting in alternation, "Freedom Now!" and "Seat Them Now!"

Next to me, a television reporter, his voice dripping with condescension, jabbed his microphone in Mary Allen's face and asked, "Don't you think you've disrupted this convention long enough?"

"This seat is rightfully mine," she said proudly, "and I plan to stay in it as long as I can. I want for the people back home in Mississippi to know we's here where we belong."

6

I woke up Wednesday morning still thinking about the issue Lenny and I had spent half the night debating: why liberals never stood on ground of their own choosing, but instead jumped in whatever ditch that separated contending sides and called it good. I expected more of the same waffling as I walked to the Union Temple Baptist Church. Apparently Humphrey felt that his prestige had been sullied when the MFDP rejected the two-seat offer out of hand the day before, so he had talked the big guns of the Civil Rights Movement into firing one more salvo at our position to see if the MFDP delegates might yield.

"First they screw the MFDP," I told Lenny, getting a perverse pleasure out of feeling so righteous, "then they expect gratitude. Humphrey wants the MFDP to grant him absolution from guilt so he can feel pure and innocent again—the happy liberal."

The mood at the church was ominous. From the drained faces in the room, I could tell that I wasn't the only one who hadn't slept much the night before. The SNCC veterans in particular looked wound up tight enough to snap. The MFDP delegates, on the other hand, were comparatively calm, with a brooding seriousness in their eyes that indicated they understood that they had arrived at a crucial crossroads.

Jack Pratt of the National Council of Churches, the same man who had warned us at orientation about free love on warm summer nights, spoke with a bubbly glee that was totally out of keeping with the dominant tone:

"The credentials committee has made a landmark decision," he enthused. "It is the greatest victory for the Negro since Lincoln signed the Emancipation Proclamation!"

". . . and it gives us about as much freedom," Ella Baker caustically remarked.

"But, but it really *is* important," he struggled on, deeply flustered. "It is a hammer to hold over the heads of the Democratic Party."

"We don't want to hold a hammer over their heads," Moses said with his characteristic sensitivity to metaphor. "We want to light a fire under their feet."

Martin Luther King's face remained an impassive mask; in contrast, his sonorous baritone voice was filled with a passionate anguish that conveyed how deeply divided he felt. "The Civil Rights Movement needs a victory," he said. "From the sharecropper's shack in the South to the teeming tenements of our northern cities, there is a terrible feeling of desolation and desperation. As our people curse the dark, they cry out for a small candle to light their way. It is important for Negroes all over America to see the MFDP win. It will help me in my work for voter registration in rural Georgia and in my effort to keep Harlem from igniting. I have spoken to Hubert Humphrey and Walter Reuther, and they have promised me that a new day is dawning. If the compromise is accepted, Humphrey assured me that the Civil Rights Commission will finally hold hearings in Mississippi, the Democratic Party will abolish segregation from its ranks, and President Johnson will personally meet with you to discuss your problems.

"At the same time I realize that this compromise is inadequate; it offers precious little in view of how much you have suffered; it is small recompense for your pains. Indeed, were I one of you, had I undergone what you have had to endure, I do not know what I would do. On balance, I believe you should accept, because I believe it does represent a victory for the Civil Rights Movement, but the decision is up to you."

Bob Moses rose from his seat in the back of the room and walked slowly forward. I was swamped with emotions it was hard to define—remorse and regret, anger and frustration. *Why couldn't we have had a chance, at least once, to sit down and talk?* For all that I admired him, he remained an enigma. I noticed something steely in his eyes that I hadn't seen before. He had calmed down from that frantic moment in the hall yesterday, but underneath, I could see that he was still simmering. My own cheeks were burning.

"They say that we're not legal," he said in a hoarse whisper. "Well I say that Mississippi is not legal. They are outlaws down there. If we don't abide by their laws, it's because they don't abide by the laws of the United States. But to face the fact that Mississippi is not legal is to raise questions that could rip this country apart. No one wants to travel that road. And so they have decided to say that we are the ones who are not legal and to deny us our seats.

"The MFDP delegates were the only free people at this whole convention. All the others had to do what somebody else said. The delegates who were sympathetic to us couldn't act on their instinct to support us because Johnson told them not to. That's politics. We're not here to bring politics into the Civil Rights Movement but the Civil Rights Movement into politics. We're here because the black people of Mississippi have been wronged. Issuing two seats can't fix that. It is a moral situation. This compromise is dangerous. People are getting killed in Mississippi. If we accept this compromise, more people might be murdered. We have petitioned the Democratic Party for a real voice and a real place and the answer has come back—'no room.' Now we must seek our own objectives, outside the political system if necessary, and let the chips fall where they may."

I could see faces harden as Moses spoke. Any thought of accepting the compromise had vanished before he finished. It didn't take the delegates long to make a decision. They came out looking elated and relieved; they had rejected the compromise sixty-four to four.

"We didn't come all this way for no two seats," Fannie Lou Hamer explained, "when all of us is tired."

She led us one more time in "We Shall Overcome," but no one crossed arms or held hands and the SNCC veterans stopped singing when we came to *"black and white together."*

I felt my heart sink. *Had all our shared effort come to nothing? Would we all now go our separate ways, forgetting entirely the dream of a beloved community and the interracial ideal that had inspired us? What kind of country would we become if black and white together became a bad joke?* It seemed to me at that moment that the whole project had been a flash in the pan, a mere glimmer of hope that was now flickering out. The air was thick with recriminations. Nobody looked anybody in the eye.

That night, Bob Moses and eight other SNCC guys invaded the convention again, standing in front of the Mississippi section and holding up protest signs. I watched on television back in my room as an NBC television crew zeroed in on Moses. I envied the fact that their anchorman, John Chancellor, could interview him. Moses freely admitted that he had reached the floor with borrowed credentials.

"Is that legal?" Chancellor asked.

"I believe it is moral," Moses replied.

"Would you compromise?" he asked.

"What is compromise?" Moses asked back. "We are here for the people and the people don't want symbolic votes. They want to vote for themselves."

"But hasn't it already been democratically decided that your delegation was not legally entitled to those seats?"

"This convention hasn't made one vote," Moses responded. "It's a convention by acclamation. No one was allowed to state a personal preference for any candidate. When you say we're not legal, what you're really saying is that they have the power. Or that they don't want us to have it."

Chancellor looked more than a little puzzled by that answer.

"What do you plan to do then?" he asked.

"We intend to stand here with our signs 'One Man—One Vote,' telling our story."

7

The papers Thursday morning spoke of the substantial victory the MFDP had won, dominating national attention and gaining recognition for their moral case, but to me it felt like a defeat. From the point of view of politics as usual, I suppose, the compromise was a remarkable accomplishment, but given our desire to redeem American society, two seats "at large" was at best a slap on the wrists of the Mississippi regulars and a pat on the head of the MFDP delegates. *Politics may be the art of the possible,* I reflected, *but sometimes what is politically feasible is morally unforgiveable.* The media might claim we had touched the conscience of the nation, but I felt that we had been given the brush-off. We had been able to state our case on national television, but if eloquence settled issues, the Indians would still own America. They were the ones who spoke poetry at the treaty negotiations, but who ended up with the land? In fact, I thought of all the wonderful heartfelt speeches I had heard from gifted black orators over the past year, but what had all their words of wisdom accomplished?

"What are you going to do?" I asked Lenny as we walked over to say good-bye to Esther and Feelgood, who were returning to Mississippi. "We could share an apartment in Cleveland and you could go to Case Western Reserve too."

"I don't want to spend the best years of my life in the stacks of some musty old library. You're the one who thinks that gals go for guys with long dossiers."

Esther and Feelgood were sitting out on the porch of the Gem Hotel waiting for the arrival of the chartered bus.

"I've got a business proposition for you, Feelgood," Lenny said with a wicked twinkle in his eye.

"What's that?" Feelgood looked up. Since the beating, he moved with the stiffness of an old man. "I'm listenin'."

"Soul dildos!" Lenny announced gleefully. "Twelve inches of polished ebony. Available at retail stores everywhere. It will make your fortune."

I waited for Feelgood's reaction with trepidation, especially after the tension of the last few days. But he laughed heartily.

"Babies, that's a gas!" he said, turning his head away from the sunshine. "We got soul, why not profit from it? You the ones that's disadvantaged. Ain't that right, Esther?"

"You guys are such assholes," Esther said, scowling at Lenny. "I've come to the conclusion that there are smart smart-asses and smart-ass asses. Which are you?"

"Don't let him bug you," I said. "He was only joking."

Esther looked at me warmly, her face free of irritation.

"That's right," Lenny said. "I need my daily supplement of irony to survive. See, my identity problem is I know who I am. You can't cure a personality. You have to take me as I am."

"What if we can't?" I went on, just to humor him.

"Then ship me off to the rubber room at the funny farm, strap me in a plastic chair, and flip on the TV."

"We may all end up in the nuthouse," Esther said.

"Are you sure you want to go back to Mississippi?" I asked her. "It's going to be rough there this fall."

"Those people trusted me enough to join the Movement," Esther said. "I can't back out now. I have to see it through."

I felt like a soldier who had made a separate peace when there was still a war to be won. To be near Esther, I was willing to walk down more dusty roads and face more danger, but Feelgood stood in the way of that.

"If you're gonna be in the Movement," Feelgood said, "you gotta keep movin'. If it takes more deaths to keep this Movement alive, that's the price we gotta pay. When you're dead, you're done—they drop you in a hole and throw dirt in your face—but until that day the Man's gonna have to *contend* with me, you dig? And if he comes after me with a gun, I *know* what I'm gonna do."

"If you kill somebody, Feelgood," Lenny said, "the state will wire your ass and up your wattage free of charge."

"That's the chance I'll take," Feelgood said.

"What happens next?" I asked, still feeling the anguish of the day before. "Everybody's going to be demoralized after this defeat."

"You still don't get it, do you?" Feelgood said. "We didn't *want* to win this one. We wanted people to see this evil system in action. They wasn't a chance in hell they was gonna seat a bunch of po' niggers at the expense of rich white folks. Now that that has been made clear, people are ready to move to the next stage: liberation— by any means necessary."

"That isn't what Moses wanted." I felt strangely exhilarated to be speaking in his name. "Only moral means can achieve moral goals."

"Bob Moses is a saint," Feelgood explained wearily. "He thought love could change the world. But now I do believe he's beginnin' to see the light. He saw how our so-called allies turned against us and sold us down the river. They were not worthy of trust. Appeals to conscience didn't mean shit when interests were at stake. They used us, man, and we ain't never gonna let that happen again."

The bus arrived for the long trip back to Mississippi. I helped Esther and Feelgood stow their bags and hugged them good-bye.

"If you really need a shrink," Esther called in a teasing voice to Lenny from the bus window, "I'll be only too glad to recommend one."

"No need," Lenny said. "My psychiatrist can lick your psychiatrist any day."

"Fuck you, Lenny." Esther laughed. "Strong letter to follow."

"I'm going to miss you, Esther," I cried.

"I know you understand why I have to go back." Esther smiled through tears. "You're a good man, Tom. I'll miss you more than I can say."

She was still smiling when the bus pulled away in a cloud of exhaust fumes.

A few of the MFDP delegates had decided to stay around for the end of the convention. In the afternoon I saw E. W. Steptoe and Hartman Turnbow at Averell Harriman's reception for Mrs. Kennedy at the Deauville Hotel. They were standing beside a huge cut-glass punch bowl, sipping from a tiny goblet in one hand, nibbling a smidgen of pastry in the other, and talking to a curious crowd of delegates. Meanwhile, Jackie, in white silk brocade, held out her slim perfectly tanned arm and white-gloved hand to an endless line of guests, including Lenny and me.

"Nice to see you," she said in a soft whisper that I thought, for a second, was a parody of Marilyn Monroe.

"Thas the biggest crock of wine I ever seen," Mr. Turnbow said to me, "but look at them itty-bitty dippers they got to ladle it out in."

"Well, you're entitled to all you want," I said.

"You know," Turnbow said, looking very serious, "I used to think Mississippi Negroes was the only peoples in the world who was always afraid of losin' they jobs. But that ain't so. Even the president of the United States is afraid of losin' his job. He knew we had justice on our side, but he was scared. That's why he didn't do right by us."

I nodded, as I tasted my glorified thimbleful of punch.

"I like this," I said. "Want some more?"

"I already licked up three," Turnbow admitted. "It's terrible good. But I better not. If I takes too much, I'm afraid the Mississippi in me will show."

"That's what we're here for," I smiled, handing him another. "Let it show!"

I wandered around the reception feeling like I was floating in space and time. Everything was over; it happened long ago; and yet here I still was, pretending life was real. In the hotel auditorium Fredric March and his wife were reading selections from JFK's favorite poets. Clearly all this was calculated to make LBJ look uncouth by comparison. What I had heard was that JFK read James Bond novels, not Elizabethan sonnets.

My notion that the Kennedys liked to see themselves as a refined royal family driven into exile by barbarian hordes was reinforced as I watched the last evening of the convention on television. When Bobby Kennedy stepped forward to introduce the memorial film devoted to his brother, the delegates, who hadn't been allowed to express themselves all week, went wild. They screamed and cheered for twenty thunderous minutes while Bobby, with a hint of a half-smile on his lips, tried to speak. Although he was dressed in black, as befits a man in mourning, and tried to keep a solemn expression, the crowd's tumultuous ovation must have thrilled every political cell in his body.

"When I think of President Kennedy," he finally said, his voice nearly cracking, "I think of what Shakespeare said in *Romeo and Juliet*:

> *"When he shall die,*
> *Take him and cut him out in little stars,*
> *And he will make the face of Heaven so fine*
> *That all the world will be in love with night,*
> *And pay no worship to the garish sun."*

After a week under LBJ's crass and tacky Big Top, I had no doubt whom "the garish sun" referred to, but the stolid delegates apparently missed the allusion as they cheered some more and then settled into their seats.

With Richard Burton singing in the background *"once there was a fleeting wisp of glory . . . called Camelot,"* the short film was packed with shots of JFK at his most winsome: the perfect Dad, plucking a buttercup and handing it to John-John and then scrambling with him into an abandoned rowboat on the beach; the decisive leader, calling for civil rights legislation, signing the Test Ban Treaty, facing the Cuban Missile Crisis; and the witty bon vivant accepting an honorary degree: "It might be said that I now have the best of both worlds—a Harvard education and a Yale degree." Then the cortege, the coffin, the eternal flame. And as Mr. Swift had predicted, Bobby's face was nowhere to be seen.

No question, it was powerful stuff—LBJ had good reason to hold off this unruly emotional storm until his nomination was secured. The fact that I didn't shed a tear I took as evidence that my tour of duty as a summer soldier in Mississippi had hardened me beyond the pull of sentiment—a self-congratulatory delusion that lasted all of ten minutes, until Adlai Stevenson delivered a tribute to Eleanor Roosevelt.

There was something vaguely reminiscent of Shakespeare in Stevenson's high, pale, alabaster forehead and hawk-nosed, sad-eyed face, but his delivery was tired and uninspired, with an undertone of melancholy. Nevertheless, his words touched me deeply:

"There is, I believe, a legend in the Talmud that tells us that in any period of man's history, the heavens themselves are held in place by the virtue, love, and shining integrity of twelve just men, who go about their humble chores unaware that the rooftree of creation is supported by them alone. And I think perhaps there are times when nations or movements or political parties are similarly sustained in their purposes and being by the pervasive, unconscious influence of a few great men or women. Can we here in the Democratic Party doubt that Eleanor Roosevelt, throughout her selfless life, had in some measure the keeping of the party's conscience in her special care?

"She was a lady—a lady for all seasons. She saw herself as an 'ugly duckling,' but she walked in beauty in the ghettos of the world. Falsity withered in her presence. Hypocrisy left the room. She believed in the human heart because she knew her own, and she proved by love what all the despairs of a despairing time will never disprove—that hope is more powerful than fear. She trained herself from the beginning of her life to face the realities, however unwelcome they might be. She would tell us today to look at our great cities and ask whether, in the midst of overwhelming affluence, we can afford such misery, such squalor, such hopelessness. She would urge us to build the Great Society not only in terms of America, but of all God's children."

The applause at the end was polite, but perfunctory; the convention wanted to get on to the next item of business. I sat in front of the television set with tears streaming down my face. I wasn't a big fan of Eleanor—I always associated her with upper-class ladies doing ineffectual charity work and that kind of ghoulish attraction liberals have to lost causes—but there was something about that legend from the Talmud that reminded me of Bob Moses working quietly in Mississippi. Maybe he was one of the twelve just persons who sustained the world. *But what if he had a change of heart? What if he gave up? What then?*

Moses and five other SNCC veterans had infiltrated the convention one more time, but they refused to speak to reporters. They simply stood silently in a circle, a band of brothers, arms on each other's shoulders, paying their respects to JFK and reminding the nation that two token seats for Mississippi were not enough. *Say it with your life, Bob,* I thought. *Say it with your life.*

"Moses is the walking understatement of the century," I said. "I wonder what he's feeling. He looked cold as stone yesterday."

"Many are cold, but few are frozen," Lenny said. "He'll be okay."

"I hope so," I said. "He's indispensable. I don't know what the Movement would do without him."

What would I do without him? I wondered. I felt as if all summer long I had been waiting for a word from Bob Moses that now I knew would never be spoken.

LBJ had arranged for his nomination to fall on his birthday, and he was determined to make the most of it. That evening the boardwalk was awash with marching bands, drum and bugle corps, precision drill teams, and folk dancers in bright multicolored ethnic costumes. Tons of fireworks turned the night into an aurora borealis of exploding stars, scintillating orange palm trees, flashing and fizzling flares, sputtering pinwheels and rainbow cascades as the swelling booms and bangs of detonating rockets split the sky to the "Ohs" and "Ahs" of the crowd. Drifting powder smoke became so thick it was hard to see, and cardboard shreds of firecracker casings floated down like confetti. The smell brought back the cordite fumes after the Freedom House was bombed; I thought of all the other bombings and how close so many had come to death in the Movement and how a few had died for their beliefs. Our heads may not have been clear or our hearts pure, but at least we had stolen a moral march on our complacent countrymen. Sweating out a summer for racial equality had given me both a spiritual high and a sense of lasting bitterness. Mr. Swift had remarked that young people should be sued for breach of promise, but really, wasn't it America that broke its promises and devoured its children? Wasn't Fannie Lou Hamer right when she said, "I question America"? While I was sunk in such gloomy reflections, a huge pyrotechnic portrait of President Johnson, bleeding red, white, and blue sparklers, ignited with a breath-taking grand-finale whoosh, casting an unholy glow over all faces. I knew then that most of us, the children that Bob Moses led, would leave Atlantic City with an idea, terrible in its simplicity, that would haunt us through the years: *America was Mississippi; Mississippi was America; from sea to shining sea.*

Tom Morton
Afterword: 1972

Ella and Eddie Mays still own their farm; Buster plans to enter the University of Mississippi in the fall. Jasmine and Ledell Simmons were married in 1966 at the Blessed Redeemer Baptist Church, Midnight Grimes presiding. They moved to San Francisco the following year so that Ledell could enter the Afro-American Studies program at Stanford; their two children, a boy and a girl, are named Robert and Miscelia. Esther Rappaport and Raymond Fleetwood were married in 1965 and divorced in 1967; Feelgood was found dead of a drug overdose in an automobile in Newark in 1969; Esther now works in Washington, D.C., with the Head Start program. We write to each other on occasion. Amontillado Poe, known to his coconspirators as Sundiata, was arrested in 1968 for plotting to blow up the Statue of Liberty. Midnight Grimes was elected mayor of Tallahatchie, Mississippi, in 1970. Gayl Norris received her law degree from Tulane University and now practices in McComb. Lenny Swift's nominating speech of Pigasus in Grant Park outside the 1968 Democratic Convention in Chicago, where Fannie Lou Hamer was seated as a delegate, is still talked about in yippie and SDS circles; he disappeared into the Weathermen underground in 1969 as commandant of a cadre known as "Bo Dah and the Incensed." I completed my doctorate in American Studies from Case Western Reserve University in 1969; my first book, *Authentic Edens in a Pagan Sea: Melville in the Marquesas,* will be published soon by the University of Hawaii Press; I now teach American literature at Transylvania College in Lexington, Kentucky.

The last I heard, Bob Moses had changed his name and was teaching school somewhere in Tanzania.

Acknowledgments

In writing this novel I have tried to be faithful to the spirit if not always the letter of what the historical characters (Bob Moses, Fannie Lou Hamer, Martin Luther King, E. W. Steptoe, et al.) said and did. On the other hand, my fictional characters (Tom, Lenny, Esther, Feelgood, Jasmine, Midnight Grimes, et al.) are exactly that; they are not based on anyone, living or dead. Tallahatchie, for example, is a made-up place and all events set there are fictional, although they are similar to the kinds of things that happened during Freedom Summer. McComb, however, is a real town and the bombings described in my novel actually occurred, but I have changed dates and many details of those events for dramatic purposes. Although several towns in Mississippi held a Freedom Day during the summer of 1964, the Freedom Day in Liberty and the events surrounding it in the Voter Registration section of the novel are fictitious. The descriptions of canvassing, while drawing on typical experiences from Freedom Summer, are not based on any people or events in the McComb and Liberty area, and Craw Dad Bottom, a site of one canvassing episode, is a completely made-up place. As for the characters, they do not represent and should not be confused with the real-life civil rights workers who were in McComb in 1964.

This narrative draws upon facts and events which were complex and whose "truth" may be obscure or open to argument. The novel transforms events through the perspective of various characters, many of whom were civil-rights workers, and should not be mistaken for a literal account of specific events of 1961 through 1964.

In order to create a seamless whole, so that history has the drama of fiction and fiction the ring of truth, I spent time doing extensive research. For ten years it has been my privilege and pleasure to immerse myself in the literature of the Civil Rights Movement, especially the primary sources. The Social Action Collection at the State Historical Society of Wisconsin, in Madison, has gathered documents from the participants in Freedom Summer. Their affidavits, field reports, letters, diaries, journals, interviews, etc. are a treasure trove of information about daily experiences and what it felt like to try to "crack" the segregated world that was Mississippi. I would like to thank Harry Miller, Ellen Burke, Joann Hohler, and the rest of the Archives staff for their generous assistance, and the many Summer Project volunteers, whose courage and eloquence were a constant inspiration, for making this distinctive collection available. The voice of E. W. Steptoe is directly indebted to an interview conducted with him by Miriam Feingold, Tape 528A; the descriptions of the Herbert Lee and Louis Allen killings rely on investigations conducted by Robert Moses, Julian Bond, and Jerry DeMuth; the local FBI agent at the time, C. G. Prospere, declined to be interviewed. The Louis Allen case remains unsolved, and my account is not intended to incriminate any person living or dead.

Scholars owe a debt of gratitude to James Forman, who insisted that SNCC "field secretaries" write reports on all their activities. The result is an invaluable paper trail, most of which is accessible in the Student Non-Violent Coordinating Committee Collection (Martin Luther King Jr. Center, Atlanta, Georgia). My thanks to the archival staff for their kind help. The Voter Education Project Papers, part of the Southern Regional Council Papers, are also in Atlanta at the Atlanta University Library. The Project South

Collection, in the Stanford University Archives, contains numerous interviews, as does the Civil Rights Documentation Project, at the Moorland-Spingarn Research Center (Howard University, Washington, D.C.). My thanks to Roxanne Mylan and Esme E. Bhan at those respective libraries. I am also indebted to the Lyndon Baines Johnson Presidential Library in Austin, Texas, especially archivists Shellynee Wucher and Tina Houston; the Robert Coles and Allard Lowenstein Papers, at the University of North Carolina Library in Chapel Hill; the Oral History collection at the University of Southern Mississippi (Orley B. Caudill, Director) in Hattiesburg; the Center for the Study of Southern Culture at the University of Mississippi in Oxford; and the collection of newspaper accounts of Freedom Summer at the Alumni Office (Jean Perry, Archivist) Western College for Women, Oxford, Ohio. Steve Rockwood and his staff at the Mount Saint Mary's College library have also been very helpful.

During several excursions to Mississippi, I was especially grateful to Mr. and Mrs. Charles M. Dunigan for their hospitality and for making available to me the relevant files of the *McComb Enterprise-Journal*. Jim Abbott of the *Indianola Enterprise Tocsin* was also cooperative, as were Mr. and Mrs. Lum of Port Gibson. Some of the people that I interviewed wish to remain anonymous, but let me thank C. C. Bryant, Ernest Nobles, Alfred Knox, Linda Seese, Don McCord, and especially Robert Moses for taking the time to talk to me. The idea of having Moses narrate part of the novel originated in an interview he gave about his activities: "Mississippi: 1961–1962," *Liberation 14* (January 1970). Out of respect for Mr. Moses's privacy, I have tried to keep my focus on his public actions. A distinguished group of civil rights scholars responded generously with advice and articles to my pleas for assistance, among them Doug McAdam, who shared important primary sources with me; Steven F. Lawson; David Garrow; Joe Sinsheimer; David Chalmers; August Meier; Claybourne Carson, who sent me his annotated interview with Robert Moses; John Dittmer; Jack Chatfield; Taylor Branch; Michal R. Belknap; Jan Hillegas; Jerry

McKnight; Stan Boyd; and William Ferris. The following college students, young scholars in the making, provided copies of their research: W. Lance Conn, Larry Clark Hicks Jr., Victoria Toliver, and Kristen Dunn.

Authors thrive on praise, but they need, especially in the early drafts, constructive criticism. For cold baths of bracing advice and for saving me from innumerable pratfalls and pitfalls, I thank my good friends: Frank Bergon, Holly St. John Bergon, Toby Olson, Marshall Dunn, Jim Vincent, Tom Flynn, Robert Ducharme, Nancy Shilling, and Tom Bligh. I am also grateful to Robert Stone and Robert Coles, for their timely support; Judy Ott, for typing numerous drafts over the years with exemplary patience; The Maryland Arts Council, The Hackney Literary Award, and Mount Saint Mary's College for financial assistance; my agent, Victoria Sanders, for keeping the faith; Emilie Buchwald, Beth Olson, Dee Ready, and the wonderful people at Milkweed Editions, for bringing my book to print; and my wife, Rosér, herself a novelist (*Once Remembered, Twice Lived,* Peter Lang 1993), who has read and reread every word of every draft of this book, accompanied me on our memorable treks across the country, and persisted in loving me, even when my eyes were fixed on the computer screen and my head was back in the summer of 1964.

Excerpts from this novel first appeared in *The Monocacy Valley Review* and *Crossroads: A Journal of Southern Culture.*

The Robert Penn Warren epigraph is from his poem "Court-Martial" in *Selected Poems: New and Old 1923–1966* (Random House, 1966). Copyright © 1964 by Robert Penn Warren.

Bibliography

The following selected works deal completely or in part with Mississippi and the Summer Project of 1964: Sally Belfrage, *Freedom Summer;* Michael Belknap, *Federal Law and Southern Order;* Taylor Branch, *Parting the Waters;* Rosellen Brown, *Some Deaths in the Delta* and *Civil Wars;* Eric R. Burner, *And Gently He Shall Lead Them: Robert Parris Moses and the Civil Rights Movement in Mississippi;* Seth Cagin and Philip Dray, *We Are Not Afraid;* Will D. Campbell, *Brother to a Dragonfly;* Clayborne Carson, *In Struggle: SNCC and the Black Awakening of the 1960s;* Hodding Carter, *So the Heffners Left McComb;* William H. Chafe, *Never Stop Running: Allard Lowenstein and the Struggle to Save American Liberalism;* David Chalmers, *And the Crooked Places Made Straight;* James C. Cobb, *The Most Southern Place on Earth;* Robert Coles, *Farewell to the South, The Call of Service,* and with Jane Hallowell Coles, *Women of Crisis II;* Paul Cowen, *The Making of an Un-American;* Richard Cummings, *The Pied Piper: Allard K. Lowenstein and the Liberal Dream;* Allison Davis, et al., *Deep South;* John Dittmer, *Local People;* John Dollard, *Caste and Class in a Southern Town;* Tony Dunbar, *Our Land Too* and *Delta Time;* Charles W. Eagles, ed., *The Civil Rights Movement in America;* P. D. East, *The Magnolia Jungle;* Sara Evans, *Personal Politics;* Mrs. Medgar Evers, with William Peters, *For Us the Living;*

Leon Friedman, ed., *Southern Justice;* James Forman, *The Making of Black Revolutionaries;* David Garrow, *Bearing the Cross;* Paul Good, *The Trouble I've Seen;* Polly Greenberg, *The Devil Has Slippery Shoes;* John Howard Griffin, *Black Like Me;* David Harris, *Dreams Die Hard;* Harold Hampton and Steve Fayer, eds., *Voices of Freedom;* Tom Hayden, *Revolution in Mississippi;* Bruce Hilton, *The Delta Ministry;* Len Holt, *The Summer That Didn't End;* William Bradford Huie, *Three Lives for Mississippi;* John Oliver Killens, *'Sippi;* Mary King, *Freedom Song;* Arthur Kinoy, *Rights on Trial;* William Kunstler, *Deep in My Heart;* Steven F. Lawson, *Black Ballots;* Nicholas Lemann, *The Promised Land;* Julius Lester, *Look Out Whitey! Black Power's Gonna Get Your Mama!* and *All Is Well;* Charles J. Levy, *Voluntary Servitude;* Walter Lord, *The Past That Would Not Die;* Debbie Louis, *And We Are Not Saved;* Florence Mars, *Witness in Philadelphia;* Doug McAdam, *Freedom Summer;* William McCord, *Mississippi: The Long Hot Summer;* Neil R. McMillen, *The Citizen's Council* and *Dark Journey;* August Meier, *CORE;* Kay Mills, *This Little Light of Mine: The Life of Fannie Lou Hamer;* Nicolaus Mills, *Like a Holy Crusade;* Anne Moody, *Coming of Age in Mississippi;* Willie Morris, *Yazoo;* Victor Navasky, *Kennedy Justice;* Jack Newfield, *A Prophetic Minority;* Kenneth O'Reilly, *"Racial Matters": The FBI's Secret File on Black America, 1960-1972;* Hortense Powdermaker, *After Freedom;* Howell Raines, *My Soul Is Rested;* Anne Romaine, "The Mississippi Freedom Democratic Party Through August, 1964" (Master's thesis, University of Virginia); Mary Aickin Rothschild, *A Case of Black and White;* Cleveland Sellers, with Robert Terrell, *River of No Return;* John Salter, *Jackson, Mississippi;* James W. Silver, *Mississippi: The Closed Society;* Harvard Sitkoff, *The Struggle for Black Equality, 1954–1980;* Frank Smith, *Congressman from Mississippi;* Lillian Smith, *Our Faces, Our Words;* Emily Stoper, *The Student Non-Violent Coordinating Committee;* Tracy Sugarman, *Stranger at the Gates;* Elizabeth Sutherland, ed., *Letters from Mississippi;* Michael Thelwell, *Duties, Pleasures, and Conflicts;* Alice Walker, *Meridian;* Michele Wallace, *Black Macho and the Myth of Superwoman;* Pat Watters, *The South and the Nation,*

Climbing Jacobs Ladder, and *Down to Now;* Robert Penn Warren, *Who Speaks for the Negro?;* Stephen Whitfield, *A Death in the Delta;* Don Whitehead, *Attack on Terror;* Juan Williams, *Eyes on the Prize;* Harrison Wofford, *Of Kennedys and Kings;* Howard Zinn, *SNCC: The New Abolitionists;* Nicholas Von Hoffman, *Mississippi Notebook.*

A native of Poland, Ohio, a graduate of Hiram College, and a participant in the March on Washington, William Heath has a Ph.D. in American Studies from Case Western Reserve University. He has taught at Kenyon, Transylvania, and Vassar. From 1979 to 1981 he was the Fulbright lecturer in American Studies at the University of Seville. His poems, stories, essays, and reviews have appeared in numerous literary magazines; he is the editor of *The Monocacy Valley Review;* and he has published one book of poems, *The Walking Man* (Icarus Books, 1994). Since 1981 he has been a member of the English Department at Mount Saint Mary's College. He and his wife, Roser, live in Frederick, Maryland, with their cat, Homer.

Designed by Will Powers
Typeset in Monotype Calisto
by Stanton Publication Services
Printed on acid-free 55-pound Glatfelter paper
by Edwards Brothers, Inc.

More fiction from Milkweed Editions:

Larabi's Ox
Tony Ardizzone

Agassiz
Sandra Birdsell

What We Save for Last
Corinne Demas Bliss

Backbone
Carol Bly

The Clay That Breathes
Catherine Browder

Street Games
Rosellen Brown

A Keeper of Sheep
William Carpenter

Winter Roads, Summer Fields
Marjorie Dorner

Blue Taxis
Eileen Drew

Kingfishers Catch Fire
Rumer Godden

Live at Five
David Haynes

Somebody Else's Mama
David Haynes

The Importance of High Places
Joanna Higgins

Circe's Mountain
Marie Luise Kaschnitz

Persistent Rumours
Lee Langley

Ganado Red
Susan Lowell

Swimming in the Congo
Margaret Meyers

Tokens of Grace
Sheila O'Connor

The Boy Without a Flag
Abraham Rodriguez, Jr.

Confidence of the Heart
David Schweidel

An American Brat
Bapsi Sidhwa

Cracking India
Bapsi Sidhwa

The Crow Eaters
Bapsi Sidhwa

The Country I Come From
Maura Stanton

Traveling Light
Jim Stowell

Aquaboogie
Susan Straight

The Empress of One
Faith Sullivan

Justice
Larry Watson

Montana 1948
Larry Watson